THE GREAT CONSERVATION DIVIDE

THE GREAT
CONSERVATION
DIVIDE

Conservation vs. Resourcism on
America's Public Lands

Dave Foreman

Third in the For the Wild Things series by
The Rewilding Institute and Raven's Eye Press

Raven's Eye Press
Durango, Colorado

Raven's Eye Press
Durango, Colorado
www.ravenseyepress.com

Foreman, Dave.
   The Great Conservation Divide/Dave Foreman
   p. cm.

1. Conservation
2. Conservation Movement
3. Wilderness
4. Wildlife
I. Title

ISBN: 978-0-9907826-1-2
LCCN: 2014952232

Cover & interior design by Lindsay J. Nyquist, *elle jay design*

Printed in the United States of America
1 3 5 7 9 10 8 6 4 2

"There are some who can live without wild things, and some who cannot. These essays are the delights and dilemmas of one who cannot."

From the Introduction to *A Sand County Almanac*
by Aldo Leopold, 1949

DEDICATION

JOHN DAVIS

My trustworthy friend, conservation conscience,
editor, and doughty wilderness warrior/companion

OTHER BOOKS BY DAVE FOREMAN

Ecodefense: A Field Guide to Monkeywrenching
(editor with Bill Haywood)

The Big Outside
(with Howie Wolke)

Confessions of an Eco-Warrior

Defending the Earth
(with Murray Bookchin, edited by Steve Chase)

The Lobo Outback Funeral Home
(a novel)

The Sky Islands Wildlands Network Conservation Plan
(lead author and editor)

New Mexico Highlands Wildlands Network Vision
(lead author and editor)

*Rewilding North America:
A Vision for Conservation in the 21st Century*

Man Swarm and the Killing of Wildlife

Take Back Conservation

TABLE OF CONTENTS
Annotated Chapter List

Acknowledgements

John Davis and Dave Foreman,
photo credit Doug Tompkins

FIRST I MUST THANK THE WILDERNESS and the many wild things I have known for over sixty years for the bliss and meaning they've given my life. Without them, I would not want to live, for there are some who can live without wild things, and some who cannot, as Aldo Leopold wrote.

Second I must thank the selfless wilderfolk with whom I've worked for over forty years to keep the wild alive and to save big wilderness for all the wild things. If I named them all, the list would look like a phone book.

I've dedicated this book to John Davis, who for thirty years has been my trusted friend in wandering the wilderness and my closest partner, other than my wife Nancy, in fighting for the freedom of the wilderness. Twelve hundred years ago, I might have written:

Getreowe freond, erde-cearu ingethanc,
boccraeft getheahta, dyhtig wildeorness gesith[1]

And I must thank Nancy for sharing my love for wilderness, for our thirty years together of fighting for wild things, and for being my best fellow wilderness wayfarer.

Insofar as writing this long-in-coming book, Susan Morgan and John Davis have been my constant editors and sounding boards. Without them, this book would not be. And I thank my friend Christianne Hinks for her proofreading. There is a reason Susan, John, and I call her Hawkeye.

Some of my friends, who share vast experience in and knowledge of the war for wild things, checked some of my chapters for accuracy. They are John Miles, Professor Emeritus of Environmental Studies at Huxley College, Western Washington University; Jim Eaton, who has fought for wilderness since the late-1960s, working for the Sierra Club, Wilderness Society, and founding the California Wilderness Coalition; and Brian O'Donnell, who, though at least a quarter-century younger than me, has worked with maybe more conservation outfits than I have, most recently the Conservation Lands Foundation. Thanks much, friends.

Thanks as always to Roxanne and Monica Pacheco of Bosque Accounting for keeping things from falling apart and always being there for me.

---

1   See the dedication page for the translation to modern English. If any readers are Old English scholars, feel free to send me a more grammatically correct rewrite.

ACKNOWLEDGEMENTS

Once again, Lindsay Nyquist of Raven's Eye Press has done a tip-top job of design and publishing this book—third in the five-book series *For the Wild Things*. For *The Great Conservation Divide*, she has worked in record speed without complaint so we could get the book out in time for the 50th Anniversary Celebration of The Wilderness Act.

Last, but far from least, I thank Caroline Gabel of the Shared Earth Foundation. Without her generous backing, I don't know how The Rewilding Institute could have published *The Great Conservation Divide*. She is also funding publication of my next book, *True Wilderness*. Thank you, Caroline.

Dave Foreman
Sandia Foothills
September 2014

Note: I apologize for there being no index in this first printing of *The Great Conservation Divide*. We just did not have time to get it in in time for the 50th anniversary of The Wilderness Act. An index will appear in future printings. If you bought this first printing and would like a copy of the index, please email TRI@rewilding.org.

THE GREAT CONSERVATION DIVIDE

Quick, Quirky Word Hoard

Below are the meanings for some words, phrases, and technical terms the reader may not at first understand.

Cannot – One who, like Aldo Leopold, cannot live without wild things; a conservationist

Conservationists – those who work to save wild things from development or from domination by Man

Deor – animal

Earthling – any living being on Earth

Good(s) – value(s)

Good – good-in-itself in Ethics

Grassroots – those for whom conservation is a calling; not *only* a job for hire

Grassroots Conservation – nonprofit conservation clubs; not government agencies

Kind – species of animal, plant, etc.

LAND (AND/OR SEA) – environment, ecological community

LANDSCALPERS – those who irresponsibly plunder Earth and its wild things with no thought for the morrow

MAN, MEN – when capitalized, humans; uncapitalized, male humans

RESOURCISM – the domestication and allegedly "wise use" of wild things (resources) by expert technicians for the benefit of Man

TREE OF LIFE – Nature, biodiversity (see Wild Things)

WILDEOR – wild animal, untamed, undomesticated (see Deor)

WILDERFOLK – wilderness and wildlife conservationists (see Cannot)

WILDERNESS – self-willed land, sea (not dominated by Man)

WILD HAVEN – protected area, such as a National Park, Wilderness Area, Biosphere Reserve…

WILDLIFE – undomesticated animals, plants, and other life kinds

WILDLOVERS – wilderness and wildlife conservationists (see Cannot)

WILD NEIGHBORHOOD – ecosystem, natural community, land community

WILD THING – wildlife; also ecological processes, landscapes, geological features, weather, and so on that is free of Man's will

WILD THINGS – Nature, biodiversity (see Tree of Life)

INTRODUCTION

Will of the Land v. Will of Man

I call the years 1785 to 1890 in the United States the "Frontier Century." I believe it is a clear timespan in American history. Through those years, with ax, saw, cattle, sheep, plow, gun, and steam engine, Americans conquered the wilderness between the Alleghenies and the Pacific and between Canada and Mexico. I write "conquered" but "scalped" would better name our work. We scalped the Great Eastern Forest, the towering White Pine Forest of the Lake States, the Great Plains, and dry grasslands farther west. We killed fifty million bison, over two billion passenger pigeons, and untold numbers of other wildlife and "game" birds. The United States at the end of the Frontier Century looked nothing at all like the United States at the beginning of the Frontier Century.

Toward the end of the Frontier Century, a backlash grew against what I call *landscalping*. That backlash called itself *conservation*, but from its beginning there were two stand-apart conservations cleaved by how each valued wildland and wildlife and how each drew the long tomorrow of wild things. It was not a single conservation movement.

[1]

Historians and others have branded that cleavage as *resource conservation* vs. *Nature conservation* and have personalized it as Gifford Pinchot, "father" of the US Forest Service, against John Muir, the embodiment of the Sierra Club. I shall follow that frame; indeed, this book is about the battle between resource conservation (or *resourcism*) and Nature conservation over the leftover wilderness in America throughout the "Public Lands Century" from 1891 to 2001.

To show how far apart these two conservations were and are in how they value wild things, let me quote a clear-throated spokesman for each:

The late Canadian naturalist John Livingston wrote in 1981 that *wildlife conservation* is

> *The preservation of wildlife forms and groups of forms in perpetuity, for their own sakes, irrespective of any connotation of present or future human use.... In essence, wildlife conservation is the preservation of nonhuman beings in their natural settings, unaffected by human use or activity, uncontaminated by human antibiosis, emancipated from human serfdom.*[1]

The same can be said about land or sea—wilderness. In this, I believe Livingston spoke for most of us who would not want to live without wild things.

Set against Livingston, a Bureau of Reclamation cheerleader wonderfully laid out the innermost belief of resourcism when the heyday of dam building was getting underway:

> *The destiny of man is to possess the whole earth, and the destiny of the earth is to be subject to man. There can be no full conquest of*

---

1   John A. Livingston, *The Fallacy of Wildlife Conservation* (McClelland and Stewart Limited, Toronto, Ontario, 1981), 17-18.

the earth, and no real satisfaction to humanity, if large portions of
the earth remain beyond his highest control.[2]

Yes, two campaigns both called conservation but so far away from one another.

In the Frontier Century, the quashing of wilderness and wildlife was carried out by individual and corporate landscalpers: settlers, trappers, market hunters, loggers, miners, cattlemen, railroaders, and irrigators, to name the best known. In the Public Lands Century, though the landscalpers were busy, the main camp answerable for the snuffing of wilderness was the resourcists in federal and state government agencies: the Forest Service, Fish and Wildlife Service, Bureau of Reclamation, and state game and fish departments, to name only a few. The other conservation movement—Nature conservation—has been the great foe of the resourcists and their drive to tame wild America.

The unending fight with the Forest Service and other resource agencies, however, goes beyond the underlying cleavage in Weltanschauung (worldview) and how the wild is valued. Resourcism, maybe most of all within the Forest Service, is deeply rooted in arrogance. David Clary, retired chief historian of the Forest Service, closes his no-holds barred book, *Timber and the Forest Service*, with:

> *The [Forest Service] also adopted the belief that any opponent was*
> *perforce in the wrong, whether from ignorance or from evil intent.*
> *Ignorance could be corrected with "information and education";*
> *evil simply resisted....When outsiders challenged the Service,*
> *they challenged its professional ego.... Criticism from within was*

---

2   J. Widtsoe, *Success on Irrigation Projects* (New York, 1928), 138. Quoted in Donald Worster, *Rivers of Empire: Water, Aridity & The Growth of The American West* (Pantheon, New York, 1985), 188.

unlikely, because the shared culture of the agency was pervasive. Criticism from without was not to be acknowledged as legitimate.[3]

This, then, was what wildlovers were up against in the Public Lands Century, 1891 to 2001. It is what I have given my life to fighting since 1970. *The Great Conservation Divide* is about that fight between wildlovers and resourcists during the Public Lands Century. It gives those who love wild things the must-have knowledge and understanding they need to carry on the fight into tomorrow.

My dear friend and fellow warrior for the wild, John Davis, writes:

Greater than the ideological wall between Republicans and Democrats, deeper than the rift between conservatives and liberals, more fundamental than the differences between atheists and believers is the moral divide between resourcists and conservationists. In the United States of America, this conflict over ethics smolders like a brushfire most widely on the federal public lands. Though the lines sometimes blur and waver, on one side generally are resourcists and landscalpers who fail or refuse to see inherent value in the land and its community of life. On the other side are conservationists who, like Aldo Leopold, have succeeded in expanding their circle of concern, their ethical reach, to embrace the whole biotic community.

Therefore, in this book—*The Great Conservation Divide*—I argue that the cleaved ethics of resource conservation and wilderness conservation are about the deepest, most important question of *Homo sapiens*: do other kinds of life and the wild neighborhoods in which they dwell have as much right to exist as we do? And, if so, how do we

3   David A. Clary, *Timber and the Forest Service* (University Press of Kansas, Lawrence, 1986), 196.

change our behavior quickly so that they can continue to live before we humanize the whole world for the good of only one species?

—Dave Foreman
Somewhere on the Sheenjek River,
Arctic National Wildlife Refuge Wilderness Area,
Alaska, July 2014

CHAPTER 1

Wilderness: Self-Willed Land

2014 IS THE 50ᵀᴴ ANNIVERSARY of the passage of the 1964 Wilderness Act, the strongest and most visionary step in history for keeping some lands free of Man's dominion and leaving them as wild neighborhoods for the wild things who dwell in them. Over these fifty years, the acreage of federal land in the United States set aside in the National Wilderness Preservation System has grown from some 9 million to over 109 million. Folks from all nooks of America have worked selflessly to gain this win for wild things. The Wilderness Act and its sister law for wild things—the Endangered Species Act—stand with the Declaration of Independence and Bill of Rights as great gifts from the United States to the world.

As we make merry for the Wilderness Act, let us keep the hard truth in the forefront: Protected areas, the tougher the better, are the best way to keep and to hand on the Tree of Life and its ongoing evolution into the eternity of tomorrow. They are also the best way to rekindle our love for the wild from which Man sprang and to keep us all aware that we need a taste of wildness to stay healthy in our minds, bodies, and societies.

WILDERNESS AND WILL

The beating heart in the clash between Nature conservationists and resource conservationists (resourcists) is wilderness. And the ways of thinking about wilderness in this brawl swirl around *will*. Whose will? Man's will over the land—domesticating, plundering, blighting? Or will of the land—wilderness, Nature? Man's will over animals— taming, yoking, killing? Or self-willed animals—*wildeors*, wildlife?

After forty-four years in the fight for wild things, I've come to believe that conservation boils down to how far and deep Man's will should spread over Earth and its wild things. In the first half of this book, I'll unfold the American tale as the taming and slaughter of wild things. In the latter half, I'll draw the fight over wildlands and wildlife in the twentieth century between Nature conservation and resourcism as a struggle over whether Man's will should break or bring to heel the last wildlands and wildlife.

In our slacker time, when toughness in thought and standards becomes too much to hope for, we often get into a snarl because of badly cast words. Bud Man on his motorized tricycle[1], academic grandees, and just about everybody in between sling the word *wilderness* in sloppy ways, muddying the wrangle about land. One who is not sloppy, historian Roderick Nash, writes that the word *wilderness* comes from the Old English *Wil-deor-ness:* "place of wild beasts."[2] *Wil:* Wild, or willed. *Deor:* Beast. *Ness:* Place, or quality.

In a 1983 talk at the 3rd World Wilderness Conference in Scotland, philosopher Jay Hansford Vest, another thoughtful and careful scholar, also sought the meaning of wilderness in Old English and further back in

---

1   Now on four wheels, I know.
2   Roderick Nash, *Wilderness and the American Mind* (Yale University Press, New Haven, CT 1967), 1-2.

Old Gothonic tongues. He believed that wilderness means "'self-willed land'...with an emphasis on its own intrinsic volition." He interpreted *der* as *of the*, not as coming from *deor*. "Hence, in wil-der-ness, there is a 'will-of-the-land'; and in wildeor, there is 'will of the animal.' A wild animal is a 'self-willed animal'—an undomesticated animal—similarly, wildland is 'self-willed land.'" Vest shows that this willfulness is up against the "controlled and ordered environment which is characteristic of the notion of civilization." These early northern Europeans were not driven to wholly lord over wild things; thus, wilderness "demonstrates a recognition of land in and for itself."[3]

In Old English an animal was a *deor*, which holds on today as *deer*, only one of many deors. After the Norman Conquest, deor was shoved aside by *beast* (Norman French), which was later mostly swapped for *animal* (Latin). Each of these word-steps was a further jump away from the breathing being and thus holds less feeling for it—and for the beat of free life within it. Today, we call someone a "beast" or an "animal" as a slur. With deor, we likely think well of the being; but through beast then animal, we steadily think less of it as it becomes more abstract. Beast and animal show far less heedfulness for worth than does deor; the word wildeor more than deor holds an understanding of the free self of a wild thing. Wildeor is a word we need today if we are to find inborn good in wild things. It acknowledges that another has a freestanding self and calls for us to think well of it, unless we are to show ourselves as unworthy wights.[4] The meaning of wildeor teaches us how we must deal with other Earthlings lest the dominion of Lord Man—now called the Anthropocene by some—harshly prunes the Tree of Life of leaves (species), twigs (genera), and even hefty, outspread limbs (families and

---

3   Jay Hansford C. Vest, "Will of the Land," *Environmental Review* (Winter 1985), 321-329.

4   *Wellthoughten* (thought well of) is Old English for *honored, respected*. *Wight* lingers yet from Old English to mean an *individual,* Man or deor.

orders).[5] Lovers of wild things should take the word wildeor to heart and to tongue. The zeitgeist of this book is that the struggle between wilderness/wildlife conservationists and resourcists in the twentieth century has been over will in Earth. Indeed, the whole tale of Man is over such will. The answer to *whose will?* is not only two sides in the American public lands fight, but the underlying question before Man in its behaviorally modern kind of the last 50,000 years.

It is, I wholeheartedly believe, *the existential question* for the tomorrow of both Man and all life.

Founder of The Wilderness Society Bob Marshall saw will of the land in wilderness. In 1930, he wrote that wilderness has "its entire freedom from the manifestations of human will."[6] Two hundred years ago, George Gordon, Lord Byron, understood this, too:

Where things that own not man's dominion dwell,
And mortal foot hath ne'er or rarely been ... [7]

This self-willed-land meaning of wilderness overshadows all others. Wilderness means land beyond Man's will.[8] Land beyond Man's will is a slap in the face to the arrogance of humanism—elitist or common man, capitalist or socialist, first worlder or third—and for

---

5   Some who overstate how fully Man dominates Earth today say we are therefore in a new geological era, which they call the "Anthropocene" to claim that we are now in control of our world and all it holds. I challenge the Anthropocene ideology—truly, just resourcism repackaged—in the epilogue and in my next book, *True Wilderness.*

6   Robert Marshall, "The Problem Of The Wilderness," *The Scientific Monthly,* February 1930, 145.

7   Quoted in Paul Shepard, *Man in the Landscape: A Historic View of the Esthetics of Nature* (University of Georgia Press, Athens, 2002), 181.

8   Aldo Leopold defined "land" as a community of soils, waters, plants, and animals, in other words as an ecosystem. Aldo Leopold, *A Sand County Almanac* (Oxford University Press, Oxford, UK 1989 [1949]), 204.

the new *über*arrogance of the Anthropoceniacs; for all these snobbish wights, it is also something to fear.[9]

WILDERNESS AND EVOLUTION

More than sixty years ago, Aldo Leopold saw wilderness as the "theater" for the "pageant of evolution."[10] Evolution is self-willed because it is not driven from the outside; nor is it teleological (goal-driven). The land where evolution can happen is self-willed land, outstandingly for big wildeors—grizzly bears, musk oxen, tigers, elephants…. Ecologically, Wilderness Areas are "self-regulating ecosystems" in the words of Michael Soulé, the conservation biologist who may best know and understand wilderness.[11] Self-willed land is another way of saying self-regulating ecosystems.

Among the more thoughtful ecologists of our time were two National Park Service biologists, George Collins and Lowell Sumner. In 1952, they flew into the eastern Brooks Range in Alaska to weigh that little-known landscape of millions of acres without roads or hamlets. Though the eastern Brooks Range never became a National Park, in 1960 after a long back-and-forth it was set up as the nearly 10 million-acre Arctic National Wildlife Range (now Refuge) by President Eisenhower. Aldo Leopold thought Sumner the best field naturalist he knew, but Sumner with his friend Collins was also a wilderness thinker at Leopold's top rung on the ladder. It's a shame neither of them wrote books. After wandering the landscape and talking around the campfire that summer, Sumner and Collins called for northeastern Alaska to

---

9   Among those who think we should now call our geological age the Anthropocene, are some who grieve over how far we've gone in wounding and taking over Earth and all Earthlings, and some who make merry over our new-gained godlike might and lick their lips at being free to remake Earth to their wishes and wants. This latter bunch I call *Anthropoceniacs*—a blend of Anthropocene and maniac.
10   Leopold, *Sand County Almanac*, 199.
11   Michael Soulé, pers. corres.

be set aside as a wilderness—foremost a landscape-big wilderness where evolution could have "freedom to continue, unhindered and forever if we are willing, the particular story of Planet Earth unfolding here... where its native creatures can still have the freedom to pursue their future, so distant, so mysterious."[12] Here they built on Leopold's thought of wilderness as where "the pageant of evolution" played.[13]

The most holy and burning job of conservation, I believe, is to keep the building blocks of evolution, and to set aside big, wild landscapes where that unforeseeable, uncanny tumble and bubble of life can play out unhindered. Evolution as a keystone of conservation has faded from sight since its heyday in the 1950s; we need to bring it back to the fore as the highest good for conservation.

The tie between evolution and self-willed life and land is strong, indeed it is the deepest way of seeing wilderness.

---

12   Roger Kaye, *Last Great Wilderness: The Campaign to Establish the Arctic National Wildlife Refuge* (University of Alaska Press, Fairbanks, 2006), 21. Kaye quotes Lowell Sumner, "Arctic National Wildlife Refuge Address," which Sumner sent to be read at the 25th Anniversary of the Refuge. Sumner, by the way, retired to Glenwood, New Mexico, where it was my great, good luck to be his neighbor.

13   Leopold, *Sand County Almanac*, 199.

CHAPTER 2

The 1964 Wilderness Act: Four Definitions of Wilderness

THE CIVILIZED WORLD'S greatest welcoming for self-willed land came in the 1964 Wilderness Act in the United States.[1] This legislation came at the end of eight years of long listening, coaxing, and rewrites in Congress and in public hearings across the nation. Hikers, horse-packers, canoeists, hunters, anglers, climbers, birders, naturalists, biologists, and even garden clubs boosted it. The Wilderness Society's *Living Wilderness* magazine carefully followed the whole tussle—citizen and agency, industry and Senator, for and against.[2] The Wilderness Society's man in Washington, Howard Zahniser, wrote the first bill in 1956 and the later sixty-five drafts. His literary skill gave the Act the uplifting words and phrases that rest so cozily in our minds for recall.

---

1   Public Law 88-577 (16 U.S. C. 1131-1136) 88th Congress, Second Session, September 3, 1964. Contained in Jay Watson, ed., *The Wilderness Act Handbook Third Edition (revised)* (The Wilderness Society, Washington, D.C. 1998).

2   There is no conservation publication like *The Living Wilderness* today. Wild Earth came out of The Living Wilderness frame but could not grab enough readers to stay in business.

The Wilderness Act holds at least four definitions of Wilderness. I believe that all four are in keeping with the meaning and feeling of self-willed land.[3] I say this even though Zahniser and other backers made what they thought would be their "strongest argument" for Wilderness as "an appeal to the national interest, not an appeal to the intrinsic value of nature, the scientific imperative of protecting wilderness, or a minority's right to enjoy wilderness."[4] I will make this point later in Chapter 13 that oftentimes wilderfolk have ballyhooed what they think is the strongest argument for wild things (the one that will speak to decision makers and opinion shapers) and not what they believe is the deepest good of what they want to save from development or destruction.

Although the Wilderness stewarding agencies have worked tirelessly since 1964 to make quantitative checklists out of these definitions, *feeling* whether or not a landscape is wilderness is more in keeping with how the Wilderness Act was written.

The First Definition: Purpose

The first definition is found in the statement of purpose for the Wilderness Act in Section 2(a):

> *In order to assure that an increasing population, accompanied by expanding settlement and growing mechanization, does not occupy and modify all areas within the United States and its possessions, leaving no lands designated for preservation and protection in their natural condition, it is hereby declared to be the policy of the Congress to secure for the American people of present and future generations the benefits of an enduring resource of wilderness.*

---

3   Better than marking off a checklist of characteristics is having the skill or soul to *feel the self-willed being of land.*

4   James Morton Turner, *The Promise of Wilderness* (University of Washington Press, Seattle, 2012), 28-29.

Here and throughout the struggle for wilderness, the drive has been to keep land from development—from being "spoiled" as conservationists once said. Aldo Leopold, Benton MacKaye, Bob Marshall, and others who cobbled together the Wilderness Area Idea in the 1920s-1930s foremost wanted to shield the backcountry from cars and roads. The title of Paul Sutter's path-finding book shows this well: *Driven Wild: How the Fight Against Automobiles Launched the Modern Wilderness Movement.*[5] The grand old man of conservation historians, Samuel Hays, writes, "[W]ilderness proposals are usually thought of not in terms of perpetuating some 'original' or 'pristine' condition but as efforts to 'save' wilderness areas from development."[6] Wilderness Areas, then, are lands walled off from industrial civilization's wrecking crew: "increasing population…expanding settlement…growing mechanization." Hays wrote against the "wilderness deconstructionist" misunderstanding that Wilderness Areas come out of a romantic/literary wish for a "pristine America." Hays grounded his thinking in having been a grassroots booster of the 1983 Eastern Wilderness Areas Act and having read many newsletters, alerts, and pamphlets from wilderness clubs. Section 2(a) thus teaches wilderness defenders that first of all Wilderness Areas are the best tool to keep lands and waters from being "developed"—or put under the will of Man. Throughout this book, I will further draw out the way wilderfolk have wielded that tool.

THE SECOND DEFINITION: IDEAL

The second definition is the *ideal*:

---

5   Paul S. Sutter, *Driven Wild: How the Fight Against Automobiles Launched the Modern Wilderness Movement* (University of Washington Press, Seattle, 2002).

6   Samuel P. Hays, "The Trouble with Bill Cronon's Wilderness," *Environmental History*, Vol. 1, No. 1, January 1996, 30.

A wilderness, in contrast with those areas where man and his works dominate the landscape, is hereby recognized as an area where the earth and its community of life are untrammeled by man, where man himself is a visitor who does not remain. Section 2(c).

Howard Zahniser of The Wilderness Society, who, as a professional editor and writer, well understood picking the right word, wrote this definition that lines up with self-willed land in both of its key phrases: "untrammeled" and "visitor who does not remain."

Wilderness is where the works of man do not *"dominate* the landscape."[7] Zahniser then chose the little-known word "untrammeled" carefully, and not just because it slips off the tongue sweetly. Others earnestly chewed on Zahnie's ears to get him to switch to another word because they thought *untrammeled* was little known and would be read by many as *untrampled.* It is still often wrongly said as untrampled. Nonetheless, untrammeled stayed in the Act, thanks to Zahnie's knowledge and feeling for words. *Trammel* is a fish net and also a hobble for a horse. As a verb, *trammel* means to hinder the freedom of something.[8] *Untrammeled,* then, means that the will of something is not hobbled; it is self-willed. Untrammeled land is the ground for evolution.

In his writings about exploring unmapped and unknown Alaska from 1929 to 1939, Bob Marshall used *untrammeled* "repeatedly in reference to the Brooks Range," writes Arctic National Wildlife Refuge wilderness specialist Roger Kaye.[9] Polly Dyer, a Seattle wilderness leader still going strong in her nineties, knew the word from Bob

---

7   This does not mean there are no works of Man in the landscape, only that they do not go over the line to "dominate" it.

8   T. F. Hoad, *The Concise Oxford Dictionary of English Etymology* (Oxford University Press, Oxford, UK, 1993), 501.

9   Roger W. Kaye, "The Arctic National Wildlife Refuge: An Exploration of the Meanings Embodied in America's Last Great Wilderness," *Wild Earth,* Vol. 9, No. 4, Winter 1999/2000, 97.

Marshall and gave it to Zahniser as he began writing the Wilderness Act in the mid-1950s. *Untrammeled*, then, might be little known to most, but was well known to the in-crowd of wilderness folks. It was the word Zahniser wanted. Untrammeled land is land whose ecosystems are self-regulating. Moreover, as James Turner shows in his new book, *The Promise of Wilderness*, Zahniser liked untrammeled because it was a fuzzy, not sharp word.[10] Thus, it lent itself more to feeling than to a checklist. In his thorough article on Zahniser's wielding of "untrammeled," longtime Boundary Waters Wilderness champion Kevin Proescholdt quotes Zahnie on why he wanted this word:

> We describe an area as wilderness because of the character it has— not because of a particular use that it serves. A wilderness is an area where the earth and its community of life are untrammeled by man. (Untrammeled—not untrampled—untrammeled, meaning free, unbound, unhampered, unchecked, having the freedom of the wilderness.)[11]

James Turner writes that Zahniser wouldn't be budged because "the point of his definition was its flexibility; he wanted to insure that the wilderness system could protect a broad range of lands, both in the East and in the West."[12] We'll later see (Chapter 20) how the Forest Service would ignore this flexibility and say flatly that there was no Wilderness in the East. Wilderfolk, though, were able to convince Congress that the flexibility of the Act meant to have Eastern areas

---

10   James Morton Turner, *The Promise of Wilderness: American Environmental Politics Since 1964* (University of Washington Press, Seattle, 2012), 35-37. Turner does an outstanding job of showing why Zahniser wanted "untrammeled." *The Promise of Wilderness*, by the way, is the best study of the wilderness struggle after the Wilderness Act (1964). Read it.

11   Kevin Proescholdt, "Untrammeled Wilderness," *Minnesota History*, Fall 2008, 117.

12   Turner, *Promise of Wilderness*, 37.

in the National Wilderness Preservation System. (Zahniser, after all, drafted the Wilderness Act mostly from his Adirondack cabin.)

The last phrase in the untrammeled sentence also gives some folks heartburn: "where man himself is a visitor who does not remain." Men and women are only visitors or wayfarers in Wilderness Areas; we have no permanent settlements. Many kinds of Wilderness Area foes bristle at this banning of dwelling. Philosophy professor J. Baird Callicott, a friend with whom I sometimes spat, has a hissy fit over this "*received* idea of wilderness."[13] However, I believe this lack of long-lasting settlement is the key to wil-der-ness (will of the land). Where humans dwell long, we trammel or fetter the willfulness of the land around our living spots and outward by stamping down our will. How far? This hinges on the population size and technological might of the band.[14]

Think of Wilderness Areas as wild neighborhoods (*earth and its community of life*) and we *Homo sapiens* who go into them as mild, friendly wayfarers wandering through. We should follow the path of

---

13   J. Baird Callicott, "A Critique of and an Alternative to the Wilderness Idea," *Wild Earth*, Winter 1994/95, 54. I deal with such worries and misunderstandings in my forthcoming book True Wilderness.

14   World-renowned field biologist George Schaller once told me that when Amazonian tribes were armed only with blowguns and bows, monkeys could be found half a mile from villages. After the coming of the shotgun, monkeys were not found within five miles of settlements. Jim Tolisano, an ecologist who has worked for the United Nations in many far-off lands, has told me of like shifts in Papua New Guinea. Tropical ecologist John Terborgh tells me the same. See also Clare D. Fitzgibbon, Hezron Mogaka, and John H. Fanshawe, "Subsistence Hunting in Arabuko-Sokoke Forest, Kenya, and Its Effects on Mammal Populations," *Conservation Biology*, October 1995, 1116-1126; Malcolm Hunter, Jr., "Benchmarks for Managing Ecosystems: Are Human Activities Natural?" *Conservation Biology*, June 1996, 695-697; and Bruce Winterhalder and Flora Lu, "A Forager-Resource Population Ecology Model and Implications for Indigenous Conservation," *Conservation Biology*, December 1997, 1354-1364.

"minimum impact" to be good neighbors.[15] We also should be good naturalists so we know who our neighbors are in the wild.[16] Even if we hunt and fish and gather berries for subsistence, we are still wayfarers and not dwellers, notwithstanding how some think Alaskan natives "inhabit" Wilderness Areas.[17]

Etymologically, ecologically, legally, these definitions for wilderness in section 2(c) agree: will of the land is at the heart of wilderness.

THE THIRD DEFINITION: WORKING OR PRACTICAL

The third definition of Wilderness is the *working* or *practical* definition of Wilderness Areas under the Wilderness Act and sets out the entry criteria for candidate areas:

> *An area of wilderness is further defined to mean in this Act an area of undeveloped Federal land retaining its primeval character and influence, without permanent improvements or human habitation, which is protected and managed so as to preserve its natural conditions and which (1) generally appears to have been affected primarily by the forces of nature, with the imprint of man's work substantially unnoticeable; (2) has outstanding opportunities for solitude or a primitive and unconfined type of recreation; (3) has at least five thousand acres of land or is of sufficient size as to make practicable its preservation and use in an unimpaired condition; and (4) may also contain ecological, geological, or other features of scientific, educational, scenic, or historical value.* Section 2(c).

15   I show how being a good neighbor is the root for seeing others as good-in-themselves in Dave Foreman, "Five Feathers for the Cannot Club," in Peter H. Kahn, Jr. and Patricia H. Hasbach, eds., *The Rediscovery of the Wild* (MIT Press, Cambridge, MA, 2013), 181-206.

16   Dave Foreman, "Talking to Wild Things," in Thomas Lowe Fleischner, ed., *The Way of Natural History* (Trinity University Press, San Antonio, 2011), 101-102.

17   Dave Foreman, "Inhabited Wilderness?" *Around the Campfire with Uncle Dave,* Issue 23, July 14, 2009.

Although in keeping with self-willed land ("undeveloped," "primeval character and influence," "without permanent improvements or human habitation," "natural conditions"), this is a practical definition acknowledging that even mostly self-willed land may not be pristine ("generally appears," "affected primarily," "substantially unnoticeable"). Indeed, the word *pristine* is not in the Wilderness Act. As with the word *untrammeled,* the entry criteria are thoughtfully fuzzy and thwart being put into a checklist, although the agencies have done their darnedest to do so.

This down-to-Earth outlook about Wilderness answers the often-silly question, "What is natural?" It understands that *natural* is not a dot on a line against the dot of *unnatural.* Rather, it sees that land falls on a span from wholly yoked by Man's will to altogether self-willed. Somewhere along the way land stops being mostly overlorded by Man; somewhere else, land comes more under the sway of evolutionary will. There is a wide gray swath in between, where Man and wild both throw weight. After the wild comes out on top, the land is self-willed. Because we ground apes have sundry and often scanty understandings of ecology as well as depths of wisdom, we may find the switchover to self-willed land at a bevy of spots on this unnatural-natural line. Yet we still can rightly say, "This landscape or seascape is mostly natural." Let us not fall into the woolly-headed trap of thinking that naturalness is all in our heads, even if we feel it more than quantify it. Wildness *is* out there. A falling tree in a wood needs not a Man's ear to be.

Nonetheless, it can be hard to see what is wild and what is not. Long ago Mencius, the Chinese philosopher, asked:

To these things [logging and then browsing by goats and cattle] *is owing the bare and stripped appearance of the mountain, and when people now see it, they think it was never finely wooded. But is this the nature of the mountain?*

Geographer Clarence Glacken wrote, "Few statements have summed up more lucidly than has this question of Mencius the difficulties of distinguishing a natural from a cultural landscape."[18] Tough though it may be, an ecologically educated eye today is better skilled to see what is the nature of the mountain than are other eyes. Aldo Leopold warned, "One of the penalties of an ecological education is that one lives alone in a world of wounds."[19] Indeed, an ecological education gives our feelings about naturalness bedrock on which to stand.

A good guide for knowing whether land is wild comes from University of Wisconsin geography professor emeritus Thomas Vale. He believes that land can be called "natural, or 'in a wilderness condition' if the fundamental characteristics of vegetation, wildlife, landform, soil, hydrology, and climate are those that result from natural, nonhuman processes, and if these conditions would exist whether or not humans are present."[20] This is no quantitative checklist, however, and it is far from being a pristine goalpost.

Some kinds of wilderness scathers wrongly believe that conservationists see wilderness as pristine (an absolute word). Many anticonservationists and resourcists, so as to thwart setting aside Wilderness Areas, say that lands must be pristine to qualify as Wilderness Areas. Neither gospel is true. Working conservationists have always understood that Wilderness Areas are seldom, and do not have to be, pristine. More than seventy years ago, Leopold said that for a wilderness system to be nationally representative, Wilderness Areas

18   Clarence J. Glacken, "Changing Ideas of the Habitable World," in William L. Thomas, Jr., ed., *Man's Role In Changing The Face Of The Earth* (The University of Chicago Press, 1956), 70.

19   Luna B. Leopold, ed., *Round River: From the Journals of Aldo Leopold* (Oxford University Press, New York, 1953), 165.

20   Thomas R. Vale, "The Myth of the Humanized Landscape: An Example from Yosemite National Park," *Natural Areas Journal*, Vol. 18 (3), 1998, 232.

would have to vary in size and degree of wildness.[21] Senator Frank Church of Idaho, who was the floor manager for the 1964 Wilderness Act, said, "This is one of the great promises of the Wilderness Act, that we can dedicate formerly abused areas where the primeval scene can be restored by natural forces, so that we can have a truly National Wilderness Preservation System."[22]

No land or water is now pristine—utterly free of Man's impact. This conservationists have known for at least seventy years, although wilderness bashers such as Michael Nelson, Charles Mann, Emma Marris, and Peter Kareiva each seem to think that it is a new insight that just went off like a light bulb in their head alone. By so thinking, they show how little they know or understand about the last one hundred years of defending wilderness. Oh, it is irksome to word-tangle with those who don't even know that they don't know what they are bickering about.

In Section 2(c) of the law, we find two definitions of wilderness twined about each other. One is a definition of a wayfarer's experience in Wilderness Areas ("appears," "unnoticeable," "solitude," "a primitive and unconfined type of recreation," "educational, scenic, or historical value"). The other is an ecological definition ("undeveloped," "primeval character and influence," "forces of nature," "ecological," "scientific"). These ecological meanings in the Wilderness Act belie the time and again rap that the Act and the National Wilderness Preservation System made by it are only about scenery and recreation. Even some conservationists and scientists have scolded the Wilderness Act for an overwhelming tilt to recreation. We must understand that recreation is not the only end of the Act, although federal agencies have often managed Wilderness Areas as if it were, and have mostly picked lands

---

21 Quoted by James Buckley, "Eastern Wilderness Areas Act," *Congressional Record Senate,* January 11, 1973.

22 Hearing Before The Subcommittee On Public Lands Of The Committee On Interior And Insular Affairs United States Senate On S. 316, February 21, 1973, U.S. Government Printing Office, Washington: 1973, 49.

for Wilderness designation because of their non-motorized recreational draw. On the other hand, Wilderness Areas are the best spots for recreation.

The two things we need to learn from Section 2(c) are that Wilderness Areas do not need to be pristine, and that the ecological worth of Wilderness Areas is well acknowledged along with experiential values. Ecological protection and recovery are underlying goals of the Wilderness Act.

THE FOURTH DEFINITION: CARETAKING

This definition comes with a yardstick for caretaking land after it comes under the Wilderness Act:

> *Except as specifically provided for in this Act, and subject to existing private rights, there shall be no commercial enterprise[23] and no permanent road within any wilderness area designated by this Act and except as necessary to meet minimum requirements for the administration of the area for the purposes of this Act (including measures required in emergencies involving the health and safety of persons within the area), there shall be no temporary road, no use of motor vehicles, motorized equipment or motorboats, no landing of aircraft, no other form of mechanical transport, and no structure or installation within any such area.* Section 4(c).

Elsewhere, the Wilderness Act makes room for a handful of exceptions to the above prohibitions, such as firefighting, rescue, livestock grazing, and prospecting for minerals until 1984, all of which were political compromises that backers of the Wilderness Act had to swallow before a few Western members of Congress would go

23 This banning of commercial enterprise includes commercial timber cutting, but not guiding and outfitting.

along with passage. Thus, the Wilderness Act is somewhat flawed and sometimes at odds with itself.

It is this fourth definition that has legal weight—not for how lands must be *before* being set aside under the Wilderness Act, but how they must be cared for *after* being set aside under the Wilderness Act. If more folks understood this before-and-after cleavage, there would be far less muddled thinking about Wilderness Areas.

The use prohibitions try to keep the land untrammeled (self-willed). They are stronger than the entry criteria in Section 2(c). For one, the Wilderness Act does not say that *candidate* Wilderness Areas must be roadless or unlogged, but Section 4(c) holds that they must be kept as roadless *after* they are put in the National Wilderness Preservation System. In other words, earlier roads, if any, must be shut down and no further logging may be done after designation of a landscape as Wilderness. There are many once-roaded or earlier-logged wildlands now in the National Wilderness Preservation System—even some of the classic big Wilderness Areas in the West.[24] This after-designation, stewardship definition lends itself to a checklist much more than do the other three definitions. Rightly so.

If what wilderness means and what the Wilderness Act says were carefully and truthfully worded in clashes, many misunderstandings about wilderness should melt away much as Bob Marshall's south-facing snowbank in June. However, muddying the meaning of wilderness is often not due to lack of knowledge, but is a witting dodge by anticonservationists and even agency resourcists.

The brawl over conservation is at heart about whether we can abide self-willed land. The Wilderness Act says we can and must.

---

24   I go into this in depth in *Rewilding North America*. Dave Foreman, *Rewilding North America* (Island Press, Washington, DC, 2004), 192-197.

CHAPTER 3

Scalping the Land and its Theology

TODAY'S GOTTERDAMMERUNG FOR WILD THINGS began at least 50,000 years ago when skilled Stone Age hunters of our species spread out of Africa into the new (to them) lands of South Asia, Australia, Europe, East Asia, Siberia, America, and sea islands.[1] Likewise, in my lifetime, the Forest Service's ransacking of big woods with trees hundreds of years old and, since 1994, the Jacobin-right raid on conservation law are within a long American tradition, one we can track back to British fishermen off the Georges Banks years before Columbus.

I call the squandering and slaughtering of wildland and wildlife "landscalping," for it scalps the land and the wild things living there as a flint (or steel) knife scalps a skull. By following the saga of landscalping and by digging into the feelings and folklore in which it is tightly rooted,

---

1   In *Rewilding North America* (Island Press, Washington, DC, 2004), I
     scroll out the long, gory tale of how we Men have wreaked an extinction
     slaughter on the Tree of Life for 50,000 years. *Gotterdammerung*, from
     Wagner's operas, literally means *twilight of the gods,* in other words a
     catastrophic collapse so bad it has no precedent. To me, it bests names
     the unspeakably grisly mass extinction we are inflicting on Earth.

we can better understand today's anticonservation gaggle. In later chapters, we will see how two backlashes to landscalping have bloomed, both hinged on the public lands and the public ownership of wildlife. These backlashes were *Nature Conservation* (such as the Sierra Club and the New Mexico Wilderness Alliance) and *Resource Conservation,* better-named *Resourcism* (such as the United States Forest Service and most state game and fish agencies[2]). In my earlier book, *Take Back Conservation,* I set out how conservation and resourcism are not the same. Here in *The Great Conservation Divide,* I will go deeper into that cleavage. In this chapter and the rest of Part I, though, I will spread out the background for understanding conservation and resourcism by looking at the Weltanschauung behind landscalping and then at the side-by-side tales of the beginning of American public lands and the great landscalping binge in the Frontier Century from 1785 to 1890.

Princeton professor Lee Clark Mitchell frames our tale in the preface to his worthy, but overlooked, book, *Witnesses to a Vanishing America,* "Propelled across the continent by notions of 'rugged individualism,' 'course of empire,' 'inexhaustible resources,' and 'manifest destiny,' pioneer Americans soon discovered that such slogans masked the other side of progress: empire building required the destruction of a wilderness."[3]

THE MYTH OF SUPERABUNDANCE

What did they see?

And what did they think about what they saw?

I tussle with these questions as I shuffle through the fallen leaves of my family tree.[4] I wonder about them as I look out over a gray

2   Though some state game and fish agencies come frightfully close to landscalping. Those of Idaho and South Dakota come to mind.
3   Lee Clark Mitchell, *Witnesses to a Vanishing America: The Nineteenth-Century Response* (Princeton University Press, Princeton, NJ, 1981), xii.
4   Thanks to my late cousin, Elaine Dodson Thomas, for gathering the tales about my mother's forebears and giving it to the Dodson family in

Chesapeake Bay from Maryland's Calvert Cliffs State Park. Fall flocks of ducks fly in from the north. I tease at them as I seek scattered plots of big woods along Virginia's Rappahannock River.

My father's first forefather in the raw English settlements of the New World was Robert Tyler, who died in 1674 in Calvert County, Maryland. I wonder how he saw this fresh new world. What did he think about the wealth of the Bay—the foot-long oysters stretching in beds for miles, the fish so thick they could be scooped out in baskets, the ducks blotting out a fall sun?

First in my mother's line in the New World was John Crawford, who was born about 1600 in Ayrshire, Scotland, to a noble family and, as a cavalier and foe to Cromwell, came with his young son William to Jamestown, Virginia, in 1643. It seems that he was hung as a would-be leader of Bacon's Rebellion in 1676. Charles Dodson was another early settler on my mother's side. Born in Scotland in 1649, he came to the tidewater of Virginia sometime before 1670 and farmed along the western bank of the Rappahannock River—only thirty or forty miles away from Tyler. What did he think about the big woods? The trees that rose and rose before their first branches? Trees greater than any he believed could be as a boy in Scotland? Trees so big that it took the linked arms of three or four men to reach about the trunks?

What did they think about a Nature so big, so far beyond their mind's eye on the other side of the Atlantic?

Their thoughts have not come down the kinship line with their names. And so I wonder. My forebears came to a world far from the cutover woodlots of the British Isles, far from the sheep-packed fields, far from wolfless and bearless hills and bergs.[5] If we walk these

---

1993. My aunt Betsy Shields gave me her work on the Foreman kindred before her death. My aunt Barbara MacDonald has shared what she has gathered on the Crawford side of my mother's family.

5   Forsooth, the wolf lingered in the fastness of Scotland until 1743. However, they were so few by the 1600s, the British Isles were wolfless and bearless in whole. Bears had been gone from Britain for over one

backpaths, these seaside Atlantic paths dim and misty from more than three hundred and fifty years' time, we find thoughts and feelings about the land that are with us still, that overbear our land and wildlife wrangles today.

Maybe the first take on the New World was amazement at the wealth of wood, fish, game, and farmland. The Western Europe from which the first explorers and later settlers sailed to the New World was an old world—overcrowded, overgrazed, overlogged, overfarmed, overfished; it was a land fearing a stark resource shortage with an energy crisis, a land whose carrying capacity had been overshot—a land and a civilization waning owing to land squandering and overpopulation. This is why the first tales back from the edge of the world were fat with the fullness of the new land and sea.

John Cabot, on his first voyage of exploration for Great Britain in 1497, was keen to bring back tidings on the mighty white pines—so fit for ships' masts—which he found.[6] But before Cabot, before Columbus, no later than 1480, British fishermen sailing out of the western harbor of Bristol had yearly brought back whopping hauls of cod and other fish from the fat waters off what was to become Canada.[7] After his 1497 sailing, Cabot wrote that the Grand Banks were so "swarming with fish [that they] could be taken not only with a net but in baskets let down [and weighted] with a stone." French explorer Jacques Cartier in 1535 found that the St. Lawrence River "is the richest in every kind of fish that anyone remembers ever having seen or heard of."[8] Feeding on the wealth of cod and other fish were endless throngs of seals, whales, and seabirds. Among them was the great auk, a big, flightless bird much like a penguin (but not near kin at all—penguins are found only in the

thousand years. Clive Ponting, *A Green History Of The World* (St. Martin's Press, New York, 1991), 162-163.

6   Carl O. Sauer, *Northern Mists* (University of California Press, Berkeley, 1968), 41.

7   Sauer, *Northern Mists*, 57.

8   Farley Mowat, *Sea of Slaughter* (Bantam Books, New York, 1986), 166.

southern hemisphere). A French sailor in the 1530s wrote of the great auks on their nesting grounds, "This island is so exceedingly full of birds that all the ships of France might load a cargo of them without anyone noticing that any had been removed. We took away two barque loads to add to our stores."[9]

One hundred years later, south in Massachusetts Bay Colony, the Reverend Francis Higginson wrote in 1630, "The aboundance of Sea-Fish are almost beyond beleeving, and sure I should scarce have beleeved it except I had seene it with mine owne eyes." William Wood wrote, "If I should tell you how some have killed a hundred geese in a week, fifty ducks at a shot, forty teals at another, it may be counted impossible though nothing more certain." (A "shot" was not one firing of a blunderbuss, but hunting from one spot.)[10]

The overwhelming wealth of tall timber, fish, seabirds, and ducks drove the making of the Myth of Superabundance. But another, in even thicker-crammed swarms, left the settlers from Massachusetts to Carolina speechless and benumbed. It was the embodiment of Superabundance. Historian William Cronon writes, "Nothing so astonished Europeans about New England as the semiannual flights of the passenger pigeons. John Josselyn [1675] measured their numbers in the 'millions of millions,' and spoke of flocks 'that to my thinking had neither beginning nor ending, length nor breadth, and so thick that I could see no Sun.'"[11]

Linger here for a little while. Read the above again. Put your feet up and head back. Then close your eyes and through your mind's eye see what Josselyn saw in his eyes. The flight of the pigeon. Noonday dusk beneath their wings. A quilt of flying birds over your world and beyond what edges you could see. What a mindboggling sight! What

9   Mowat, *Sea of Slaughter*, 23. It took 300 years, but enough "barque loads" were taken and the great auk was gone from Earth.

10   William Cronon, *Changes in the Land* (Hill and Wang, New York, 1983), 22-23.

11   Cronon, *Changes in the Land*, 23.

a fright when first you beheld it. Ahh, but did you smack your lips over the wild wealth when you saw the pigeons fly again?

Aldo Leopold once wrote about how a landscape or any kind of wild neighborhood had its "numenon," a living being that was the soul of that land.[12] If the Great Eastern Forest thick with chestnut, oak, hickory, beech, and other mast-bearing trees had a numenon or soul it was unquestionably Josselyn's passenger pigeon. That storm of life gave being and definition to the big woods from Atlantic shores to the other side of the Father of Waters. In other words, the passenger pigeon was the keystone of keystone species in the Mixed Mesophytic Forest (to call it by its ecological handle) of eastern temperate North America. It was its voice, its heart, its maker, and caretaker.

Cronon also writes that these early New Englanders could see as many as one hundred deer while walking a mile during spring and that the deer were so many that they could be hunted throughout the year.[13]

As for the forests, in 1632, Thomas Morton wrote of spruce trees in northern New England that were twenty feet about.[14] Cronon says of the white pine: "The average height of a mature grove might be well over a hundred feet, with a few trees as much as five feet in diameter and 250 feet in height."[15] Think of that: New England with pines almost as tall as the tallest Douglas-firs in Oregon and Washington.

Farther south, where the Tylers and Dodsons settled, the natural wealth was no less. Captain John Smith bragged, "We had more Sturgeon than could be devoured by Dog and Man."[16] In 1633, the Calverts of Maryland wrote, "Of birds diversely colored there are infinite. Eagles,

12   Aldo Leopold, *A Sand County Almanac* (Oxford University Press, New York, 1949), 137.
13   Cronon, *Changes in the Land*, 24.
14   Cronon, *Changes in the Land*, 25-26.
15   Cronon, *Changes in the Land*, 30.
16   Peter Matthiessen, *Wildlife In America* (Viking, New York, 1987), 55. *Wildlife in America* is the best overview of the slaughter of wildlife in the United States.

bitterns, swans, geese, partridge, ducks...and the like."[17] White-tailed deer were thick in Virginia and Maryland; woodland bison and eastern elk roamed east of the Appalachians from New York to Georgia.

Scattered between the early settlements (often found on cleared Indian fields left empty after epidemic disease brought by the earliest European seafarers in the Americas) and stretching west seemingly forever, was a temperate deciduous forest beyond my forebears' dreams and without a match in all the world. More species of trees grew in Virginia and Maryland than in Europe from Ireland to the Urals. And what trees! They were Brobdingnagian in those days. The tulip poplar grew over 200 feet tall and more than twenty feet about. The American chestnut spread its great limbs over a quarter of an acre (think of four trees shading a whole football field). Sycamores were thick-trunked and rose high along rivers, mighty oaks climbed the Piedmont to the Blue Ridge where tall white pines, spruce, and fir came down the heights from the north. No wonder the tale grew of how a squirrel could run from the Chesapeake west 750 miles to the Mississippi River without ever laying a foot on the ground.

Game. Furs. Fish. Fat land for farming. Firewood. Lumber. Room to stretch. New World resources staggered the minds of Europeans. They were without end. They were "inexhaustible." There was always more land, more fish, more wood, more game just up the river, just over the hill, just a little farther out to sea. Trap out one beaver-river and head over to the next one.

There was always a next one.

The Myth of Superabundance became one of the European settlers' earliest, most unshakable, most tightly-clutched-to-the-chest beliefs. It became Gospel. To doubt it was un-American. Maybe even unGodly. It is with us still. Listen to the doctors of economics in our great universities. Listen to the Oregon logger. Listen to the statesmen in the well of the United States Senate.

17   Matthiessen, *Wildlife in America*, 56.

Disbelieving in limits is a mark of immaturity. The Myth of Superabundance was thereby bewitching to European settlers. Their lack of responsibility for their deeds—whether overfishing, careless landtilth that withered the land, killing Indians to take their land—wrapped in a twofold swirl about the belief that resources were endless in the New World. It was a spellbinding song of freedom, of the freedom to become and stay a spoilt two-year-old child again and forever.

THE MYTH OF SATAN'S KINGDOM

Even as the Tylers, Dodsons, and Crawfords were drawn to this wealth of Nature, did they also come to fear it? From New England to the Tidewater, Indian tribes, grown more and more embittered by the overbearing English, began to fight back from beyond the edge of white settlement. (The Pamunkey Indians killed David Crawford, son of James, in 1710.) Slinking through the deep woods with all the good animals (meat and fur) were gray wolves, cougars (called catamounts in New England and panthers in Virginia), bobcats, black bears, and rattlesnakes. Clearing the land was hard, backbreaking work. In New England the ground was rocky, the soil stingy, the winters long and withering. I do not know what my great-great-great-great-great-great-great-great-great grandfathers and –mothers thought, but I can guess from what other settlers of their time wrote.

The overall frontier fear of wilderness slithered out of the minds of New England's Puritans, who came to see the howling wilderness as Satan's Kingdom on Earth. In 1662, Michael Wigglesworth scratched out in verse:

a waste and howling wilderness,
Where none inhabited
but hellish fiends, and brutish men
That Devils worshipped

Wigglesworth wrote that "the dark and dismal Western woods" were "the Devil's Den."[18] Fear was becoming loathing.

Cotton Mather, the Puritan divine known for fanning the Salem witch madness, crafted the harebrained fears of superstitious settlers into a theology that saw North America as Satan's stronghold and the natives as "not merely heathens but active disciples of the Devil," writes Roderick Nash.[19] The Puritans also pulled North American wildlife into this Hell-spawned pantheon, both living—wolves and snakes— and make-believe—dragons and "fiery flying serpents."[20]

This bogeyman take on the wildwood is another mark of immaturity—akin to a child's dreaming up monsters under the bed. (Think of the Puritans as Gary Larson's fat little flat-topped kid wide- eyed and sweating in bed as fiends beneath plot the gruesome ripping of his flesh.) Listen to Cotton Mather in 1707, "the *Evening Wolves,* the rabid and howling *Wolves* of the *Wilderness* [which] would make... Havock among you, *and not leave the Bones till the morning.*"[21] Never mind that there is no case of wolves killing any New England settlers, and no well-founded tales of healthy, wild wolves killing anyone in the United States. Nonetheless, as Peter Matthiessen writes, in 1630 "the Massachusetts Bay Company established the first New World bounty system" on wolves.[22] This was but a handful of years after the first European foot had stepped onto Plymouth Rock. Virginia swiftly followed.

Overwrought fear of slavering wildeors and fear of village witches both came from a fear of things beyond human will, and both came from immature, childish minds. The Salem witch trials were as much

---

18   Roderick Nash, *Wilderness and the American Mind* (Yale University Press, New Haven, CT, 1967), 36.

19   Nash, *Wilderness and the American Mind,* 36.

20   Nash, *Wilderness and the American Mind,* 29.

21   Nash, *Wilderness and the American Mind,* 29.

22   Matthiessen, *Wildlife in America,* 57.

about fear and loathing of wilderness—self-willed land—as they were about witchcraft.

With this fearful outlook on the North American wilderness, the settlers stormed into the bloody takeover of the wild with all the fire their faith could enkindle. Edward Johnson in 1654 wrote that "the admirable Acts of Christ" had transformed Boston from "hideous Thickets" where "Wolfes and Beares nurst up their young" into "streets full of Girles and Boys sporting up and downe."[23]

Mather's theology gave a blessing to—no, it roared for, prayed for, lusted for—the takeover and taming of the new continent and the ruthless killing of its native Men and wildeors. Such theology stirred a holy crusade to break the wilderness to the will of God and Man, to wrest it out of the hands of Satan, Indians, and wildness and yield it unto the fold of the godly. Puritan fear and loathing was the grandfather of Manifest Destiny's juggernaut against the wilderness.

Delving ever deeper into the great wildwood over the next two hundred years, the settlers believed that the dark, gloomy glades of endless tall trees had to be hewn down—on two grounds, utilitarian and spiritual. First, the forest had to be opened to let in sunlight and grow crops; and, second, because the trees harbored savages, wildeors, dragons, and Satanic thoughts and lusts, the wildwood had to be cast down in a holy-ghostly way as well.

After the War of Independence, the setting up of the public domain—millions of acres of federal land open for the taking west of the Alleghenies—let Americans take over and take down that wildwood all the way to the Pacific.

---

23   Nash, *Wilderness and the American Mind*, 37.

CHAPTER 4

Oh, Give Me Land

WHILE SPAIN TOOK OVER the New World for the Three Gs (God, Gold, and Glory), settlers from England, Scotland, Holland, Sweden, and Germany came to North America for religious freedom, economic opportunity, and…LAND.

Listen to the cowboy sing the song of America:

Oh, give me land,
Lots of land,
Under starry skies above.
Don't fence me in.

Don't Fence Me In would be more befitting as a national anthem than *The Star-spangled Banner* or any other song. It uncloaks the American soul.

Let me tell a little story about land and the American soul. My grandma never cussed in her life, never took the Lord's name in vain.

Not even mild little oaths such as "Good Lord!" or "Oh, for God's sake." No, what I heard her say was "Lands sakes alive," "Good Lands," "Oh, for Land's sake," "Dear Lands," and "Oh, my Lands!" The way I heard these exclamations, "Land" sounded capitalized just as "God" or "Lord" would be. Slipping in *Land* to stand for *God* or *Lord,* says much about how we yearned to have land of our own. I know other pious folk from a long line of American farmers said the same things. What an underlining to our tie to land of our own.

LAND HUNGER

We came with a hunger for land. This hunger for land—and the freedom to slake that hunger—is at the heart of the American national selfhood. We wanted land to clear, crop, build homes, rear families. We saw land as a way to pile up wealth. For many, there was an even deeper hunger for land—for the freedom to roam, to not be hemmed in, and to get away from lords, kings, and sheriffs. All these hungers were fed by an oddly American hallmark—that of *public land.* Open land. Up-for-grabs land. Federal government land. The way the United States brought into being the thought and work of public land shaped our settlement layout from the Alleghenies to the Pacific and led to the flaying of the land. On the other hand, it later bequeathed to us the world's best conservation birthright and lore. For the first hundred years of public land—the Frontier Century, the aim was to give it away and sell it so as to build the nation and, in smoky backrooms, to make the politically mighty wealthy. Only in the second century of public land did a more greathearted belief—that of keeping and stewarding land in public ownership for the good of all Americans—come into being.

To understand today's land, water, and wildlife clashes, we must go back to the beginnings of public land, back even before the United States.

At the end of the Seven Years' War in 1763,[1] King George III decreed that his subjects could not settle west of the Appalachians. This royal order was meant to stop the headstrong, out-of-hand spread of settlers west where their ties and loyalty to the crown frayed and then unraveled more and more. George III was pretty much setting aside the trans-Appalachian country for Indian tribes. Notwithstanding the King's bidding and the threat of Shawnees, Miamis, and Cherokees shielding their land, my Scottish and English forebears on the far-western edge of European society looked hungrily over the mountains at the land and the freedom, and at the pigeons, bears, buffalo, and elk. Even more hungrily, maybe, George Washington and other land speculators looked west to the buckraking happenstance of selling land to Dodsons and Foremans. As historian Louis M. Hacker has written:

The west was not opened up by the hardy frontiersman; it was opened up by the land speculator who preceded even the Daniel Boones of the wilderness. When the young Washington surveyed the lands around the waters of the upper Potomac in 1748 he was doing so as the representative of a great colonial landlord and as the scion of a rich land-owning family; and when he bought up soldier bounty claims in the decade following he was only pursuing the same line of interest already marked out by the Fairfaxes, the Lees, and the Mercers.[2]

Then, in 1774, came the Quebec Act, setting up civil government for the "French-speaking, Roman Catholic inhabitants of Canada and the Illinois country. The law extended the boundaries of Quebec to include the French communities between the Ohio and Mississippi rivers. It also granted political rights to Roman Catholics and recognized the

1   Called the French and Indian War in Britain's North American colonies.
2   Louis M. Hacker "The First American Revolution," (1935) in Esmond Wright, ed., *Causes and Consequences of the American Revolution* (Quadrangle Books, Chicago, 1966), 123.

legality of the Roman Catholic Church within the enlarged province," wrote the authors of *A History of the United States to 1877.*[3] This land between the rivers (now Illinois, Indiana, Ohio, Michigan, and much of Wisconsin and Minnesota) was seen by the thirteen colonies as their natural path for booming growth. Indeed, some of the seaboard colonies had earlier been granted land claims by the crown in the land now given to Quebec.

Shutting off the west to frontiersmen and land speculators was enough for dashed-hope anger, but among the colonists were many also given to paranoid conspiracy theories, who saw this backing away from deviling Catholics as a sign that the Anglican and Catholic churches were coming back together after a two-hundred-year-old split, and that "a plot was afoot in London for subjecting Americans to the tyranny of the Pope."[4] Remember this. A dark American thread stretches all the way from 1774 to Oklahoma City and Timothy McVeigh—as well as to today's hick fears that conservation groups are agents of the New World Order and part of a plot for fettering Americans to the tyranny of the United Nations.[5] And, yes, Cliven Bundy and the treasonous militia goons drawn to his teapot revolution are the latest end of the unbroken thread reaching back to 1774 and before.

For both the colonial upper crust and the backwoods pioneers, the ban on western settlement became one of the "repeated injuries and usurpations, all having in direct object the establishment of an absolute tyranny over these States,"[6] which led to independence and war. Public-lands scholar Bern Shanks writes in his classic study of the public lands, *This Land Is Your Land,* "Personal freedom, especially freedom

---

3   T. Harry Williams, Richard N. Current, and Frank Fiedel, *A History of the United States to 1877* (Alfred A. Knopf, New York, 1965), 134-135.

4   Williams, Current, and Fiedel, *A History of the United States to 1877,* 134-135.

5   In *The Nature Haters* I'll show how this paranoid strain today shores up the anticonservation movement and the Tea Party.

6   Thomas Jefferson, John Adams, and Benjamin Franklin, *The Declaration of Independence.*

to use frontier land, was an important issue in the Revolution."[7] The Continental Congress came to see the western land as wealth to fund the war and to pay off the growing national debt. Western land was brought into play to spur enlistments: 100 acres to a private, 500 for a colonel. British soldiers were promised land west of the Alleghenies if they deserted.

THE NORTHWEST ORDINANCE

Following the War of Independence, seven of the thirteen states held sweeping colonial land claims between the Appalachians and the Mississippi River. Shanks writes that the six states without land claims, led by Maryland, "feared the size and potential economic power of the larger states" like Virginia. Maryland "boldly argued that frontier lands were won with the 'common blood and treasure of the thirteen colonies'" and would not sign the Articles of Confederation unless the lands were ceded to the new federal government. When Virginia gave up its lands south of the Ohio in 1784, "it put two conditions on the gift. First, western public lands were to be considered a common source of wealth for the use and benefit of all the nation's people. Second, the ceded territory would eventually be divided up into states and admitted to the union with standing equal to the original states. This agreement was codified in the Northwest Ordinance," writes Shanks.[8]

Virginia had earlier ceded its lands north of the Ohio River to the Confederation, in 1781. Other states followed in handing over their western land claims. These were the first public lands of the United States.

This "public domain" stretching from the Appalachians to the Mississippi came to 370,000 square miles, or 236,825,000 acres.

---

7   Bernard Shanks, *This Land Is Your Land* (Sierra Club Books, San Francisco, 1984), 21.

8   Shanks, *This Land*, 22.

Shanks writes, "Land, not paper or laws, was the instrument to unite the nation. ... It was the only tangible source of federal wealth and power."[9]

Congress passed the Land Ordinance of 1785 to handle sale of the new public domain. Harvard historian Frederick Merk wrote in his *History of the Westward Movement*, "A first principle was that survey must precede sale in any federal wilderness." A north-south, east-west grid, in "townships" of six miles square (making up thirty-six square miles or "sections") was laid out through miles of wild, heretofore unmapped land. The sections (square miles) were regularly numbered in each township. One section in each township was set aside for public schools. Merk believed that this law "was one of the most important and admirable measures ever enacted by an American legislature."[10]

This township-and-section surveying pattern was used for nearly all the land later brought into the Union. While it brought an even and well-thought-out way to set down land lines for private ownership, it pounded an abstract grid of Man-will into that land, a grid that paid no mind to the natural lay of the land—rivers, watersheds, mountains, or swatches of vegetation. In its Enlightenment abstraction, in its cold rationality, its mathematical Weltanschauung, the Ordinance of 1785 meant to quell *wil-der-ness*, to overcome once self-willed land and all that it held. It was the first step for taming wilderness and for making it unwelcome for wildeors. Nature was boxed by Man with tidy, square lines on paper; the corners of those paper squares were hacked with hatchets into "witness trees" on the land. The township surveying, to be sure, made it more straightforward to sell land, and to carefully tally who owned what.

In 1967, Paul Shepard wrote that "the American land survey was the world's most extensive example of the rationalized landscape" and

9   Shanks, *This Land*, 23.
10   Frederick Merk, *History of the Westward Movement* (Alfred A. Knopf, New York, 1980), 102-103.

"a uniform, mechanical treatment of the universe...." He called the survey grid "Topophobia."[11]

After many years of careful looking at National Forest and topographic maps with their neat, little squares, I have this section layout in my head. It shows how deeply an abstract overlay can cut, how strongly it can shape the way we see land. Now, when you fly over the Great Plains, you see the section squares in the land as fence lines and roads and often as different hues from plowing and irrigation and sundry crops. Likewise, over Montana you may see the straight lines of square-mile clearcuts slicing up and down mountainsides—the mark of private timberlands from railroad grants checkerboarded in the National Forests. But for me, and I think others who have looked so long at National Forest maps, our minds project the section lines even onto wild, rugged landscapes. The Ordinance of 1785 has become a *frame* embedded in our minds.

---

11   Paul Shepard, *Man in the Landscape: A Historic View of the Esthetics of Nature* (University of Georgia Press, Athens, 2002), 234.

CHAPTER 5

Making the Public Lands

LAND SPECULATION

While prostitution may the oldest profession in the world, land speculation is the oldest profession in the United States and in the British colonies before it. The earliest colonies were set up on land grants given to darlings of the court, such as Sir Walter Raleigh. We have a romantic folk-memory of homesteaders building a nation out of the public domain, but, warned Professor Merk, "The chief beneficiaries... were the land speculators who later sold to settlers....They were usually a jump ahead of settlers in buying up the choicest locations." In Kentucky's Blue Grass country, Robert Morris, bankroller of the American Revolution, owned 600,000 acres, and the father of Chief Justice Marshall had 140,000 acres.[1]

Farther south, land sales were even shadier. Merk wrote:

1   Frederick Merk, *History of the Westward Movement* (Alfred A. Knopf, New York, 1980), 84.

In Georgia… the greatest speculation and greatest legislative scandal in American history took place. Practically all the state's western land in what is now Alabama and Mississippi—about 35 million acres, much of it exceptionally rich—was in 1795 sold by the legislature to four land-speculating companies for the sum of $500,000. Every member of the legislature except one had been bribed to make the sale.

Although the next legislature revoked the sale, the U.S. Supreme Court turned down the revocation. "Chief Justice John Marshall, who had a strongly developed sense of the rights of private property and who was a land speculator on a big scale, led the Court in ruling… that Georgia could not revoke a sale once made…."[2]

Thus was set the framework for dealing out the public domain.[3]

MANIFEST DESTINY

The growing swarms of new Americans piling up on the Atlantic coast, the untiring tramp west, the hunger for more land, endless game for the shooting, and elbow room beyond the sight of your neighbor's chimney smoke led to the Louisiana Purchase and then to a new national theology. This theology drew deeply on the Myth of Superabundance and on the religious drive to civilize the wilderness; it was a theology that lay bare God's wish for the United States: Manifest Destiny.

Given the name by a New York newspaper editor, John L. O'Sullivan, in 1845, Manifest Destiny meant that "the United States was preordained to control all of North America." Williams, Current, and Fiedel wrote in *History of the United States:*

2   Merk, *Westward Movement,* 115.

3   Although we should be aware of the historical truth of land speculation in the United States, it is unfair to use it to smear the whole character of Washington and other signers of the Declaration of Independence who happened to be speculators.

There is significance in the mechanistic implications of Manifest Destiny. Expansion, supposedly, was not just something that human beings willed; it was created by certain forces, historical, geographical, cultural, beyond human control. Although expansion could be defended logically... it did not, being partly superhuman, particularly need justification.[4]

I think this is a bright, true insight into American hallowed-belief, and shows how greatly historical determinism helped to shape us.

In 1874, William Gilpin, the stock Western boomer, wrote, "The American realizes that 'Progress is God.' He clearly recognizes and accepts the *continental* mission of his country and his people. His faith is impregnably fortified by this vision of power, unity, and forward motion."[5]

Only a little more than one hundred and fifty years after Cotton Mather preached that it was our job as Christians to wrest the Berkshire wilderness out of the hands of Satan, our nation came to understand that God wanted us to take over all the way to the Pacific. Keep Gilpin's thunder in mind; it is a window into the thinking of landscalpers and resourcists who later came, yea, who are with us yet today.

THE LOUISIANA PURCHASE

However, after the War of Independence, the United States only reached to the Mississippi River. Spain had Florida and the Gulf Coast, thereby taking in the mouth of the Mississippi at New Orleans. Spain also claimed all the land west of the Mississippi to the Pacific Ocean, although Great Britain and Russia also had claims on the northern

---

4   T. Harry Williams, Richard N. Current, and Frank Fiedel, *A History of the United States to 1877* (Alfred A. Knopf, New York, 1965), 515-516.

5   William Gilpin, *Mission of the North American People, Geographical, Social, and Political,* 2nd rev. ed. (Lippincott, Philadelphia, 1874), 40, quoted in Mark Stoll, *Protestantism, Capitalism, and Nature in America* (University of New Mexico Press, Albuquerque, 1997), 120.

Pacific Coast above San Francisco Bay. By the time of American independence, Spain had had settlements in New Mexico for nearly two hundred years (though with a twelve-year gap after being shoved out by the Pueblo Revolt in 1680). Spanish missions, presidios (military outposts), and pueblos (colonial settlements) had been dropped into Arizona, California, and Texas throughout the 1700s.[6]

France had earlier claimed the Louisiana country, stretching from New Orleans west of the Mississippi to the headwaters of the Missouri River in what is now Montana. In 1763, after France's loss in the Seven Years' War, Great Britain took Canada (Quebec), and Spain took Louisiana. In 1800, however, Napoleon strong-armed Spain to hand back all of Louisiana to France. This was hush-hush as Napoleon wanted no one to know that France was back in the New World. In 1802, President Jefferson learned of the deal. That fall, the Spanish doing France's bidding in New Orleans shut the port to American shipping (notwithstanding words in the 1795 Pinckney Treaty). The American West thus "faced economic ruin, for there was no feasible route by which they could carry their crops directly over the mountains to the ports and markets of the East," write Williams and fellows.[7] Napoleon was widely believed to be behind the shutdown. The frontiersmen of the West howled for a rough answer, even war against France.

Jefferson sent James Monroe to Paris to negotiate buying New Orleans. Napoleon instead put up all of Louisiana. Why? T. Harry Williams and his coauthors write, "*mosquitoes* and *ice*." Yellow fever had killed General Leclerc and thousands of French soldiers sent to take

6   Through the wide sweep of what is now Texas, New Mexico, Colorado, Utah, Arizona, Nevada, and California, only a few square miles were truly under the control of Spain and only a few thousand Spaniards lived there: 3,000 in Texas, 3,500 in California, fewer than 1,000 in Arizona, and 30,000 in New Mexico, or less than 37,500 Europeans overall. John Francis Bannon, *The Spanish Borderlands Frontier 1513-1821* (University of New Mexico Press, Albuquerque, 1974), 231.

7   Williams, Current, and Fiedel, *A History of the United States (to 1877)*, 266.

back Haiti after the slave revolt led by Toussaint L'Overture. An early winter iced in the Dutch harbor from which French reinforcements were to sail to Haiti and from there take over Louisiana. To these setbacks Napoleon pretty much said, "To hell with it," and made up his mind to get France out of North America.[8]

For $15 million, the United States grew twofold in land. The new territory was to be dealt out along the straight lines of the Northwest Territory. Public Land. Lots of land. Over the next fifty years, driven by land hunger and the belief in Manifest Destiny, the rest of what are now the contiguous forty-eight United States was taken by purchase (Florida from Spain in 1819), war (the Southwest from Mexico in 1848), and treaty (the Pacific Northwest from Great Britain in 1846 and southern Arizona from Mexico in 1853). Other than Texas, which came into the Union in 1845 after being an independent Republic, and for scattered Spanish and Mexican land grants in the Southwest, it all became federal public land at first. It was a hell of a lot of public land. Merk writes, "Land in the area to the Mississippi River, amounting to approximately 233 million acres, was turned over to Congress during the Confederation period by the original states with western land claims. Between 1803 and 1853 the public lands grew to approximately 1,413,333,000 acres...."[9] That is nearly one and a half *billion* acres—more than fivefold the acreage of the public lands before the Louisiana Purchase. A lot of land.

Dealing Out the Land

Dealing the public lands from the Alleghenies to the Pacific into private ownership built the nation in the years between the Land Ordinance of 1785 and the shutting of the frontier as marked by the Census Bureau in 1890. I believe that this 105 years is a standalone

8   Williams, Current, and Fiedel, *A History of the United States (to 1877)*, 267.

9   Merk, *History of the Westward Movement*, 229.

time in our nation's history, a time that I call the Frontier Century. In our folk history it was good, hardworking, and hardy families who homesteaded this land—the "Little House on the Prairie" myth. What happened is another tale, though. As we have already read, historians warn us that the land speculators were always a jump ahead of the pioneers. Furthermore, hundreds of millions of acres went into the pockets of railroad, mining, and logging businesses through giveaway laws and swindles.

Also please understand that "homesteading" did not come along until the 1862 Homestead Act. In the Ordinance of 1785, settlers had to put cash on the barrelhead. Shanks writes that the always-there fear of frontier rebellion goaded Congress in the early 1800s to give credit and to cut the acreage that could be bought down to 160, or a quarter section.[10]

However, the Land Act of 1820 flipped the catbird seat back to the speculators. Credit was done away with, and land was to be sold for cash to the highest bidder at public auctions. Frontier families, such as my forebears, turned a deaf ear to Congress and leapfrogged surveyed land and settlements to squat farther west. Great debates stormed in Congress between the East and West over "pre-emption"—forgiving squatters for unlawful settlements and giving them first rights to buy the land they had cleared.[11]

The frontier at long last won with the 1862 Homestead Act signed by President Lincoln. Horace Greeley called it "a magnificent national democratic triumph—a bold but noble promise." Shanks writes, "The act permitted any person, citizen or not, to settle on 160 acres of land and either purchase land at a minimum price of $1.25 per acre or acquire title free after five years of residence and cultivation. It was the most progressive land law in history." By the end of Lincoln's

10   Bernard Shanks, *This Land Is Your Land* (Sierra Club Books, San Francisco, 1984), 39.

11   Merk, *History of the Westward Movement*, 229-239; Shanks, *This Land Is Your Land*, 39-40.

presidency, 3.4 million acres had been homesteaded. This sounds mighty high-minded. But, in that same time, 74.4 million acres of public land were given to railroad businesses.[12] So for every acre the homesteaders got, the railroads got *twenty*. Even one hundred and fifty years ago, in carving up the commonwealth, big business got twenty-fold to the citizens. *Commonwealth*, please understand, is the common wealth of the nation—of all the citizens of the nation—until it is dealt out to private hands.

Over the years, to be sure, much public land was homesteaded. Some of my Dodsons, Frizzels, and Crawfords homesteaded in eastern New Mexico in 1907. Other kinfolks did so in Oklahoma, Colorado, and Montana. However, giveaways to corporations and swindles by Big Men led to many more acres passing out of the public domain. Overall, some 223 million acres were granted to railroads to foster the laying of lines to the Pacific, and to other corporations through such special-interest legislation as the 1873 Timber Culture Act and the 1872 Mining Law ("basically drawn up by, and for, miners and the mining interests of the mountainous areas west of the Great Plains," writes Merk).[13] For some fast-buck hustlers, congressional giveaways were not fat enough. Millions of acres passed into private hands through scams. Big cowmen used cowboys and timber lords used loggers as "dummy entrymen" to claim acreage that the dummies then handed over to their bosses. Some of the great empires of the West were built in this way. This is how the redwood forest of California and the mighty Douglas-fir forests of Washington became privately owned. Others did not even bother with these games. Livestock kings hired gunmen to keep homesteaders off the public land the big ranchers wanted to graze (the stuff of great Western novels and movies like *Shane*), and cut-and-run timbermen

---

12   Shanks, *This Land Is Your Land*, 41. For the story of the 1864 grant of 40 million acres to the Northern Pacific Railroad, see Derrick Jensen, George Draffan, and John Osborn, *Railroads and Clearcuts* (Inland Empire Public Lands Council, Spokane, WA 1995).

13   Merk, *History of the Westward Movement*, 415.

stripped the public lands of timber and moved on ahead of the agents of the General Land Office. The 1877 Desert Land Act let settlers buy 640 acres for $1.25 an acre if some of it was irrigated. Merk wrote, "It has been estimated that 95 percent of titles obtained under the Desert Land Act were fraudulently obtained by or for corporations."[14] Stories were told of cattle barons pouring a glass of water or pissing on the land and then boasting they had irrigated it. Indian reservations were raided with the 1887 Dawes Act, and "26 million acres were transferred to corporate or private ownership. Tribe after tribe lost the majority of its land," Shanks writes.[15]

As new states came into the Union, they were given sundry fat acreages of public land (some grants were rich indeed—Alaska got a third of all the federal land there). Since both federal and state lands were slated for sale and not for keeping and stewarding, the granted state lands were not in blocks but scattered through what was still federal land. Likewise, the grants to railroads were given in every other section so many miles on either side of the rail line. It was thought that all of these lands would be sold at some time, so why worry about the layout. This is how it went in the well-watered East and Midwest. But most federal and state lands in the West were too dry for homesteading or sale and thus were left in federal or state hands. As for the railroad lands in the dry West, they were kept in the hands of the railroads or spun-off land and cattle companies while the "checkerboarded" public lands were not sold, either. This is why when you look at a standard land ownership map in the West, you see a checkerboard of colored squares: yellow for Bureau of Land Management, green for National Forest, blue for state, white for private.

Overall, however, from the Alleghenies west to the Pacific, the bulk of the public domain passed into private or state ownership. In the next chapter, we'll learn what happened to the leftover public lands in the West.

---

14   Merk, *History of the Westward Movement*, 464.

15   Shanks, *This Land Is Your Land*, 48.

CHAPTER 6

The Great Barbecue I:
Wildlife Slaughter

EATING OUR WAY WEST

Outfitted with the Myth of Superabundance and Mather's wilderness-conquering theology, settlers scalped the land as they scalped the Indians. All too soon, the endless land-wealth began to run out. Poorly husbanded farms lost their high yield. Overhunting of deer was such that "in Massachusetts a closed season was enforced by 1696, and by 1718 a closed term of three full years became necessary." So much for 100 deer in a mile. Ducks and geese fared no better: "Massachusetts, in 1710, prohibited the use of boats, sailing canoes, and camouflaged canoes in the pursuit of waterfowl," writes Peter Matthiessen.[1]

Never mind. There was more just over yonder. Westward ho!

The lines of my family seemed to go through a farm about every generation and then moved on to richer soil, yet-uncut trees, and teeming wild meat. By the 1740s, the Dodsons had left the Virginia

---

1   Peter Matthiessen, *Wildlife In America* (Viking, New York, 1987), 65.

tidewater for the edge of settlement in southwestern Virginia. Before 1796, they were hacking away at virgin forest in middle Tennessee. My father's family, Tylers, Foremans, and Shieldses, were trekking, too— first to the Shenandoah Valley and then following Daniel Boone over the Wilderness Road into Kentucky after the Revolutionary War.

They were barely in time. Elk were going fast east of the Appalachians and the last bison east of the Appalachians was killed in 1801 at Buffalo Cross Roads in Pennsylvania.[2] West of the Appalachians all was well, however. Boone recalled Kentucky where he "found everywhere abundance of wild beasts of all sorts, through the vast forests. The buffalo were more frequent than I have seen cattle in the settlements."[3]

Beaver had been trapped out of New England as early as 1650. By the late 1830s, after the mountain-man trapping hooray, only a few were left even in the farthest hidey-hole streams of the West.[4] This killing-off of one of the most overflowing and widespread wildeors of North America (biologists think there were some sixty million beavers in North America before Columbus[5]) has had far-reaching ecological outcomes. Beavers are a *keystone species*, which means they "enrich ecosystem function in a unique and significant manner through their activities, and the effect is disproportionate to their numerical abundance."[6] The beaver, through its dam building, had shaped much

---

2   Matthiessen, *Wildlife In America*, 63.

3   Matthiessen, *Wildlife In America*, 82.

4   Lisa Mighetto, *Wild Animals and American Environmental Ethics* (The University of Arizona Press, Tucson, 1991), 29.

5   Adrian Forsyth, *Mammals of the American North* (Camden House, Camden East, Ontario, 1985), 233.

6   Brian Miller, Richard Reading, Jim Strittholt, Carlos Carroll, Reed Noss, Michael Soulé, Oscar Sanchez, John Terborgh, Donald Brightsmith, Ted Cheeseman, and Dave Foreman, "Using Focal Species in the Design of Nature Reserve Networks," *Wild Earth*, Winter 1998/99, 81-92. Biologists now call keystone species *highly interactive species* and have shown that to have their ecological effectiveness, their populations must be big enough. Too few or too scattered, such species cannot play their key role in an ecosystem. Michael E. Soulé, James A. Estes, Joel Berger,

of North America. Dozens of other species needed the beaver-crafted landscape—from kingfishers and flycatchers to otters and mink. With the swift slaughter of the big water-squirrels,[7] Americans and Canadians withered the land. Wetlands dried up, many wildeors lost their wild neighborhoods, stream dynamics were upset, floods went up, water flows went down in dry months. No one has fully reckoned all the ecological harm from the early loss of the beaver.

In 1808, my great-great-great grandfather William Frizzell settled in Belmont County, Ohio, where wolves and panthers were "abundant." In 1809, the bounty for wolves was one to three dollars a head. The panther bounty was somewhat less.[8] Mind you, two hundred years ago, a dollar was worth something. The heftiness of these bounties shows how much big wild hunters were loathed, and what a nitty-gritty chore it was at the edge of settlement to rid the land of them. The settlers felt they needed to kill wolves and cougars as much as they needed to cut down the big woods. The task was to tame the wilderness—the hallowed work of Americans.

Passenger pigeons darkened the skies above William Frizzell, as they did the skies o'er my forebears south of the Ohio. In 1810, early American ornithologist Alexander Wilson reckoned that a brawny flight of pigeons in Kentucky had 2,230,272,000 birds. That's more than two *billion* birds.[9] What John Josselyn had seen nearly 150 years earlier had not withered. Thirty years later, when my great-grandfather David Foreman was born in Kentucky, there was as yet no end to the meaty birds. I wonder if he hefted a gun in the great pigeon hunts when millions were killed on their nesting grounds, salted down for

and Carlos Martinez del Rio, "Ecological Effectiveness: Conservation Goals for Interactive Species," *Conservation Biology* 17, No. 5 (October 2003), 1238-1250.

7   David W. Macdonald, ed., *The Princeton Encyclopedia of Mammals* (Princeton University Press, Princeton, NJ, 2009), 140.

8   Elaine Dodson Thomas, *The Ancestry and Descendants of Mary Belle Frizzell and Elvas Aaron Dodson* (privately printed, July 1993).

9   Matthiessen, *Wildlife in America*, 119.

shipment to the cities, or left on the ground for the thousands of hogs herded in for the fattening binge. As late as 1857, the state of Ohio saw no grounds to slow the slaughter: "The passenger pigeon needs no protection. Wonderfully prolific, having the vast forests of the North as its breeding grounds, traveling hundreds of miles in search of food, it is here to-day and elsewhere to-morrow, and no ordinary destruction can lessen them or be missed from the myriads that are yearly produced."[10] Ahh, Superabundance!

However, in 1810, well before David Foreman was born, maybe about the time his father Benjamin was born in Kentucky, Daniel Boone had told John James Audubon:

Sir, what a wonderful difference thirty years makes in the country! Why, at the time when I was caught by the Indians, you would not have walked out in any direction for more than a mile without shooting a buck or a bear. There were then thousands of buffaloes on the hills in Kentucky; the land looked as if it would never become poor; and the hunt in those days was a pleasure indeed. But when I was left to myself on the banks of the Green River, I daresay for the last time in my life, a few signs only of deer were to be seen, and, as to a deer itself, I saw none.[11]

Ol' Dan'l did the smart thing. He packed up and headed west all the way beyond the Mississippi to Missouri. Not long after, the Crawfords in Kentucky, Frizzells in Ohio, and the Dodsons down in Tennessee followed him and settled in Dade and Bolivar counties where the oak-hickory forest begins to thin into the Tallgrass of the plains.

---

10 Matthiessen, *Wildlife in America*, 158.
11 Matthiessen, *Wildlife in America*, 112.

THE FRONTIER CENTURY

The Frontier Century between 1785 and 1890 saw the greatest wasting of wilderness and wildlife in history (until today). With the theology of Manifest Destiny, America swept west—the get-rich-quick 49ers, oak-girdling sod-busting pioneers like the Dodsons and Crawfords, bloody market hunters like Buffalo Bill Cody, and newly rich and mighty corporations like the Northern Pacific Railroad, Weyerhaeuser, and Phelps-Dodge.

After the Civil War, landscalping blew up into a giddy free-for-all of bloodletting—The Killing Decades. In the twenty gory years following Appomattox, 30 to 50 million bison were shot, skinned, tongues hacked out, and mostly left to rot; over a billion passenger pigeons were shot down to fewer than a million; most of the Great Eastern Forest from the Appalachians to the Great Plains and Gulf Coast to the Great Lakes was sawed down, burned, and cleared for farms. Even the swift, dreadful ransacking of rainforests in Africa, the Amazon, and Southeast Asia in the last forty years barely matches the wasted or gobbled flesh and stumps in the United States between 1865 and 1885 or so. It seems that American manhood didn't get enough blood at Antietam and Gettysburg.

EXTINCTION OF THE PASSENGER PIGEON

David Day, author of *Vanished Species,* writes, "As late as 1860 any naturalist or layman might easily have argued that the Passenger Pigeon was, in biological terms, the most successful species of bird on earth."[12]

In 1871 in south-central Wisconsin, 136 million passenger pigeons nested in an area seventy-five miles long and ten to fifteen miles wide. That newfangled contraption, the telegraph, drew thousands of hunters in the upper Midwest to the great barbecue waiting for them. Peter Matthiessen writes in *Wildlife in America,* "The area was laid waste. Hundreds of thousands, indeed millions of dead birds were shipped

12   David Day, *Vanished Species* (Gallery Books, NY, 1989), 32.

out at a wholesale price of fifteen to twenty-five cents a dozen...."[13] Superabundance still gleefully, drunkenly frolicked in Americans' minds.

Only seven years later (1878), though, in Petoskey, Michigan, came the last big nesting. After the jubilee of killing there, never again did millions of passenger pigeons come together. In 1896, a nesting of only 250,000 pigeons, near Mammoth Cave in Kentucky, drew droves of hunters. (In other words, for every pigeon in this flock, there had been ten thousand pigeons in the flock Wilson saw eighty-six years earlier.) It is thought that only 5,000 pigeons fled the slaughter. Forty thousand were left broken and torn on the forest floor for hogs. Ahh, but 200,000 were loaded on boxcars and shipped east.

A derailment up ahead on the line stopped the shipment. They rotted on the tracks and were dumped into a gulch.[14]

The last of the living storm.

My great-grandfather, David Foreman, living only a few miles away, was fifty-five years old, and my grandfather, William Foreman, who later dandled me on his knee, was thirteen. I hope they were not among the hunters, but I fear they could well have been.

On March 24, 1900, in Pike County, Ohio, a passenger pigeon was shot. It was the last known passenger pigeon in the wild.[15] All hail the man or boy who shot it. He stands as the true soul of the American pioneer.

At 1:00 PM, September 1, 1914, in the Cincinnati Zoo, a passenger pigeon named Martha died.[16] She was the last of her kind in all the world. You can see her today, stuffed with cotton, behind glass at the Smithsonian. The last little puff of a whirlwind of life had ended. I

---

13 Matthiessen, *Wildlife in America*, 159-160.
14 Day, *Vanished Species*, 36-37.
15 I think sometimes about this pigeon—how unspeakably lonely she must have been, given the dawn to gloaming flocks she was born to.
16 Errol Fuller, *Extinct Birds* (Facts on File Publications, NY, 1988), 116.

wonder when last she blinked her eyes, if a sweet memory of flying with millions of others flickered blissfully before the dark blew in.

Why? How? We shot them and ate them and left them to feed hogs or to rot. Big city hucksters were selling as many as 18,000 birds a day in the 1850s. Shooting clubs would go through 50,000 birds in a week's shooting match.[17]

Even after the last slaughter, we could not believe they were gone. Excuses were made. *We* could not have done it. They had flown to Australia. They had flown to the moon. They dove to the bottom of the sea. Truly.[18]

On May 11, 1947 (when I was seven months old), the Wisconsin Society for Ornithology put up a monument to the passenger pigeon in Wyalusing State Park. Aldo Leopold wrote about it:

> *Men still live who, in their youth, remember pigeons. Trees still live*
> *who, in their youth, were shaken by the living wind ... .*
> *There will always be pigeons in books and in museums, but these*
> *are effigies and images, dead to all hardships and to all delights.*
> *Book-pigeons cannot dive out of a cloud to make the deer run for*
> *cover, or clap their wings in thunderous applause of mast-laden*
> *woods ... .They live forever by not living at all.*[19]

While some of us have heard of the passenger pigeon and its careless slaying,[20] very few have heard of another bird of the Great Eastern Forest—the Carolina parakeet. We are taken aback today to learn that there was a parrot in the United States; indeed, it may have

---

17   Day, *Vanished Species*, 36.

18   I do not make these up. Truly, such outs were offered.

19   Aldo Leopold, *A Sand County Almanac* (Oxford University Press, New York, 1949), 108-109.

20   With the passenger pigeon was also lost the passenger pigeon chewing louse—an extinction unknown until recently when dead lice were found in the feathers of museum specimens of pigeons.

been the teeming-most parrot on Earth. This foot-long, lovely, green and yellow bird flapped and squawked from Florida to Ontario and west to Missouri. It, too, was slaughtered by the gun and ax. Its wild food was seeds of many kinds, but as native plants were cleared, and orchards and grain fields planted, the parakeet turned to fruit and wheat. The "pest" was shot in flocks of over a hundred. It melted away from the wild at the same time as the passenger pigeon. The last also died in the Cincinnati Zoo—three and a half years after Martha.[21]

Near-Extinction of the American Bison

When the Crawfords trekked to western Missouri in 1838, another thundering river of life was just to the west. At the end of the Civil War, there were some 50 to 60 million bison, 40 million pronghorn (wrongly called antelope), and over two million elk grazing on the Great Plains from Alberta to Chihuahua. In 1871, Wyatt Earp, famous lawman/less-famous outlaw, stood on a hill in Kansas:

> *I could see, twenty or thirty miles in each direction. For all that distance the range seemed literally packed with grazing buffaloes... the prairie appeared to be covered by a solid mass of huge, furry heads and humps, flowing along like a great muddy river...Clear to the horizon the herd was endless.*[22]

But in 1869, the Central Pacific and Union Pacific railroad lines had met in Promontory, Utah. With fast cross-continental shuttling began the great slaughter. Railroads hired hunters to feed the rail workers. One, Buffalo Bill Cody, boasted of having personally killed 4,280 buffalo in one year. The railroad hauled meat, hides, and bones east. With the butchery flowing out from the tracks, the tens of millions of bison on the plains split into two great herds.

21   Fuller, *Extinct Birds*, 150-152.
22   Day, *Vanished Species*, 183-184.

Peter Matthiessen writes, "The southern herd was the first to go. Between 1872 and 1874, well over a million animals were shot yearly, and five years later a solitary survivor met its end at Buffalo Springs, Texas, on the cattle trail to Santa Fe." Goodness only knows what that one, lone bison thought. In its mind, did it speak to the Texan, "I knew you would come."

The northern herd lasted a little longer only because the Northern Pacific Railroad did not give rail access until 1880. Then, wrote Matthiessen:

> [D]efeated Indian tribes joined forces with the buffalo hunters. *They worked toward their own destruction willingly and well, and in 1883 a mixed company of Crees and whites trailed the remnants of the northern herd to the Cannonball River of North Dakota. There, by cutting off access to water, the hunters accomplished the destruction of the entire herd.* [23]

The buffalo was gone.

The great herds that had swept like a prairie fire from Chihuahua to Alberta had been slaughtered in a spree of gore and greed such as the world has seldom seen. A few stragglers found shelter in Yellowstone National Park in Wyoming and far up in northern Alberta on the Peace River. A handful of others hid away near Lost Park, Colorado. A few ranchers corralled one or two buffaloes or tiny herds.

1750. At least sixty million.

1869. Thirty to fifty million or more.

1884. A few hundred.

My god.

Teddy Roosevelt ranched in North Dakota in the mid-1880s. He wrote:

---

23   Matthiessen, *Wildlife in America*, 148-149.

No sight is more common on the plains than that of a bleached buffalo skull; and their countless numbers attest the abundance of the animal at a time not so very long past. On those portions where the herds made their last stand, the carcasses, dried in the clear, high air, or the mouldering skeletons abound.... A ranchman who at the same time had made a journey of a thousand miles across northern Montana, along the Milk River, told me that, to use his own expression, during the whole distance, he was never out of sight of a dead buffalo, and never in sight of a live one.[24]

At the time that Roosevelt ranched in North Dakota, my mother's grandfather's uncle, Billy Crawford, rode through the southern plains from Missouri to Albuquerque, New Mexico.[25] There were no living bison. Like Roosevelt's friend, he rode through a boneyard hundreds of miles long.

I could go on with like tales of slaughter of other wildeors— feathered, furred, and finned. But I'll stop here. It's quite enough to tell the story.

---

24 Matthiessen, *Wildlife in America*, 150-152.
25 Billy Crawford, then, would be my great-great grand-uncle. He found his end a handful of years later when, as an Albuquerque city detective, he was gunned down by a sheep rustler.

CHAPTER 7

The Great Barbecue II:
Logging, Mining, Ranching

LOGGING

Through the Frontier Century, the squirrel's endless forest from the Atlantic to the Mississippi was hewn down. The Great Eastern Forest came under a two-axed whack—from settlers hacking farms out of the wilderness and from timber companies skinning the land for fast pay dirt.

Quick shearing of the forest came first in New England. William Cronon writes, "New England lumbering used forests as if they would last forever."[1] As early as 1682, twenty-four sawmills were cutting boards in Maine.[2] Grasping as logging was, though, Cronon warns us that "the lumberer was not the chief agent in destroying New England's forests; the farmer was."[3] By the time of the Louisiana Purchase, New England but for Maine was mostly stripped. New Hampshire was 95

---

1   William Cronon, *Changes in the Land* (Hill and Wang, New York, 1983), 111.
2   Cronon, *Changes in the Land,* 110.
3   Cronon, *Changes in the Land,* 114.

percent forested in the 1600s. By 1880, tree cover was down to 47 percent, and most of this was ecologically poor—spindly second or third growth and scrub, not the lordly old growth once darkening the hills and dells. Much the same holds for Vermont and southern Maine.[4] Steve Trombulak and Chris Klyza of Middlebury College write that "the percentage of Vermont that is forested went from an estimated 95 percent in 1620, to 25 to 35 percent around 1850 to 1870....."[5] As in New Hampshire, much of this was scrawny regrowth on once-scalped fields.

As settlers spread over the ridges throughout the trans-Appalachian frontier, they, too, hacked down the forest for farms. French wayfarer Alexis de Tocqueville witnessed their feelings about the big woods on the Michigan settlement edge in 1831:

> [The pioneer] living in the wilds... only prizes the works of man. He will gladly send you off to see a road, a bridge, or a fine village. But that one should appreciate great trees and the beauties of solitude, that possibility completely passes him by. [Americans are] insensible to the wonders of inanimate nature, and they may be said not to perceive the mighty forests that surround them till they fall beneath the hatchet. Their eyes are fixed on another sight... peopling solitudes and subduing nature.[6]

The most straightforward utterance of the settlers' thoughts about the Great Eastern Forest came from the matchless American frontiersman and Indian killer, Andrew Jackson, at his presidential inauguration in 1828:

---

4 John A. Litvaitis, "Responses of Early Successional Vertebrates to Historic Changes in Land Use," *Conservation Biology* Vol. 7, No. 4, December 1993, 867.

5 Stephen C. Trombulak and Christopher McGrory Klyza, "The New Natural History," *Natural Areas Journal*, Vol. 20 (3), 2000, 267.

6 Michael Williams, *Americans And Their Forests: A historical geography* (Cambridge University Press, Cambridge 1989), 11.

[W]hat good man would prefer a country covered with forests and ranged by a few thousand savages to our extensive Republic, studded with cities, towns, and prosperous farms, embellished with all the improvements which art can devise or industry execute.[7]

Historian Michael Williams believes that over 100 million acres of the Great Eastern Forest were chopped down before 1850. Between 1850 and 1859, however, another forty million acres were cut, "equivalent to roughly one-third of all clearing carried out during the previous two centuries. It was a decade of maximum impact on the forest."[8]

After the easily reachable timber of New England and southern New York was cut in the 1700s, logging companies worked into the far backcountry of Maine and the Adirondacks. Their more swashbuckling brethren shoved the timber edge west. After the Civil War, big logging businesses took over the North Woods of Wisconsin, Michigan, and Minnesota, which gave the timber industry its age of heroic legend. From the 1870s on, the ransacking of the virgin White Pine forests in the North Woods set a new yardstick for land lust, and a mighty folk hero—Paul Bunyan—had to be crafted to match the deed. Never before had so much forest fallen so swiftly. Even some within the timber industry spooked. The owners of the Black River Falls sawmill told the Minnesota legislature, "In a few years, the wealthiest portion of the pineries will present nothing but a vast and gloomy wilderness of pine stumps." They had good reason for their worry: Logs passing Beef Slough, a Chippewa River channel above the Mississippi River, went from "12 million feet in 1868 to 274,367,000 feet in 1873. On the neighboring Black River the traffic rose from 6 million feet in 1864 to

7   Roderick Nash, *Wilderness and the American Mind* (Yale University Press, New Haven, CT 1967), 41.
8   Williams, *Americans And Their Forests,* 118.

195,398,830 feet in 1873," wrote Frederick Merk.[9] These are jumps of 23-fold in five years and 32.5-fold in nine years, respectively.

Paul and the Blue Ox did their work well for the timber kings. The Northern Hardwoods and Great Lakes Pine Forests were chopped to smithereens in a few short years. Lumbermen had run after the American forest from the Atlantic to the Great Plains over the millrace of the Frontier Century, scalping it in New England, stripping it bare in Pennsylvania, New York, and Michigan, and plundering it in Wisconsin and Minnesota. All the while they told Americans not to worry: the trees were without end.[10]

MINING AND MARKET HUNTING

The 1849 California Gold Rush became the benchmark for the early settlement of the Mountain West. Gold and silver rushes followed finds in Colorado in 1858, Nevada in 1858, Arizona in 1860 and 1862, Idaho in 1860, Montana in 1862 and 1864, Wyoming in 1867, and so on. These rushes led to tens of thousands of miners, "soiled doves," gamblers, whiskey dealers, and storekeepers throwing up towns in the wilderness. Forests were chopped down for mine timbers, streams were ripped apart and fouled with placer and hydraulic mining, and market hunters shot out the bighorn sheep, elk, pronghorn, and mule deer to feed the miners. Wiped out by the mining camp meat-slaughter was the biggest subspecies of elk, Merriam's. Roaming in herds of up to two thousand, it was thought "very plentiful" in 1876 in the Mogollon Mountains of New Mexico. The last was shot in 1906 in the Chiricahua Mountains.[11] Over half a million elk were in California—herds of two

9   Frederick Merk, *History of the Westward Movement* (Alfred A. Knopf, New York, 1980), 451.

10   Little patches and a few amazingly big tracts of unlogged forest were left behind in the logging madness. Mary Davis, before her untimely death, began to inventory all the virgin forest left in the East. See Mary Davis, ed., *Eastern Old-Growth Forests: Prospects for Rediscovery and Recovery* (Island Press, Washington, 1996).

11   Peter Matthiessen, *Wildlife In America* (Viking, New York, 1987),

thousand Tule elk were seen in the Central Valley. By 1870, they were feared extinct. In 1874, workers draining a marsh for rancher Henry Miller found one pair. Miller quickly locked them away and worked to breed them. This and only this is why the Tule elk are alive today (albeit only 2,700 animals in twenty-two small herds) and not extinct like the eastern and Merriam's subspecies.[12]

Frederic H. Wagner, a professor in the College of Natural Resources, Utah State University, has reckoned how much big game was in the West before market hunters. Pronghorn were ten to fifteen million (twenty to forty million with the Great Plains), bighorn sheep were some two million, and elk were also about two million (ten million elk with what were in the East and plains at first).[13] As the last big passenger pigeon nesting was being blown to bits and bloody feathers in Kentucky, big game herds in the West dropped to almost nothing. William T. Hornaday, head of the Bronx Zoo and one of the greats of early conservation, wrote in 1914, "[T]he remnant of game birds and quadrupeds now alive in the United States represents only about 2 per cent of the stock that existed here only fifty years ago...."[14] In other words, 98 percent had been wiped out since the end of the Civil War. The Killing Decades. Indeed.

144. Some authorities do not believe elk were common south of the Mogollons; see the *Sky Islands Wildlands Network Conservation Plan* (The Wildlands Project, Tucson, AZ, 2000), 115. The late biologist Joe Truett of the Turner Endangered Species Fund argued that Merriam's elk (and bison) were absent south of the Mogollons because of native hunting before white settlement; Joe Truett, "Bison and Elk in the American Southwest: In Search of the Pristine," *Environmental Management*, Vol. 20, No. 2, 1996, 195-206.

12 Jon K. Fischer, "Future bright for California elk," *Outdoor California* May-June 1994, 12-13.

13 Denzel and Nancy Ferguson, *Sacred Cows at the Public Trough* (Maverick Publications, Bend, OR, 1983), 116. For Pronghorn: Adrian Forsythe, *Mammals of the American North* (Camden House, Camden East, Ontario, 1985), 31.

14 William T. Hornaday, *Wild Life Conservation in Theory and Practice* (Yale University Press, New Haven, CT, 1914), 19.

RANCHING

With the outright overkill of wildlife came another stroke of the Killing Decades—livestock. Cattle and sheep were the last straw in the domestication of the big open. When whipped Johnny Rebs of the Confederate Army trudged home to Texas in 1865, they found tens of thousands of cattle gone loose.[15] A go-getting man with a fast horse, a ready rope, and a willing gun could become a cattle baron. Hungry cities in Europe and the eastern United States wanted beef. Railroad lines nosing west and the coming of refrigerated cars made shipping western cattle east workable. The all-out slaughter of the big buffalo herds and the downfall and murder of the tribes made the Great Plains and the Mountain West safe for the cattleman and sheepman. Western historians LeRoy Hafen and Carl Coke Rister wrote, "During the wild seventies and eighties the free-range industry was at its height. From 1866 to 1885 approximately 6,000,000 cattle were driven over the northern and western trails [from Texas] to Sedalia, Abilene, Dodge City, Wichita, Ellsworth, Denver, Tucson, and elsewhere."[16] This was the classic Wild West of *Rawhide, Gunsmoke,* and untold movies.

Herds were also driven to Montana, Wyoming, and Idaho from Texas and from the West Coast. Denzel and Nancy Ferguson, in their hard look at the Western livestock industry, *Sacred Cows at the Public Trough,* gave an almost unbelievable tally of the growth in livestock after the Civil War:

In 1850 the number of sheep in western states other than California was only about 514,000 but the numbers soared to nearly 20 million by 1890.

---

15   LeRoy R. Hafen and Carl Coke Rister, *Western America: The Exploration, Settlement, and Development of the Region beyond the Mississippi,* Second Edition (Prentice-Hall, Englewood Cliffs, NJ, 1950), 545.

16   Hafen and Rister, *Western America,* 350.

In 1870, the total number of cattle in the Arizona Territory was only 5,000....by 1891 the population of cattle in the territory had grown to an estimated 1.5 million.... In 1870, the cattle population in 17 western states was estimated to be 4-5 million head; by 1890, that had grown to 26.5 million.[17]

Although there were many small mom-and-pop ramshackle ranches throughout the West, the cattle industry then, as it is now, was lorded over by big outfits, often owned by outside money. Hafen and Rister again:

In 1882 the Wyoming Stock-Raisers Association's By-Laws and Reports estimated that English and Scottish investments in the West, and largely in Wyoming and Texas, amounted to ... $30,000,000. And on March 27, 1884, Representative N. W. Nutting of New York reported to Congress that foreign interests controlled more than 20,000,000 acres of Great Plains range lands and threatened to dominate the industry.

The Scottish American Mortgage Company had one ranch of 2,580,480 acres in northern New Mexico and one in southeastern Colorado of 2,240,000 acres.[18] Titled Europeans like the Marquis de Mores, Baron von Richthofen, and the Earl of Dunraven had sprawling ranches. American investments outdid the Europeans', though. The XIT ranch in the Texas panhandle was over three million acres and had a fence 781 miles long hemming it in. A Chicago syndicate owned it.[19]

Notwithstanding ownership—European nobility, American corporations, rustlers turned cattle barons, or hardscrabble toeholds of a man and his wife and their herd of children—the range was badly

---

17   Fergusons, *Sacred Cows at the Public Trough*, 14-15.
18   Each was the size of Yellowstone National Park or bigger.
19   Hafen and Rister, *Western America*, 551-553.

overstocked and overgrazed. Thunderstorms swept away the topsoil in sheets, and gullywashers turned slow, winding streams into straight-shot dry arroyos with forty-foot sheer banks. Arizona rancher H. C. Hooker recalled the San Pedro River valley in 1870, before the onslaught of livestock, as "having an abundance of timber with large beds of sacaton and grama grasses. The river bed was shallow and grassy with its banks with luxuriant growth of vegetation." It was another world thirty years later. He wrote that "the river had cut 10 to 40 feet below its banks with its trees and underbrush gone, with the mesas grazed by thousands of horses and cattle."[20]

Never mind. These were bully times. Forget about stops or edges. The mind of the range livestock industry was best told by the unanimous declaration of a west Texas cattlemen's association in 1898:

> Resolved, *that none of us know, or care to know, anything about grasses, native or otherwise, outside the fact that for the present there are lots of them, the best on record, and we are after getting the most out of them while they last.*[21]

The Texans' careless bravado was bewildering in light of what had happened in the short years earlier. The overstocked grasslands north and west had already crashed. Drought and fire hit the Montana range in the spring and summer of 1886. Nonetheless, the range was filled up with more cattle—more than a million by fall. One after another god-awful blizzards spun the northern grasslands into a killing field that winter of 1886-1887. Bay State Land and Cattle Company alone lost 100,000 head. Seventy percent of the cattle in eastern Montana died. The total loss was in the neighborhood of $20 million (in 1887 dollars).

20   Steve Johnson, "Learning to Miss What We Never Knew," *The Home Range* (Predator Project) Summer, 1997.

21   Thadis W. Box, "Range Deterioration in West Texas," *Southwestern Historical Quarterly* 71, No. 1 (July 1967), quoted in Paul Shepard, *Nature and Madness* (Sierra Club Books, San Francisco, 1982), 2.

Two years later the same dreadfulness hit the Intermountain West. Drought followed by blizzards filled the years 1889-90 with heartbreak and wretchedness. One big Nevada-Idaho cow-kingdom had only 68 head left in 1890 after branding 38,000 calves in 1885. Drought then whacked Arizona and New Mexico in 1891-1893 with 50-75 percent of all cattle dying. "Witnesses stated that a person could stand at one carcass and throw rocks to others nearby," wrote the Fergusons.[22]

In those seven years, cattle heaven fell to hell. But before it did, the landscape of the West was made a lesser world with a new hard leanness. The land had been scalped. Millions of acres had lost their topsoil, no stream was left healthy, and native vegetation was snuffed. Wealth had been turned into rubble by the cattle and sheep raiders.

THE PIONEER

The Frontier Century and the Killing Decades were best weighed by Charles M. Russell, one of America's most-loved artists, who started out in 1879 as a fifteen-year-old cowpuncher in Montana. One of his paintings of the frontier sold for $2.3 million a few years ago. A great National Wildlife Refuge on the banks of the Missouri River in Montana is named after him. After he became well-known as an artist, a booster bunch, the "Forward Looking Citizens" of Great Falls, Montana, asked to give him an award as a great pioneer. Charlie Russell stood before them and said:

> *In my book, a pioneer is a man who comes to a virgin country, traps off all the fur, kills off all the wild meat, cuts down all the trees, grazes off all the grass, plows the roots up and strings ten million miles of wire. A "pioneer" destroys things and calls it civilization. I wish to God that this country was just like it was when I first saw it and that none of you folks were here at all.[23]*

---

22 Fergusons, *Sacred Cows,* 16-19.
23 Michael Frome, *Battle for the Wilderness* (Westview Press, Boulder, CO 1984), 46.

CHAPTER 8

End of the Frontier

IT HIT AMERICA LIKE A GRIZZLY'S SLAP across the cheeks. After the 1890 census, the U.S. Census Bureau said there was no more frontier. Before, there had been a line of settlement past which was mostly wild uninhabited country.[1] That line was gone in 1890. The Killing Decades had ended the frontier. Manifest Destiny had overwhelmed the land. Miners, market hunters, railroaders, cattlemen, and sodbusters had broken the line of the big empty. Gone, too, were free Indian nations. The Battle of Wounded Knee in 1890 killed any hope for the comeback of the old ways.

THE FRONTIER, DEMOCRACY, AND THE AMERICAN CHARACTER

Americans high and low worried about whether America—a frontier nation—would stay America without the frontier. The frontier

---

1   By European- and African-rooted Americans, at least. However, natives were far from thick over most of the post-Civil War frontier. See my *True Wilderness.* The Census Bureau yardstick for "frontier" was fewer than two persons per square mile over sprawling landscapes.

had shaped our national character. Our democratic institutions had
come out of it. Could we keep our democracy? Wilderness had been
the fire into which the European was thrust and then hammered out to
make a new being—the American. Would we grow soft and weak and
sinful without the annealing fire of wilderness? In the 1890s, Harvard's
Frederick Jackson Turner built his theory of American history around
"the transforming influence of the American wilderness," wrote
Roderick Nash, who went on to say that Turner believed "democracy was
a forest product." In 1896, Turner wrote in the *Atlantic Monthly,* "Out of
his wilderness experience, out of the freedom of his opportunities, [the
American pioneer] fashioned a formula for social regeneration—the
freedom for the individual to seek his own."[2]

Turner's thesis elbowed out an earlier belief, of which David
Hackett Fischer writes, "Historians believed that the American
system had evolved from what one scholar called 'Teutonic germs' of
free institutions, which were supposedly carried from the forests of
Germany to Britain and then to America." Turner did not toss this
"germ theory," but believed the seedbed—the American frontier—had
more to do with it than the germs, or seeds, sowed. Turner and others
found the tree of liberty in the back and forth with wildland, not in
folkways from Europe.[3] Some historians and other academics have an
odd weakness: the wholesale takeover of one way of seeing by another.
I think a wiser and truer path is to see that sundry theories may each
hold slabs of the truth. In keeping with the either/or path, however,
historian William Cronon wrote twenty years ago, "Later historians
would reject this argument about the frontier origins of American
democracy, so that Turner's anxiety about the 'passing frontier' should
now be read as his own ideological construct."[4] But for some of today's

2   Roderick Nash, *Wilderness and the American Mind* (Yale University
     Press, New Haven, CT, 1967), 146.

3   David Hackett Fischer, *Albion's Seed: Four British Folkways in America*
     (Oxford University Press, New York, 1989), 4.

4   William Cronon, "Landscape and Home: Environmental Traditions in

historians to shun Turner's frontier thesis does not mean it lacks any truth, just as "Teutonic germs" have a dab of truth. Those who toss out Turner's "Frontier Myth" as if getting rid of a pile of old beer cans may be hurting from their own "ideological constructs." Aldo Leopold, by the way, lived two houses away from Turner in Madison, Wisconsin. His writings smack strongly of the salt of Turner's thought.

Theodore Roosevelt was another worried watcher, but one who had an answer. In 1899, he warned, "As our civilization grows older and more complex, we need a greater and not a less development of the fundamental frontier virtues."[5]

The far-flung wilderness was gone; left were moldering bone piles on the plains, the dimming recall of thunderous pigeon flights, and rotting stumps big enough to be a dance floor for half-a-dozen couples. Was the wealth of the land a will-o'-the-wisp like the frontier? A shade from the past ne'er to be glimpsed again?

RISE OF THE AMERICAN CONSERVATION MOVEMENT

Out of these fears—of the loss of the frontier and the crumbling of the Myth of Superabundance—the American conservation movement arose in the last days of the nineteenth century. It did not leap full-grown and ready to fight out of the Census Bureau's report, though. Conservation had roots stretching back even before the English colonies. We have seen that Massachusetts and Virginia had passed laws cutting back hunting by the early 1700s.[6] Historian Lee Clark Mitchell warns, "Issues that we assume are modern—conservation, protection of endangered species, native rights, and questioning the

---

Wisconsin," *Wisconsin Magazine of History,* Vol. 74, Winter, 1990-1991.
5   Nash, *Wilderness and the American Mind,* 150.
6   In my next book, *True Wilderness,* I show that, before the United States, both lords and tribes had locked up lands for wildlife and to keep their forests.

price of progress—actually originated early in the nineteenth century. As such they form a uniquely American legacy."[7]

Aldo Leopold and others brought out the loss of the frontier in their call to protect roadless landscapes on the National Forests as Wilderness Areas (soon renamed *Primitive Areas* by the Forest Service).

What follows in this chapter and the rest of the book is not the full history of public lands and the conservation movement. That would take a whole, long book by itself. Indeed, more than a few books have been written on this, and I draw from them here, but I also weave in my own wide and deep wilderness and wildlife understanding and work from the last forty-some years.[8] This chapter and the next two are a quick look at the beginnings of conservation and the public lands to clean up some broad misunderstandings and to shine brighter light on things often overlooked:

The public and even many conservationists and scholars are misled about how conservation and the public lands first came about. We must understand the history of the public lands to understand today's conservation struggles and to lay down a path for conservation into the twenty-first century. Without grounding in what came before, today's siblinghood of wilderfolks can only thrash away in an unknowing nothingness.

The belief that there is one conservation movement holding both Resource Conservation (the "efficient" exploitation of Nature) and Nature Conservation (shielding self-willed land) is wrong. The great sharp ridge between the two is about valuing self-willed land and wildeors.

Far from being the wardens of wild America, natural resource management agencies have worked tirelessly to tame wilderness and manage wildeors—often to death.

---

7   Lee Clark Mitchell, *Witnesses to a Vanishing America: The Nineteenth Century Response* (Princeton University Press, Princeton, NJ, 1981), xiv.

8   The key books for understanding the beginnings of conservation and the public lands are those that I cite in the footnotes of this section.

Today's conservation movement comes from many streams flowing in over the last 150 years.

Each of these streams sprang from a need to shield wildlife or wildlands from here-and-now threats.

There has not been one set of values and grounds upholding public lands and conservation. Rather, the political establishment, resource agencies, and conservationists have used sundry arguments and values to back public lands and conservation laws.

The underlying split between Nature conservation and resource conservation (resourcism) is over whether wilderness and wildeors have goodness inborn or are good only as things for Man. Should wild things be kept for their own sake or only because they have worth of some kind or other for Man?

The Falsehood of One Conservation Movement

In 1987, then-President of The Wilderness Society George Frampton wrote, "It may come as something of a shock to our current generation of committed environmentalists to discover that the modern conservation movement sprang from a highly developed philosophy of *intensive use,* that is, exploitation, of our natural resources."[9] In all kindness, I think Frampton's map is thuddingly wrong. Today's wilderness conservation movement sprang from no such thing.

The early wave against landscalping split in the 1890s, a victim of unbridgeable beliefs about wild things (Nature).[10] The two forks that came out of the split were both backlashes to landscalping, and both were grounded in the public lands and public ownership of wildlife.

---

9   George T. Frampton, Jr., "Introduction," in Gifford Pinchot, *Breaking New Ground* (Island Press, Washington, D.C., 1987), xi. Frampton later became President Clinton's Assistant Secretary of the Interior and then head of the Council on Environmental Quality.

10   Nature is a much-overworked word and one given to many tangled and often clashing meanings. Therefore, I give it a break in my writing and scribble instead wild things for a cleaner meaning.

They were, however, far away from each other in what they hoped for the public lands and how they weighed the worth of the many kinds of wildlife living throughout the United States. These forks were Conservation (mostly clubs such as the Sierra Club and The Wilderness Society) and Resourcism (mostly government agencies such as the United States Forest Service and state game and fish agencies, and their fellows in agriculture and forestry colleges). The two are deeply at odds over what they think about self-willed land. Keep in mind, however, that men and women on their own may not think the same as does their agency or club, as we shall see.

Words have might, and I believe we must take care in what we name things. Both these forks hold onto the conservation handle and this leads to a muddle. What do we call these two conservation strands? Resource Conservation vs. Nature Conservation? Conservation vs. Preservation? Gifford Pinchot said he came up with the word "conservation" and stuck it on to his "wise use" of natural resources.[11] He sneered at John Muir and friends as "preservationists." Through the twentieth century, though, the word "conservation" has become more and more tied to the so-called preservationists.

Neil Evernden at Ontario's York University called the resource conservation ideology "resourcism" in 1985, writing, "Resourcism is a kind of modern religion which casts all of creation into categories of utility."[12] In *The Idea Of Wilderness* (1991), philosopher Max Oelschlaeger shows why "resourcism" is a better tag than "conservation" for Pinchot and his followers.[13] However, before Evernden and

11   Gifford Pinchot, "The Birth of 'Conservation,'" in Roderick Frazier
      Nash, ed., *American Environmentalism: Readings in Conservation History*
      Third Edition (McGraw-Hill Publishing Company, New York, 1990),
      73-79.

12   Neil Evernden, *The Natural Alien: Humankind and Environment* (University of Toronto Press, 1985), 23.

13   Max Oelschlaeger, *The Idea Of Wilderness* (Yale University Press, New
      Haven, CT, 1991), 281-289.

Oelschlaeger, Paul Shepard in 1967 used "resourcism" for resource conservation. He warned:

> *Resourcism is the most insidious form of nature hating because it poses as a virtue, as prudent, foreseeing, and unselfish. It destroys the world and ourselves in spite of the altruism of its protagonists because they no longer operate as a face-to-face social or economic entity; while as components of corporations, governments, or other agencies they do not touch the world with their own hands. There is no blood on their fingers, but no blood in them either.[14]*

No historical, political, social, or philosophical map is a true drawing of the world, but I believe a map showing conservation and resourcism as two and unalike is much more right than the everyday one showing them as one even if in a big tent.

Although both conservation and resourcism arose against the landscalping of the nineteenth century, I think that, in the twentieth century in the United States (and likely in the rest of the world, too), resource agencies like the U.S. Forest Service and U.S. Bureau of Reclamation, and the Alaska and South Dakota Fish & Game Departments have wrecked or wounded more wilderness and threatened as many species as have even the modern-day landscalpers.[15] Howie Wolke, a backpacking guide and outfitter from Montana, writes that "the destruction of our public lands—in particular, of our wilderness—is the routine business of the agencies."[16] Government agencies entrusted with the "wise" management of our public lands,

---

14   Paul Shepard, *Man in the Landscape: A Historic View of the Esthetics of Nature* (University of Georgia Press, Athens, 2002), 236-237.

15   Following the lead of folk singer and early river runner Katie Lee, conservationists call the Bureau of Reclamation the Bureau of Wreck-the-nation.

16   Howie Wolke, *Wilderness on the Rocks* (Ned Ludd Books, Tucson, Arizona, 1991), 3.

wildlife, and natural resources (raw goods) have been too often the leading foes of conservationists, who work mostly through nongovernmental groups.

Now, some true conservationists have worked and still work for the agencies and we will meet some of them in the next chapters. Many unwavering men and women have tried to do right by the land within the Forest Service and other agencies for one hundred years, but they have nearly always been without clout. Few true conservationists have worn brass in the agencies, and resourcist underlings have undercut those few.

Resourcism has its spot, though, and is a good way to do some things. Engineers are needed. Resourcism is the best way to get and keep those gifts of Earth that Man's civilization needs. Where engineering or resourcism becomes threatening is when it becomes an ideology or religion, when it becomes the only way to do things, when it leaves no room for self-willed land. For thoughtful work in the land community (or neighborhood), careful resourcism is in the mulligan along with keeping and restoring wilderness.

CHAPTER 9

The River Wild:
The Answer to Landscalping

Unsettled feelings about the wasteful looting of North America budded early in the Frontier Century and then blossomed in the Killing Decades. I see the conservation movement as a watershed, with streams dropping from high saddles and cirques and flowing down to swirl into a river—the River Wild, let's call it. A good outlook from which to ken this watershed is that of a raven, where we can see it all spread out before us. And—since it is a raven's eye through which we see—we can think about what we see with strong wits.

The nineteenth century headwater streams that flow together to make the River Wild are wildlife keeping, stewardship, beauty, and forest protection. Downriver in the twentieth century, the streams of wilderness, ecosystem representation, carnivore protection, endangered species, landscape permeability, restoration, and rewilding flow in. For all of these side streams, hikers and their outdoors kin were at the beginning and still tote a heavy load. Nearby, but aside, is the

[79]

watershed for the river of Resourcism. Some of the headwaters of the Resourcism River come off the same ridges and peaks as those that feed the River Wild, but they flow down on another bearing. The watershed for the Environmental River is over hills from that for the River Wild and has other headwaters, though sometimes there is only a low saddle between them.[1]

All the streams feeding into the conservation movement spring from protecting land and wildlife from threats of development, plunder, and killing. Underline this. It is needed truth for understanding those who love and shield wild things and for their tale since before the Civil War. It has most often been outdoors folks—climbers, canoeists, anglers, and such—in the front lines. For each of the wild streams, I'll show how it sprang from threatened wild things. One misunderstands conservation without knowing how threats to tame or kill wild things drove all these protection streams. They did not spring from romantic/ literary wishes of regaining a pristine fantasy, as the wilderness deconstructionists have sparred.

WILDLIFE KEEPING

Saving wildlife is the first headwater stream. Most histories of conservation dwell on early campaigns to ward forests and to set up National Parks. Gifford Pinchot and Teddy Roosevelt believed and taught that it was fear of a coming timber famine that birthed conservation (both resourcism and conservation), and many historians take them at their word. In 1975, John Reiger, executive director of the Connecticut Audubon Society and a Ph.D. in history, took a shotgun to this way of thinking about how conservation began with his book *American Sportsmen and the Origins of Conservation*.[2] He shattered it

---

1   I show how wild conservation and environmentalism are different movements notwithstanding some overlapping in Dave Foreman, *Take Back Conservation* (Raven's Eye Press, Durango, CO, 2012).

2   John F. Reiger, *American Sportsmen and the Origins of Conservation Revised Edition* (University of Oklahoma Press, Norman, 1986).

like a clay pigeon: "American sportsmen, those who hunted and fished for pleasure rather than commerce or necessity, were the real spearhead of conservation."[3] Reiger wrote that "the first challenge to the myth of inexhaustibility that succeeded in arousing a substantial segment of the public was not the dwindling forests, but the disappearance, in region after region, of game fishes, birds, and mammals."[4] He thinks that sportsmen were the leaders in keeping not only wildlife, but also forests and National Parks. I think Reiger is *mostly* right. I also think that seeing both conservation and resourcism as first coming from hunters and anglers is good for how we understand conservation today, and for how wildlovers should answer our belittlers who carry a rifle or rod. I only wish that more of today's hunting and fishing clubs had the backbone and ethic of the 19th Century conservation-sportsmen. I don't see Teddy Roosevelt truckling to the National Rifle Association or Safari International. With today's knowledge, I fully believe Teddy would stand for the wolf against the yahoo gun-nuts of Idaho and other frontier-wannabees.

English aristocrat William Henry Herbert came to the United States in 1831 and brought with him the "code of the sportsman." As the woodsy "Frank Forester," Herbert fought the ransacking market hunters of his time by spurring sportsmen to band together to fight game hogs. The New York Association For The Protection of Game began in 1844. National hunting magazines started up in the 1870s, and they jumped into the fight against market hunting and fishing and for habitat protection. Sport hunters and their magazines raised a din against the crazy slaughter of the buffalo. The first national conservation club was not the Sierra Club (founded in 1892), but the Boone and Crockett Club, founded in 1887 by Theodore Roosevelt, George Bird Grinnell, and fellow hunters. The role of the Boone and Crockett Club in starting the first National Parks, wildlife refuges, and forest reserves has mostly

---

3   Reiger, *American Sportsmen*, 21.
4   Reiger, *American Sportsmen*, 22.

been overlooked by historians as well as by today's conservationists.[5] While it is true that many of these sportsmen were in the resourcist wing, many were not. Grinnell (a merry hunter) "led the fight to ban hunting in Yellowstone National Park, spring shooting, and...market hunting," writes historian Thomas Dunlap in his good book, *Saving America's Wildlife*.[6] Such work was not self-serving; Grinnell and others worked for what was right for American Nature (as understood at the time).

Saving the American Bison

1872 is a hallmark year for conservation because it was the year Yellowstone National Park was set up by law. However, 1872 was also a dark year for conservation because that year a bill to shield bison from slaughter died, although both houses of Congress had passed it.[7] The bill was written by the Territorial Delegate from Arizona, R. C. McCormick, who had watched the wasteful shooting of bison on train trips across the Great Plains. On the floor of the House, McCormick scorned and slammed the "reckless slaughter of that noble and valuable animal, the American bison or buffalo." He quoted a *Harper's Weekly* editorial that called the slaughter "neither wise nor sportsman-like." By showing letters from Army officers on the Great Plains that were against the killing and called for keeping bison, McCormick smacked down those who said that bison had to be wiped out to tame the Plains Indians.[8]

---

5   Reiger, *American Sportsmen*, 22-29.

6   Thomas R. Dunlap, *Saving America's Wildlife: Ecology and the American Mind, 1850-1990* (Princeton University Press, 1991), 11-12.

7   1872 was also the year the Mining Act became law. This way-out-of-date bit of Manifest Destiny still runs mineral giveaways on the public lands. Of all taking raw goods from the public lands, mining is the most mired in nineteenth-century, pre-public land thinking.

8   "Speech of Hon. R. C. McCormick," *Appendix to The Congressional Globe*, 42nd Congress, 2nd Session, April 5, 1872. I thank Robert Brulle at George Mason University for sending me a copy of McCormick's

Other Americans, many of them sportsmen, were also angry over what they had heard of the slaughter. Nonetheless, President Ulysses S. Grant let the bill die without his signature. Of all the things Grant did in his life, killing the bison protection bill was the worst. There were tens of millions of bison still alive in 1872. Had Grant signed the bill, the greatest animal slaughter in United States history would have been stopped and millions of bison likely would still roam o'er much of the plains as wildlife. Grant's smothering of the bison bill shoved many sportsmen into becoming conservationists.

No shield whatsoever was given bison until they were wholly gone from the Great Plains. Ah, but there was Yellowstone National Park. But for over twenty years after its establishment, Yellowstone was a "paper park" like so many in the world today. Yellowstone had no rangers, no armed wardens. After the slaughter on the Plains, poachers moved into Yellowstone where 500 big woollies had found what was hoped to be shelter.

George Grinnell and the Boone and Crockett Club led the campaign to keep Yellowstone's wildlife sheltered from poachers' hot lead.[9] The poaching in Yellowstone had cut the bison herd down from about 500 to only 200 or so.[10] The public outcry about their poaching in Yellowstone National Park prodded Congress at long last in 1894 to do something. Congressman John F. Lacey of Iowa introduced a tough Yellowstone Protection bill. It passed both houses of Congress and was

speech. The word *noble* was widely spoken and written in the nineteenth century to show that something was very good, indeed. It now hits me that perhaps the adjective *noble* somewhat held a meaning of something good-in-itself. Hint: digging into this would be a darn good thesis or dissertation topic.

9   Richard West Sellars, *Preserving Nature in the National Parks: A History* (Yale University Press, New Haven, CT, 1997), 25.

10   Sheilagh C. Ogilvie, *The Park Buffalo: Being an Account of the Role of Canada's National Parks in the Preservation of the North American Bison* (Calgary-Banff Chapter National and Provincial Parks Association of Canada, 1979), 16. I thank Canadian conservationist Harvey Locke for sending me a copy of Ogilvie's booklet.

signed by President Grover Cleveland on May 7, 1894.[11] Teeth were at last put into the no-hunting law for National Parks. The cavalry was sent in to protect the buffalo and other wildlife from the lowlife scum who had come from the blood-soaked Great Plains.

Finally the last buffalo were given shelter and a hope for life.

But oh, so, so close did the American bison come to leading the passenger pigeon and Carolina parakeet into that dark, dark night with no dawn.

Plume Hunting

In the 1890s, fashion held that women should bedeck their heads and bodies with egret plumes, whole mounted birds, and feathers from many kinds of fowl. Bird lovers, scientists, and sport hunters went after the feather trade as flocks of water birds crashed. Audubon societies sprang up in some states to shield birds from slaughter. Although wildlife management was deemed to be the turf of the states, Iowa congressman John Lacey wanted federal action. The 1900 Lacey Act brought to bear the interstate commerce clause of the United States Constitution to ban "the shipment across state lines of wild animals killed in violation of state laws." The plume trade was ended and egrets and other water birds may have been kept from extinction as the passenger pigeon and Carolina parakeet had not.[12] Lacey is truly the granddaddy of congressional conservationists.

Sport hunters and anglers, bird lovers, and good citizens saw that market hunters, game hogs, trophy hunters for the last of a species, landscalpers, and stylish Gibson Girls threatened wildlife. Good citizens stood up and spoke out.

---

11   David A. Dary, *The Buffalo Book* (Avon Books, New York, 1974), 133.

12   Dunlap, *Saving America's Wildlife*, 13-14.

STEWARDSHIP

The second headwater stream is that of Stewardship. One of the standout Americans of the nineteenth century was Vermont's George Perkins Marsh. As Lincoln's ambassador to Turkey and later Italy, Marsh took in the sights of the Mediterranean, where among the ruins of classical civilizations he found ruins of the land. The rocky, treeless hills of Greece were as much a witness to a fallen civilization as was the crumbling Acropolis. His 1864 book, *Man and Nature; or, Physical Geography as Modified by Human Action,* is one of the benchmarks of both history and science. He wrote, "But man is everywhere a disturbing agent. Wherever he plants his foot, the harmonies of nature are turned to discord."[13] Former *New York Times* foreign correspondent and later environmental reporter Phillip Shabecoff wrote, "Marsh was the first to demonstrate that the cumulative impact of human activity was not negligible and, far from benign, could wreak widespread, permanent destruction on the face of the earth."[14]

Marsh drew on his work in the Mediterranean to warn Americans of their wrecking of the land, writing that "the world cannot afford to wait till the slow and sure progress of exact science has taught it a better economy."[15]

Marsh's careful digging into Man's wounds to the land and his call for further scientific study and careful husbandry was the spring for much of later conservation and resourcism. Marsh, however, was in

13   Philip Shabecoff, *A Fierce Green Fire: The American Environmental Movement* (Hill and Wang, New York, 1993), 57.
14   Shabecoff, *A Fierce Green Fire,* 57. Geographer Clarence Glacken, however, has listed a few thinkers who became aware of Man's scalping of the land before Marsh, men who could see what was before them, men such as Mencius and Plato. (Clarence J. Glacken, "Changing Ideas of the Habitable World," in William L. Thomas, Jr., ed., *Man's Role In Changing The Face Of The Earth* (The University of Chicago Press, 1956), 70-92.) I quoted Mencius in Chapter One.
15   Shabecoff, *A Fierce Green Fire,* 58.

the early resourcist camp and more or less wanted Nature tamed.[16] As part of making sure a land's resources were not squandered, he wrote, "The sooner a natural wood is brought into the state of an artificially regulated one, the better it is...."[17]

I also see a spring called Malthus feeding into the flow in Stewardship Creek (although Marsh mostly overlooked Malthus[18]). Behind all of Man's wounds to Earth is our snowballing population growth.[19] Stewardship is needed to stop and then heal soil erosion and other careless land wounding and thoughtless gobbling up of raw goods; it also deals with the threats of Man's population growth.

BEAUTY

The third headwater stream is Beauty—setting up National Parks and other wild havens to keep unmarred their breathtaking loveliness and soul-stretching goodness. In *National Parks: The American Experience*, Alfred Runte writes that "the national park idea as we know it today did not emerge in finished form. More accurately it evolved."[20]

Here are some steps in that evolution:

In 1832, American painter George Catlin, whose work keeps a little of the Plains Indians alive on canvas, came upon a great encampment of Sioux near Fort Pierre in South Dakota. They were slaughtering bison only for their tongues, which they traded for whiskey. This foretold the end of the Great Plains wilderness to Catlin fifty years before it fully happened. But instead of only ruing the end, Catlin called for making the grassy wilderness "a *magnificent park.... A nation's Park*, containing man and beast, in all the wild[ness] and freshness of their nature's

16   William L. Thomas, Jr., "Introductory," in Thomas, ed., *Man's Role*, xxxv.
17   David A. Clary, *Timber and the Forest Service* (University Press of Kansas, Lawrence, 1986), 1.
18   Thomas, "Introductory," in Thomas, ed., *Man's Role*, xxix.
19   Dave Foreman, *Man Swarm and the Killing of Wildlife* (Raven's Eye Press, Durango, CO, 2011).
20   Alfred Runte, *National Parks: The American Experience Second Edition Revised* (University of Nebraska Press, Lincoln, 1987), 1.

beauty!"²¹ Catlin's call went unheeded. Had the mighty in Washington listened, think what might have been—and still would be.

White explorers did not find Yosemite Valley in the Sierra Nevada of California until 1851, and the mighty sequoias near it were not written about until 1852. Within a few years, however, both were drawing sightseers who wanted to bask in their still, steady awesomeness. In 1859, Horace Greeley, editor of the *New York Tribune*, came to Yosemite and wrote to his readers that it was "the most unique and majestic of nature's marvels."²² Five years later, on June 30, 1864, taking time from the burden of the Civil War, President Abraham Lincoln signed a bill handing over the wild wonders of Yosemite Valley and the Mariposa Grove of sequoias to the state of California as a public park.

In 1872, President Ulysses S. Grant signed legislation withdrawing two million acres in one of the most out-of-the-way, least-known landscapes of the West as Yellowstone National Park. Not only was a monumental wilderness being set aside, but a monumental decision for the United States and the world was being made. In saying that Yellowstone should stay the public's land for all time and not be handed over to private interests, Congress and President Grant set a new path for the Republic by starting in one fell swoop the first National Park and the beginning of the *retained* or *kept* public lands. Up until Yellowstone there had been no decision to keep some of the public domain in federal—that is, the public's—hands. The preservation of beauty underlaid the work. Thomas Moran's sketches of Yellowstone were set up for showing in the Capitol during talk about the Yellowstone bill.²³

In 1890, at the prodding of California wilderness tramp turned well-to-do orchardist and much-loved writer John Muir, Congress named Sequoia, General Grant, and Yosemite National Parks in the Sierra

21   Roderick Nash, *Wilderness and the American Mind* (Yale University Press, New Haven, CT, 1967), 101.
22   Runte, *National Parks*, 19-20.
23   Richard West Sellars, *Preserving Nature in the National Parks: A History* (Yale University Press, New Haven, CT, 1997), 9.

Nevada. With this legislation eighteen years after that of Yellowstone's, National Parks became mainstream; Yellowstone was no longer a lucky, one-time side trip from the emptying of the public domain. National Parks and public lands had made it as American institutions. Muir was happy. He thought that first and foremost the National Parks would be for preserving wilderness.

American citizens were for setting aside Yellowstone, Yosemite, and the other early National Parks mostly for beauty, although other things, such as backing from railroads, helped lead to the political settlement. Conservationists feared that all of America's natural wonders were threatened by tawdry tourist development and industrial plundering after such happened at Niagara Falls from 1830 on. Alfred Runte writes, "In the fate of Niagara Falls, Americans found a compelling reason to give preservation more than a passing thought. ... A continuous parade of European visitors and commentators embarrassed the nation by condemning the commercialization of Niagara."[24] All this holds true, as well, for the kindred National Parks work in Canada.

FORESTS

The fourth and last headwater stream is Forest Protection. It falls out of a cirque-held tarn, but splashes down only to be split by a steep sharp ridge. One side pours off into the Resourcism River with Gifford Pinchot and the other gushes into the River Wild with John Muir. (From the other three of these headwater saddles, streams had also flowed into the watershed of resourcism.)

While doing a "Grand Tour" of Europe in 1851, the great New York City newspaperman Horace Greeley was taken aback by how tamed the European landscape was. It made him understand how worthwhile and standalone the American wilderness was. He wrote home asking Americans "to spare, preserve and cherish some portion

---

24   Runte, *National Parks*, 5-6.

of your primitive forests."[25] In 1858 Henry David Thoreau wrote about his wilderness canoe trips in Maine for the *Atlantic Monthly*, in which he asked, "[W]hy should not we ... have our national preserves ... in which the bear and panther, and some even of the hunter race, may still exist, and not be 'civilized off the face of the earth'—our forests ... not for idle sport or food, but for inspiration and our own true recreation?"[26]

These early stands for threatened wildwood led others to become upset by the scalping of the Great Eastern Forest. The first to take steps here was not the federal government, but a state. There is little of which to be proud in American history for some years after the Civil War when business became the business of America, and New York City became its capital. Nonetheless, in such an age of materialism and from the city of Mammon itself came the first great day in American forest preservation. With the heartfelt backing of the New York City Chamber of Commerce, the Governor of New York signed a bill in 1885 for the Adirondack Forest Preserve in the northern end of the state. In 1894, the New York State Constitutional Convention etched in stone stewardship of the state-owned lands in the Adirondacks as "forever wild" in that state's highest law.[27]

In 1891, soon after the state of New York had blazed the path for keeping wild forests in the Adirondacks, Congress bestowed the President with the might to withdraw wooded public lands from handover to private ownership. This was done to stop landskinners' mad rush to cut down the wild, unmapped forests of the West for fast bucks. Although little-known today, easily reached pinewoods in the West had already been heavily logged. In 1891, J. G. Bourke mourned logging around Flagstaff, Arizona. "What was the forest primeval at one time has since been raided by the rapacious forces of commerce ... I cannot repress a sentiment of regret that the demands of civilization

25   Nash, *Wilderness and the American Mind*, 101.
26   Nash, *Wilderness and the American Mind*, 102.
27   Nash, *Wilderness and the American Mind*, 116-121.

have caused the denudation of so many square miles of our forests."[28] Almost as soon as Geronimo gave up his guns, sawmills rushed into the back-of-beyond Chiricahua Mountains within sight of Geronimo's surrender site.

Unhappy with such greedy logging of lands in the Rocky Mountains and the Southwest for mine timbers, railroad ties, boards, firewood, and charcoal, President Benjamin Harrison daringly withdrew 13,000,000 acres in the West as fifteen Forest Reserves under the Forest Reserve Act.[29] In world history, this is a standout political act. The political drive behind Harrison was to shield watersheds in the mountains for downstream water flow for farming, homes, and industry. More than a hundred years ago, towns downstream of the high forests of the West backed such stewardship—as did irrigators. At first, these Forest Reserves were off-limits to logging and livestock grazing, since keeping watersheds healthy was their end. For conservationists such as John Muir, Forest Reserves were the answer to the threat of wide-open, wasteful logging on the public lands. He and other conservationists, such as Enos Mills of Colorado, thought the forest reserves would preserve wilderness.

With the setting up of Forest Reserves, public lands were truly a done deal that would not be forsaken in America. More than anything else, I believe our network of public lands sets the United States off as a bulwark of conservation in the world. It was Benjamin Harrison, one of our lesser-known presidents, who drove in the golden spike to anchor the keeping of some public land as the public's land forever.

28   J. G. Bourke, "On the Border With the Crook," U.S. Geological Service Survey Paper, quoted in Kieran Suckling, "Fire & Forest Ecosystem Health In The American Southwest: A Brief Primer," Southwest Forest Alliance, May 27, 1996.

29   Nash, *Wilderness and the American Mind,* 133.

CHAPTER 10

The River Wild Swells

THE FOUR HEADWATER STREAMS flowed together to make the River Wild in the closing years of the Nineteenth Century. But after twenty years or so, many outdoors folks and scientists came to understand that more—much more—was needed if the United States was not to lose its wild things. As our knowledge about wildlife and wildland grew—along with our understanding of the threats to them—so did our conservation vision.

WILDERNESS

Down the River Wild, another stream—Wilderness—runs in. The work to set up Wilderness Areas came first from Forest Service rangers, such as Arthur Carhart and Aldo Leopold, thirty years after the first Forest Reserves. Leopold, who spoke out against "Ford dust" in the backcountry, feared that the growing automobile takeover of the National Forests would do away with the pioneer skills of early foresters. He wanted to keep alive the kind of life on horseback he knew when he came to Arizona's Apache National Forest as a new ranger out of Yale in 1909. "Wilderness areas are first of all a series of sanctuaries for the primitive arts of wilderness travel, especially canoeing and packing," wrote Leopold.[1] He called the frontier values of Wilderness Areas *split-rail* values.[2] In 1921, he wrote that wilderness was "a continuous stretch of country preserved in its natural state, open to lawful hunting and fishing, big enough to absorb a two weeks' pack trip, and kept devoid of roads, artificial trails, cottages, or other works of man."[3] In his first definition of Wilderness, then, he saw it as a recreational area where one could keep alive old-time traveling and camping skills—those without motors or wheels. After World War One, automobiles and roads threatened this back of beyond, which was once widespread in the National Forests. The roadless backcountry needed shielding were it not to slip away. In the 1930s, a growing wave of wilderfolks asked that wilderness also be marked off in National Parks; they believed the Parks were threatened by the National Park Service and the tourist industry, both of which wanted to build scenic highways for motoring sightseers. Leaders of the Park Service, however, said that wilderness was already protected in the Parks and did not need to be shown on maps.[4] Historian Paul Sutter writes, "When Aldo Leopold proposed a 'wilderness' designation for the Gila National Forest, he was quite clear that he sought to save the area not from [logging], but from improved roads and automobiles." National Park designation would not do the job Leopold wanted thanks to roads in the Parks; a new kind of public land that kept out roads was needed.[5]

1   Aldo Leopold, *A Sand County Almanac* (Oxford University Press, NY, NY 1987(1949)), 193.
2   Leopold, *Sand County Almanac,* 177.
3   Aldo Leopold, "The Wilderness and Its Place in Forest Recreational Policy," *The Journal of Forestry* 1921 in Susan L. Flader and J. Baird Callicott, eds., *The River of the Mother of God and Other Essays by Aldo Leopold* (The University of Wisconsin Press, Madison 1991), 79.
4   John C. Miles, *Wilderness in National Parks: Playground or Preserve* (University of Washington Press, Seattle, 2009).
5   Paul S. Sutter, "Driven Wild: Roads, Automobiles, and the Origins of

Leopold's brainchild of Wilderness Areas would later be broadened under the sway of the next two streams.

ECOSYSTEM REPRESENTATION

On the other side of the River Wild, right below its meeting with the Wilderness Stream, the Ecological Representation Brook trickles in.[6] As early as 1926, the *Naturalist's Guide to the Americas*, edited by one of America's leading biologists, Victor Shelford, called for finding and setting aside ecologically representative natural areas.[7] Since then, both the National Audubon Society and The Nature Conservancy have worked to buy and shield ecosystems not otherwise held by government.[8] The National Park Service and conservationists have sought to set up National Parks for all main ecosystems, but without fulfillment. The 1975 Eastern Wilderness Areas Act, which brought Wilderness Areas to National Forests east of the Rockies, was straightforwardly about ecosystem representation. Senator James Buckley, the bill's chief sponsor, said, "The point of introducing the Eastern Wilderness Areas Act today is to demonstrate that we can have a system of wilderness areas nationwide, not merely regional, in scope, representative of the diversity of our land, of its flora and fauna, and history."[9] Conservationists sought to put drylands in the Wilderness System through a Wilderness Review section in the Bureau of Land Management Organic Act in 1976. During the Second Roadless Area

Wilderness Advocacy," *Core Connections: The Newsletter of the Southern Rockies Ecosystem Project,* Fall/Winter 1997-98.

6   I discuss how ecological representation and other ecological cares were folded into work on Wilderness Areas in *Rewilding North America* (Island Press, Washington, D.C., 2004), 144-156.

7   Victor E. Shelford, ed., *Naturalist's Guide to the Americas* (Williams and Wilkins, Baltimore, MD, 1926).

8   Since 1990, however, The Nature Conservancy has been edging away from protecting natural areas. See Dave Foreman, *Take Back Conservation* (Raven's Eye Press, Durango, CO, 2012), 123-145.

9   Congressional Record—Senate, January 11, 1973, S 437.

Review and Evaluation (RARE II), the Forest Service, with backing from wilderfolk, sought new Wilderness Areas for hitherto left-out ecosystems.[10] Once again, though, development threats drove this wild stream. Had Shelford and friends not highlighted the need, the United States would have lost even tag-ends of many of the plant communities and ecosystems that embodied the soul of the North American landscape. Ecosystem representation, nonetheless, has not gotten the heed it needs. In a special report for the Department of the Interior in 1995, conservation biologist Reed Noss and his co-authors lined out our poor record of protecting representative ecosystems.[11]

PREDATOR PROTECTION

Just after the Ecosystem Representation Brook, the Predator Protection Stream splashes down as a waterfall. In "A Nature Sanctuary Plan," unanimously adopted by the Ecological Society of America on December 28, 1932, Victor Shelford wrote, "Biologists are beginning to realize that it is dangerous to tamper with nature by introducing plants or animals, or by destroying predatory animals or by pampering herbivores...." The Ecological Society said we needed to protect whole assemblages of native species, including large carnivores, and the natural fluctuations in numbers of species.[12] At that time, shielding wolves and mountain lions was—well, bold, hence my seeing it as a

10   Draft Action Plan and Instructions for Ecosystem Representation Data Collection RARE II (Forest Service, August 31, 1977); Assignment of Regional Targets (Ecosystem Representation, Landform Representation, Wilderness Associated Wildlife Representation) for NWPS (Forest Service, January 16, 1978). George Davis of the RARE II staff was behind these documents. Sadly, he is a little-known hero of the modern wilderness network.

11   Reed Noss, Edward T. LaRoe III, and J. Michael Scott, *Endangered Ecosystems of the United States: A Preliminary Assessment of Loss and Degradation,* Biological Report 28 (USDI National Biological Service, Washington, February 1995).

12   Victor E. Shelford, "The Preservation of Natural Biotic Communities," *Ecology,* April, 1933.

waterfall. Large carnivores were threatened with being wiped out in the United States. They were already mostly gone from the National Parks. The earlier wildlife protection movement was about keeping and bringing back "game" and fish and, in its ecological dimness, often called for slaughtering predators to grow herds and flocks of "desirable" or "good" game birds and mammals. Therefore, I see predator protection as its own side-stream.[13] It wasn't until the 1990s, though, that biologists in federal and state agencies, other biologists, and grassroots conservationists grew strong enough to gain wolf recovery in the Northern Rockies and Southwest. We haven't had the strength yet to reintroduce cougars and wolves into suitable habitat in the East.

ENDANGERED SPECIES

The wildlife protection movement was led by sportsmen against market hunting and game hogs. Again, its goal was hanging onto sturdy populations of game birds, fish, and mammals for hunting and fishing by true sportsmen and -women. The struggle for predators was led by scientists and was mostly targeted against "predator control," which was ridding the lower 48 states of large carnivores. Keeping endangered and threatened wildlife alive, however, should be seen as another stream flowing into the River Wild. It is grounded in a deeper understanding of the extinction crisis and is for all kinds of wildeors and plants that are up against the wall thanks to the Man swarm.

In 1935, after a trip to look at forest management in Germany, Aldo Leopold wrote that the first job for conservation in Europe and North America was to save rare species.[14] In 1936, in a landmark article

13   Michael Robinson of the Center for Biological Diversity authored an amazingly in-depth work about the early wolf-slaughter program of the federal government: *Predatory Bureaucracy: The Extermination of Wolves and the Transformation of the West* (University of Colorado Press, Boulder, 2005). If you want to understand the mad single-mindedness of predator extermination, you must read Robinson's book.
14   Aldo Leopold, "Naturshutz in Germany," *Bird-Lore,* Vol. 38, No. 2, 1936.

for *American Forests,* "Threatened Species," he wrote, "That there are grizzlies in Alaska is no excuse for letting the species disappear from New Mexico." Furthermore, he called for putting aside habitat for other fast-going beings like the ivory-billed woodpecker.[15] He was years ahead of his time.

In 1962, the Bureau of Sport Fisheries and Wildlife (today known as the U.S. Fish & Wildlife Service) started a Committee on Endangered Species, which soon became the Office of Endangered Species. In 1964—thirty years after Leopold's call, the office put out a list of sixty endangered birds, mammals, fish, reptiles, and amphibians. The 1966 Endangered Species Preservation Act appropriated $15 million from the Land and Water Conservation Fund to buy land for Endangered Species, and told federal land managers to look after Endangered Species on the lands they oversaw. Over time, more and more conservation and animal welfare clubs waded into this stream. President Nixon called for stronger care of Endangered Species in 1972, and tough steps soon followed: the Marine Mammal Protection Act in 1972, the Convention on International Trade in Endangered Species of Wild Fauna and Flora (CITES) in 1973, and the sweeping 1973 Endangered Species Act.[16] Soon thereafter, Norman Myers, Hugh Iltis, John Terborgh, and other biologists warned that we were in the midst of the greatest extinction since the end of the dinosaurs.[17]

---

15   Aldo Leopold, "Threatened Species: A proposal to the Wildlife Conference for an inventory of the needs of near-extinct birds and animals," *American Forests,* 42:3, March 1936, 116-119; reprinted in David E. Brown and Neil B. Carmony, eds., *Aldo Leopold's Southwest* (University of New Mexico Press, Albuquerque, 1995), 193-198.

16   Thomas R. Dunlap, *Saving America's Wildlife: Ecology and the American Mind, 1850-1990* (Princeton University Press, Princeton, NJ, 1988), 142-155.

17   Dave Foreman, *Rewilding North America: A Vision for 21st Century Conservation* (Island Press, Washington, DC, 2004).

CONNECTIVITY

One hundred years after the beginning of Yellowstone National Park, ecologists and population biologists began to grasp that fragmentation of the landscape by roads, dams, clearcuts, farms, cities, and other building was a big hurdle to wide-roving wildeors. Breaking up forests was blamed for the slump in forest-nesting songbirds. Moreover, the species-area relationship held that when 90 percent of an ecosystem is lost, 50 percent of the species in it are lost.[18] Conservation since 1990 or so has been driven by the knowledge that we need to keep and rebuild wildlife linkages between core wildernesses, that National Parks, Wildlife Refuges, and Wilderness Areas cannot keep all their native species when they are islands of habitat in a sea of unfriendly human settlement and other wrung-out land.[19]

ECOLOGICAL RESTORATION

Since about 1980, many wilderness lovers and biologists have grasped that it is not enough to keep what's left of wilderness and wildlife, but that we need to restore wounded ecosystems. David Brower called for global CPR—conservation, preservation, and restoration.[20] The Wildlands Project sought insight from Aldo Leopold, who saw "wounds" in the land and called on wildlovers to "heal" these wounds.[21]

REWILDING

In 1998, two of the leading conservation biologists, Michael Soulé and Reed Noss, called for a new conservation stream: Rewilding.

18   As the aforementioned Noss report documented, many of our country's ecosystems have been chopped by that amount or more. *Endangered Ecosystems of the United States: A Preliminary Assessment of Loss and Degradation.*

19   Foreman, *Rewilding North America*. Also see www.rewilding.org.

20   David Brower and Steve Chapple, *Let the Mountains Talk, Let the Rivers Run* (HarperCollins, New York, 1995).

21   Aldo Leopold, *Round River: From the Journals of Aldo Leopold* (Oxford University Press, New York, 1972), 165. Foreman, *Rewilding North America*. Also see www.rewilding.org.

Research now shows that many ecosystems need large carnivores, such as wolves and jaguars, for ecological integrity. Big wild-hunters need big wildlands for homes. Few wildernesses are still big enough to hold healthy populations of large carnivores, so linkages or *wildways* between wild places are needed. This rewilding stream stirs together all of the earlier streams of the River Wild into what I have called a Vision for 21st century conservation.[22]

These twentieth-century side streams have joined with the nineteenth-century headwater streams of the River Wild to shape a conservation movement for the twenty-first century. Although there has been a widespread welcome for the new streams, too often it is talk only, and conservation clubs have not brought such streams as representation and connectivity wholly into their thinking and Wilderness Area proposals.

Many battles were fought over each of these streams. Although the old-time landscalpers and their newer Nature-hating friends have been big dogs against taking care of wild things, much of the fight in the twentieth century was between resource agencies such as the Forest Service and wilderness and wildlife conservation clubs such as the Sierra Club. Resourcists wanted to tame wildland and to kill wildeors that seemed to be of no worth to Man. Conservationists stood athwart this road of taming wilderness and worked to keep wild things wild. In the next chapters, we'll see how this fight unfolded in manifold landscapes and over sundry wild things from the 1890s to 2001—the Public Lands Century.

---

22   Michael Soulé and Reed Noss, "Rewilding and Biodiversity: Complementary Goals for Continental Conservation," *Wild Earth*, Fall 1998, 18-28. For an in-depth look at rewilding, see Foreman, *Rewilding North America*. For the solid scientific bedrock on which Rewilding rests, see Michael E. Soulé and John Terborgh, eds., *Continental Conservation: Scientific Foundations of Regional Reserve Networks* (Island Press, Washington, DC, 1999).

CHAPTER 11

The Public Lands I

THE AMERICAN PUBLIC LANDS

One Third of the Nation's Land was the title of the report from the congressionally set-up Public Land Law Review Commission in 1970, and one-third of the nation's land is yours and mine. Not the timber companies'. Not the land and cattle companies'. Not the mining companies'. Not the rich folks'. Not the land speculators'. Ours. One-third of the acreage of the United States of America is yet owned by her citizens and overseen by the federal government—740 million acres in all. These are the National Parks, National Wildlife Refuges, National Forests, and Bureau of Land Management lands. Moreover, the sundry states own on behalf of their citizens another 197 million acres, such as grazing and oil leasing lands in the West, timber lands in the East and West Coast, and state parks, state forests, and state hunting areas in all of them.[1] All of this came out of Yellowstone National Park, Adirondack Forest Preserve, and President Harrison's forest reserves.

---

1   There are over 6,600 state parks with 14 million acres of land.

These lands are why the United States has a conservation legacy unmatched elsewhere in the world. Underline that last sentence. As I have learned more about international conservation, I've wondered why the whole game of protecting land seems easier in the United States (not that it's easy here, but alongside other countries we are better off). Our public lands are the answer. I know of no other country that has such a set-up with its citizens owning and having a strong say in the running of one-third of the country's land acreage. Two federal laws above all give citizens and their clubs sturdy handles to help guide stewardship of the public lands: the Wilderness Act and the National Environmental Policy Act (NEPA).

Canada has something like our public lands—Crown Lands—but they are not like National Forests or even BLM lands. For one thing, they are not even under multiple-use management, but are wide-open to be leased long-term to logging or mining companies. For another, although Crown Lands are owned by the nation of Canada, the provinces, not the feds, run them. The mighty woe of this is that if acreage is to be set aside, it is the province alone who can do it— or not do it. (However, the federal government can set up National Parks, which they run.) There are Provincial Parks throughout Canada, but they are not like our National Parks; they are much more like our National Forests. Australia has a set-up much like Canada's. Moreover, willingness to set aside land as parks or such hangs on the political party running the province or state in their parliamentary set-ups. Neither country has the kind of federal laws the US has such as the Wilderness Act, National Environmental Policy Act (NEPA), Endangered Species Act, and others for the whole country and that give citizens a mighty hand in helping to shape policy. (Canada does have an endangered species law, but it is not as tough as that of the US. However, Canada's National Parks are a match for those in the US.) Mexico is even worse in having almost no public lands. Nearly all lands in our neighbor to the south are privately owned or owned by *ejidos*, communal lands for underwriting a village. Mexico's National Parks are often on private or ejido land and mean little. One such is the Toluca Nevada National Park; an ejido owns all but a few thousand acres on top of the volcano owned by the federal government and only those lands are protected by park guards (to keep divers from looting artifacts from the two Toltec sacrifice lakes).[2] Only a few such as Pinacate in Sonora south of Arizona are truly federal lands.

In no other nation do citizens have as many handles on the gears of political conservation as do those of the United States and none have anything like our federal public lands. The United States is a standalone nation for conservation most of all for the public lands and a steadily more open door for citizen input on their stewardship. Our matchless system of U.S. public lands is the key for our gains in conservation notwithstanding the economic, political, and philosophical might of those fighting protection of public lands in the United States: resource agencies, corporations, politicians, landscalpers, motor-bound brats, Nature haters, and conspiracy nuts. Indeed, though the slaughter of wild things goes on, in the United States at least, conservationists have done one heck of a job against the mighty landscalpers of dollar-fat businesses ransacking the land with political help from agency managers who love the sound of drill rigs and chainsaws. Public lands have not been given the acknowledgment for this that they are owed, although much of conservation has been and will go on being about how to steward public lands.[3]

---

2   Brian Miller, pers. corres.
3   The key books for understanding the public lands as a whole are Ber-
     nard Shanks, *This Land Is Your Land* (Sierra Club Books, San Francisco,
     1984); Dyan Zaslowsky and T. H. Watkins, *These American Lands* (The
     Wilderness Society and Island Press, Washington, 1994); and William
     K. Wyant, *Westward In Eden: The Public Lands and the Conservation
     Movement* (University of California Press, Berkeley, 1982). There are
     also guidebooks to the National Parks, Wildlife Refuges, and Wilderness
     Areas, as well as websites for the sundry agencies.

Back in Earth First! in the 1980s, I puzzled over why Canada and Australia were able to mobilize many more folks for civil disobedience than we could in the United States. At last it dawned on me that wildlovers in Canada and Australia did not have the legislative handles to lawfully sway or thwart government ransacking of wildlands or snuffing of wildlife that we had in the United States—the Wilderness Act, National Environmental Policy Act, Endangered Species Act, Clean Water Act, and National Forest Management Act, to name only a few. Therefore, they often had no way to fight landscalping but to stand in front of the bulldozers or chainsaws. After the breakup of Earth First! in 1990, some former Earth First!ers started tough, uncompromising teams such as the Center for Biological Diversity to work within the system to make federal agencies follow the law to shield wild neighborhoods and list Threatened and Endangered Species. Thanks to our (US) public lands and the laws dealing with them, such "paper monkeywrenching" worked better than direct action overall against harmful grazing, logging, drilling, and other exploitation.

When I think about it, I have to chortle that the set-up to pay off the war debt of the American Revolution had the unforeseen witchery to bring about our unmatched conservation heritage. Death tales from the Killing Decades and the awfulness of landscalping in the US notwithstanding, we have a gift of great worth in our public lands. Without them, wild things would be in far worse shape than they are in the US. We conservationists should never brook mistaken catcalls from "new conservationists" that our hoary conservation path has failed owing to the weight we give to set-aside public lands.

Mind you, I am not saying that America's public lands are flawless or the best they can be. They are far from that. After all, the shortcomings of our public lands are what this book is about. But we have them! And that is wonderful and worth more than we often think.

THE PUBLIC LAND SYSTEMS

Public lands are not of one kind. This rather jumbled line-up of managing agencies is another way the United States stands out in conservation—since the Federal Lands Policy and Management Act (FLPMA) in 1976, which was the "organic act" for the Bureau of Land Management and which once and for all did away with disposal. Public lands are now all stacked into one of the *systems* of public lands. These systems are under sundry managing agencies, with a jumble of mandates. Many state lands are also dealt out into two or more state systems under different agencies. This chapter and the next are about the federal systems of public lands, how each came about, and how each is cared for.

Most federal land is overseen by one of four government agencies, each part of a cabinet-level department:

U.S. Forest Service (USFS or FS)—Department of Agriculture: National Forests (NFs), National Grasslands, some National Recreation Areas (NRAs), and a few National Monuments. 193 million acres in forty-three states and Puerto Rico. These are "multiple-use" lands—unless designated Wilderness Areas—mostly open to commercial timber cutting, livestock grazing, mining, energy drilling and digging, dams, power-line and pipeline rights-of-way, road-building (the USFS is the world's biggest road-managing agency with over 400,000 miles, from two-tracks to paved), off-road vehicle (ORV) play, firewood gathering, built campgrounds, outfitter camps, privately owned cabins on leased NF land, trapping, and hunting and fishing. National Forest lands can also be leased by businesses for ski areas and other resorts, though the Forest Service must, with our input, write Environmental Impact Statements to say how such are to be run. Ranchers graze livestock in many NF Wilderness Areas—an unhappy compromise for getting the Wilderness Act through Congress. The "line officer" hierarchy is Chief, Regional Foresters, National Forest Supervisors, and District Rangers.

National Park Service (NPS)—Department of the Interior: National Parks (NPs), National Monuments (NMs), National Seashores and Lakeshores, National Recreation Areas (NRAs), National Preserves, and other areas, including historical and cultural sites. Almost 80 million acres in all fifty states and some overseas territories. NPS lands are on the whole not open to hunting, livestock grazing, logging, mining, or energy gobbling, and vehicles must stay on roads or designated routes; but there are striking exceptions. Parks are not shielded from development, however. Industrial tourism can have a big and often nasty footprint in Parks: paved highways, hotels, stores, cruise ships, overflights, helicopter tours, snowmobiles, even ski areas, and other plush, tawdry, or thrilling merriments can leave wild things tattered. The line officer hierarchy is Director, Regional Directors, and National Park Superintendents.

U.S. Fish & Wildlife Service (USFWS or FWS)—Department of the Interior: National Wildlife Refuges (NWRs). 150 million acres in every state and in many island possessions of the US. Although NWRs are for wildlife production and habitat stewardship, some are open to logging, mining, energy extraction, livestock grazing, speedboats, and ORVs. Many NWRs also have public hunting and fishing areas. Moreover, few are taken care of mainly for threatened or rare species; nearly all were set up to make sure there would be plenty of ducks and geese and big game for hunting. However, refuge managers were on the whole more for Wilderness Area designation on their refuges than were managers in other agencies. Not only are some of the wildest and best-cared-for Wilderness Areas on National Wildlife Refuges but also some of the best Wilderness boundaries are on NWRs thanks to the way refuge managers backed Wilderness. The Arctic National Wildlife

Refuge in Alaska may be the best-stewarded Wilderness Area in the US. I think of it as the Flagship of the National Wilderness Preservation System. Alas, the biggest and wildest refuge in the lower 48 states, Cabeza Prieta in western Arizona on the Mexican border, has had its once-untracked Sonoran Desert flats shredded by unlawful immigrants, drug smugglers, and U.S. Border Patrol vehicles running amuck in designated Wilderness, to the deep unhappiness of refuge staff.

Bureau of Land Management (BLM)—Department of the Interior: National Conservation Areas (NCAs), newly set-up National Monuments (since the late-1990s), and undesignated public lands. 268.5 million acres in twenty-eight states (thirteen of these states outside the West have rather piddling acreages). These are multiple-use lands, like the National Forests, but often with even less oversight from the agency. Strong steps were taken by Interior Secretary Bruce Babbitt and President Bill Clinton at the end of Clinton's administration by wielding the Antiquities Act to withdraw large areas for National Monuments in many western states. For the most, these new Monuments were kept under the BLM and not shuffled over to the National Park Service. A good fallout from this is that it gave BLM a big acreage of semi-protected land to care for and called for more BLM staff given to land caring instead of resource exploitation. However, these National Monuments are only as good as the management plan for each. BLM set up the National Landscape Conservation System for these National Monuments, along with Wilderness Areas, Wilderness Study Areas, Wild & Scenic Rivers, and such under BLM jurisdiction. The line officers are Director, State Director, District Manager, and Area Manager.

OTHER FEDERAL LAND

Millions of acres of other federal lands are under the Air Force, Army, Navy, and Marine Corps of the Department of Defense:

reservations, ranges, test sites, forts, ports, and bases. These lands are almost always not open to the public, but some have outstanding natural areas and homes for Endangered and Threatened Species. Sometimes these lands and wildlife are well sheltered and cared for under good stewardship plans. Make no mistake, however, the "mission" of the base always comes first. Military lands are most often not thought of as public lands. Some other federal agencies such as the Bureau of Reclamation and Army Corps of Engineers have recreational lands in small bits, and the Department of Energy and some others manage land but not for public use.

These systems did not leap from Uncle Sam's forehead fully made, nor did they grow in a thoughtful way, but came about in a willy-nilly tumble, with business keeping as much sway over them as it could for as long as it could, while conservationists and some agency people tried to run them for the good of all the people and even for the good of the land. The endless tug of war between dollar-driven businesses and thrill-driven motorheads, federal resourcists, and wild-loving citizen conservationists shaped and made the public lands what they are today.

As much as the Bill of Rights, our public lands define who we are as Americans and have been key to what gains wildlovers have made in the United States.

In the next chapter, we'll delve more deeply into the federal public land systems.

CHAPTER 12

The Public Lands II

ALTHOUGH MANY KEY CONSERVATION LAWS—The Wilderness Act, National Wild & Scenic Rivers Act, National Environmental Policy Act, Endangered Species Act, and others—apply to the four federal land systems, each also has laws specific to it as well as different regulations, history, organization and style.

NATIONAL PARK SYSTEM

The first public lands withdrawn for conservation were National Parks: Yellowstone in 1872 and Yosemite, Sequoia, and General Grant (later folded into Sequoia) in 1890.[1] Other early National Parks set up by acts of Congress were Mount Rainier, Washington, 1899; Crater Lake, Oregon, 1902; Mesa Verde, Colorado, 1906; Petrified Forest, Arizona, 1906; Grand Canyon, Arizona, 1908; Zion, Utah, 1909; Olympic, Washington, 1909; Glacier, Montana, 1910; Rocky

---

1   I say "for conservation" since the first withdrawals from the public lands were for army and navy forts and ports, post offices, canals, and other public works.

Mountain, Colorado, 1915; and Hawaii Volcanoes, Hawaii, 1916.[2] Behind most of these Parks was a champion like John Muir, Enos Mills (Rocky Mountain), or Judge William Steel (Crater Lake), and a struggle with boomers seeking a fast buck.

In 1906, Congress passed the Antiquities Act to halt the wholesale looting of Indian ruins on the public lands. This legislation forbade taking "objects of antiquity" from public lands. It also gave the President authority to withdraw public lands from disposal so as to protect "objects of historic and scientific interest."[3] Such withdrawals were named *National Monuments*. Theodore Roosevelt set aside the first National Monuments in 1906: Devils Tower (Wyoming), El Morro (New Mexico), and Montezuma Castle (Arizona). Twenty such National Monuments had been brought into being by executive orders of presidents Roosevelt, Taft, and Wilson by 1916. Many of our best known National Parks were first administratively set up as National Monuments and later were made into National Parks by Congress: Lassen Peak (California), Grand Canyon, Olympic, Zion, Carlsbad Caverns (New Mexico), and Death Valley (California), for starters. Historian Hal Rothman writes, "The real achievement of the Antiquities Act of 1906 was that it allowed the establishment of a system of preservation without the approval of Congress. Prior to its existence there had been few mechanisms through which the federal government could permanently and easily preserve the public domain."[4] However, thirteen out of the twenty-eight National Monuments in 1911 were run by the Forest Service, no friend to land set-asides at that time. Indeed, in 1915, President Woodrow Wilson, under the sway of the Forest

2   Dyan Zaslowsky and T. H. Watkins, The Wilderness Society *These American Lands* (Island Press, Washington, DC, 1994), 1.
3   Hal Rothman, *America's National Monuments: The Politics of Preservation* (University Press of Kansas, 1989), 47.
4   Rothman, *National Monuments*, xvi-xvii.

Service, undid most of Mt. Olympus National Monument so it would be open for logging.[5]

In *These American Lands*, Dyan Zaslowsky and Tom Watkins write, "By 1916, then, one might charitably say that a national park system was in place—but if so, it was a system without system. It was, first of all, headless; nowhere in official Washington could 'an inquirer find an office of the national parks or a single desk devoted solely to their management....'"[6] In 1916, after a citizens' campaign, Congress passed an "organic act" for the National Parks and a system was started to be run by the National Park Service in the Department of the Interior.[7] The Park Service was told "to conserve the scenery and the natural and historic objects and the wildlife therein, and to provide for the enjoyment of the same in such manner and by such means as will leave them unimpaired for the enjoyment of future generations."[8] (Canada, by the way, beat the United States out of the blocks, and set up a National Park agency in 1911.[9]) Today, the NPS stewards 90 million acres, in every state and in several territories (over 52 million acres are in Alaska).

---

5   Alfred Runte, *National Parks: The American Experience* Second Edition, Revised (University of Nebraska Press, Lincoln, 1987), 98. Wilson was no friend of wild things; Coolidge and Hoover were both better conservationists. Indeed, since 1892, Wilson is the only President from the Democratic Party as uninterested in conservation as is Barrack Obama. However, Republicans William McKinley, Warren Harding, Ronald Reagan, and George W. Bush were far worse than Wilson and Obama. Small praise, indeed.

6   Zaslowsky and Watkins, *These American Lands*, 21.

7   J. Horace McFarland and the American Civic Association, the Department of Interior, and the railroads were stout backers. The Forest Service was a strong foe. Also against was former USFS Chief Gifford Pinchot, who had been given the boot by President Taft in 1910. Runte, *National Parks*, 97-103.

8   Zaslowsky and Watkins, *These American Lands*, 24.

9   J. B. Harkin, *The History and Meaning of the National Parks of Canada* (H. R. Larson Publishing Company, Saskatoon, Saskatchewan, 1957), 5.

NATIONAL FOREST SYSTEM

The second public lands system is the National Forest System.[10] Little heed was given the few words riding the General Revision Act of 1891, which authorized the President to "set apart and reserve … public land bearing forests … or in part covered by timber or undergrowth, whether of commercial values or not, as public reservations."[11] This provision, which was the beginning of the National Forest System, was the brainchild of President Benjamin Harrison's Secretary of the Interior, John W. Noble, and of Bernhard Fernow, head of the Division of Forestry. When its full meaning and weight were later grasped, this rider was called the Forest Reserve Act. The day Harrison signed the bill into law (March 3, 1891) is truly a red-letter day in our history, and Harrison's signing led to the coming look of our landscape and to the ongoing free soul of the American folk as have only a few other things. Noble, Fernow, and Harrison should be acknowledged as great early conservationists. The three also stand more rightfully as the daddies of the National Forests than does Gifford Pinchot.

On March 3 we should have a picnic in a nearby National Forest, roast weenies or whatever, and toast John, Bernie, and Ben with the best champagne we can afford. Be sure to take whatever kiddies you can round up. March 3 should be an American holiday (holy-day).

There are three widespread misunderstandings about the Forest Reserves withdrawn under the 1891 law's authority. One is that land was withdrawn only on the utilitarian grounds of keeping watersheds from harm. Two is that reserves were mostly uncared-for after being withdrawn. Three is that these early Forest Reserves were open to logging, mining, livestock grazing, and other make-a-buck uses. James

---

10 We can bicker over this statement. Yellowstone National Park came twenty years before the first Forest Reserves, but the *system* of Forest Reserves and its upgrade to the National Forest System came before the National Park System by twenty-five, seventeen, or eleven years, hinging on which law you pick—1916 vs. 1891 or 1897 or 1905. Your choice.

11 Section 24 of the Act of March 3, 1891.

Muhn sets things straight in his chapter for the worthy anthology, *The Origins of the National Forests*. In truth, from the beginning, Forest Reserves were chosen for scenery, recreation, and wildlife habitat, as well as for watershed protection. Notwithstanding a lack of funding and few field agents, steps were taken to shield the reserves, and all grazing, mining, and logging was banned from them.

Secretary of the Interior John Noble ordered that the reserves would "preserve the fauna, fish and flora of our country, and become resorts for the people seeking instruction and recreation." Muhn wrote, "He also expressed willingness to withdraw those areas of 'great interest to our people because of their natural beauty, or remarkable features.'"[12] Noble is an unsung American hero and visionary—a twentieth-century man who lived in the nineteenth century.

Under the following Cleveland administration (Harrison was a Republican and Cleveland was a Democrat), Noble's great work could have been undone, but the new Secretary of the Interior, M. Hoke Smith, built further on Noble's framework and put out regulations on April 14, 1894, that were published "in local newspapers and posted along forest reserve boundaries....No one, it announced, could 'settle upon, occupy, or use any of these lands for agricultural, prospecting, mining, or other business purposes.' They could not 'cut, remove, or use any of the timber, grass, or other natural product,' fires were forbidden, and the grazing of livestock was 'strictly prohibited.'"[13]

Sheepherders, a low breed of men then, in California's Sierra Forest Reserve swiftly tore down the notices. Sheep were brazenly driven into Oregon's Cascade Reserve, as well. Timber cutters also trespassed. Not backing down, Smith went after wrongdoers in the federal courts. He

---

12   James Muhn, "Early Administration of the Forest Reserve Act: Interior Department and General Land Office Policies, 1891-1897," in Harold K. Steen, ed., *The Origins of the National Forests* (Forest History Society, 1992), 260.

13   Muhn, "Forest Reserve Act," 265.

won with a federal court ruling in Oregon in the fall of 1896.[14] Congress
and two presidents and Secretaries of the Interior from clashing parties
had stood up for the making of a new system of public lands withdrawn
from disposal and under amazingly tough stewardship. Now the federal
courts said not only were the withdrawals constitutional but so also was
bold, tough stewardship for keeping the Four Horsemen of the Frontier
out—settlers, grazers, miners, and loggers. Such stewardship went
against the whole thrust of Manifest Destiny and the holy belief that
land and raw goods were good only if put to work for Man. Hoke Smith
also is more rightfully another daddy of the National Forests than is
Pinchot. And, so, don't forget to raise a glass to Hoke and Grover, too,
when you do so for John, Bernie, and Ben. Thank them for what we
have today.

But, on June 4, 1897, a management act for the forest reserves
was passed as an amendment to another bill. This Forest Organic Act
authorized the Secretary of Interior to "regulate the occupancy and
use" of the reserves, but gave little direction as to what that should be.[15]
However, the reserves were now open to livestock grazing, logging, and
mining. The high hopefulness of wilderness set-asides for the forest
reserves was shelved. But the forest reserves under federal management
stayed, notwithstanding the setback in stewardship.

In 1905, the 65 million acres of forest reserves were shifted to
the Bureau of Forestry (renamed the Forest Service in 1907) in the
Department of Agriculture. All the withdrawn forests at that time
were from public lands in the West. In 1911, the Weeks Act authorized
"the purchase of eastern forests to protect the headwaters of navigable
streams."[16] The 1924 Clark-McNary Act extended permission to
buy any lands in the East for National Forests.[17] Thus came a truly

14   Muhn, "Forest Reserve Act," 265-267.
15   Zaslowsky and Watkins, *These American Lands,* 68.
16   Named after the bill's sponsor, Representative John W. Weeks of
      Massachusetts.
17   Alfred Runte, *The National Forest Idea: Public Lands, Public Heritage*

National Forest System, which today totals about 193 million acres in 176 National Forests and Grasslands in 44 states, Puerto Rico, and the Virgin Islands.

NATIONAL WILDLIFE REFUGES

With an executive order, Theodore Roosevelt set up the first National Wildlife Refuge in 1903—Florida's Pelican Island—to shield wading birds from market hunters killing them for their plumes (used to pretty-up the hats of Gibson Girls). There are now 561 National Wildlife Refuges, with at least one in every state and territory. The total acreage is 93 million (76.3 million acres are in Alaska). There was not, however, a National Wildlife Refuge System until the signing of the National Wildlife Refuge System Improvement Act in 1997. That's right—1997. The U.S. Fish & Wildlife Service oversees the refuges; they are often seen as the poor sister to the service's other programs. Refuge managers long have been unhappy with the service's caring for the refuges. Not until October 1998 had there ever been a national meeting of refuge heads.[18] A full-on organic act is needed for a National Wildlife Refuge System run by its own agency free of the Fish & Wildlife Service, which, as we shall see, has often been a feckless and shameful steward of the other Earthlings living in the United States.

BUREAU OF LAND MANAGEMENT

Although the Bureau of Land Management (BLM) oversees the greatest acreage of federal land of any of the agencies (268 million acres, mostly in the 11 contiguous western states and Alaska), the agency and its lands are the least known. Indeed, its holdings have been called "The Lands No One Knows," the forgotten lands, and the lands no one wanted. There is not even a popular name for BLM's lands.

(Roberts Rinehart Publishers, Niwot, CO, 1991), 55, 60.
18   Jamie Rappaport Clark, *Director's Priorities FY 1999-2000* (U.S. Fish & Wildlife Service), 4.

THE GREAT CONSERVATION DIVIDE

"National Resource Lands" was tried and fizzled like the Edsel. "Public Lands" is right, but can also be for any federal lands. Most folks say the redundant "BLM lands."

For these are the leftovers. Left over, that is, after the land wheeler-dealers and railroads and timber outfits and big ranchers and homesteaders got theirs, fair and square or through swindles. After the states took their big slices. After the wooded mountains went to the Forest Service and the jaw-dropping scenery to the Park Service and the duck grounds to the Fish & Wildlife Service. This still left a lot of nobody's land in the West and Alaska owned by the federal government, grazed by local ranchers without true oversight, and picked over and trashed by prospectors and miners.

In 1934, the biggest, politically most-brawny ranchers got together behind the Taylor Grazing Act, outwardly to bring order out of the dark swirl of unregulated public lands grazing, but behind closed doors to rope in their overlordship of grazing rights. Bern Shanks writes, "It established a system of grazing preferences that favored large and established ranchers—the old western range aristocracy."[19] Taylor did, however, stop homesteading and most other ways to get rid of the public lands. In 1946, the Grazing Service, begun by Taylor, was blended with the General Land Office, which had sold or given away the public lands since 1812, to make up the Bureau of Land Management. This was a toothless caretaker agency that ranchers and miners slapped into the corner whenever it sat up to do its job.

The Public Land Law Review Commission was set up to study these unwanted lands, and, with their report in 1970, called for keeping them as federal lands run for multiple use. In 1976, President Ford signed an organic act for the BLM, the Federal Land Policy and Management Act (FLPMA). Thus ended an era. Between 1872 and 1976, the United States grappled for an answer of what to do with public lands other than

---

19   Bernard Shanks, *This Land Is Your Land* (Sierra Club Books, San Francisco, 1984), 81.

sell them or give them away. From Yellowstone to FLPMA, the nation slowly made up its mind to keep a heritage of land for the people. As I earlier wrote, these public lands set the United States off by itself and laid the groundwork for much of the way we do conservation. By and large, the conservation movement in the United States has worked on the public lands.

THE NATIONAL WILDERNESS PRESERVATION SYSTEM

Although there is no stand-alone "Wilderness Bureau" to care for Wilderness Areas (Wilderness Areas are kept under their earlier agency: Forest Service, Park Service, BLM, or Fish & Wildlife Service), they make up a system under one law—the 1964 Wilderness Act. Since the end of World War Two, wilderness has been at the heart of the three-sided struggle between conservationists and resource agencies like the Forest Service and the latter-day landscalpers. Until World War Two, though, Wilderness set-asides were something upon which conservation clubs and the Forest Service often saw eye-to-eye. As we've seen, the Wilderness Area idea came out of the Forest Service. Since 1945, however, the Forest Service has been the biggest stumbling block to new Wilderness Areas, notwithstanding all its swank about being the first friend of Wilderness Areas. (Though one could argue that since the mid-1990s with their growing overall loss of intelligence, reason, prudence, and true patriotism, Republican office-holders in the West have become the leading foes of Wilderness and other kinds of conservation. That, though, is the topic for another book.)

On December 6, 1919, two Forest Service staffers worried about the speedy loss of roadless, uncluttered wilderness met in Denver. They were Arthur Carhart, a Forest Service landscape architect ("beauty engineer"), and Aldo Leopold, from the Albuquerque regional office of the Forest Service. Both wanted to keep some of the slipping-away wilderness of the West. Leopold had heard about Carhart after Carhart wrote a report against a road and summer cabin lots around Trapper

Lake, in the Flat Tops of western Colorado, so as to keep whole the lake's wilderness feeling. (Carhart had been sent by the White River National Forest Supervisor to plan where the cabin lots should be.) From that meeting, Leopold went on to propose the Gila Wilderness Area in southwestern New Mexico, designated in 1924, and Carhart went on to put forward protection of the much-loved canoe lakes and pinewoods in the Superior National Forest of Minnesota, set up as the Superior Primitive Area in 1926 (later renamed the Boundary Waters Canoe Area and, in 1978, the Boundary Waters Canoe Wilderness Area).[20]

Aldo Leopold spoke at the second National Outdoor Recreation Conference in 1926. Three things he said there later became big roots for the National Wilderness Preservation System. First, he acknowledged that the National Parks should be players, and called for two kinds of wilderness recreation—one with guns in National Forests and one without guns in National Parks. Second, he called for wilderness to be set aside in the East in both National Forests and National Parks then being named there. And third, he worked to move folks away from the alpine aesthetic. Not only should mountainous landscapes be shielded as Wilderness Areas, but so should "swamps, lakelands, river routes, and deserts."[21] By calling for the protection of "river routes," Leopold was forty-two years ahead of the National Wild and Scenic River System (which will be the next system I deal with in this chapter).

In 1927, the Chief of the Forest Service, William B. Greeley, took heed of Leopold and Carhart's work and asked other regions of the Forest Service to think about keeping some Wilderness. He wrote, "The

20   Carhart lived long and started the Conservation Library partly to house his papers. The Conservation Library now takes up two floors of the Denver Public Library and has, among other key collections, The Wilderness Society papers. It will also house my archives, which I am slowly getting up there.
21   John C. Miles, *Wilderness in National Parks: Playground or Preserve* (University of Washington Press, Seattle, 2009), 50-51.

frontier has long ceased to be a barrier to civilization. The question is rather how much of it should be kept to preserve our civilization."[22] In 1929, Greeley put out Regulation L-20, which gave the go-ahead for "Primitive Areas" on the National Forests. This was in the Forest Service's "custodial" time, after the Forest Service had been set up as a lasting agency and before an all-out timber-selling and road-building mindset took over. Nonetheless, even in those early days, timber was uppermost in the minds of Forest Service brass. The regional office for the Pacific Northwest wrote "every Primitive Area has of course been selected with the idea of using lands with little or no value for timber or other commercial uses, unless it might be grazing."[23] Some Forest Supervisors and District Rangers were happy to keep roadless the backcountry they liked best for pack-trips and for hunting and fishing. Thus, sixty areas, mostly rugged, breathtaking high country with "jewel-like" lakes and rocky spires, came to be named as Primitive Areas by 1935. The Forest Service was a horse-and-mule outfit longer than any other government agency except maybe the National Park Service (though park rangers were more likely to hike than were forest rangers).

We have to give a big tip of the hat, though, to the National Park Service for the Forest Service's quick embrace of Primitive Areas. Horace Albright's biographer, Donald Swain, wrote that "Mather and Albright deserve credit for goading the Forest Service into recognizing the concept of preserving natural beauty, once described by Pinchot

22 Michael Frome, *Battle for the Wilderness* (Westview Encore Reprint, Boulder, CO, 1984), 121. Frome's book, first published in 1974 for The Wilderness Society, then updated in 1997, is the best history of down-to-earth Wilderness Area protection. It is strong in underlining how folk wildlovers were key for shielding agency-proposed Wilderness Areas and also working hard to set up new ones not wanted by the agencies. Frome highlights how citizens fought hard, often drawn-out struggles with the Forest Service and Park Service to keep them from wrecking potential wilderness. Revised Edition (University of Utah Press, Salt Lake City, 1997).

23 David A. Clary, *Timber and the Forest Service* (University Press of Kansas, Lawrence, 1986), 99.

as 'sentimental nonsense.'" [24] The Forest Service was gripped with a fear that the Park Service would "steal" its loveliest landscapes. This led Forest Service brass to boost Primitive Areas and wave them around to say we have our own system for keeping America's best scenery and recreation areas.

Chief Forester Roy Stuart called the FS brass in for a meeting on Primitive Areas in 1932. The foremost argument given for setting up Primitive Areas was that they could be roadblocks to National Park Service looting the National Forests for new Parks. A year after this meeting sixty-three Primitive Areas with 8.5 million acres had been set up. But what paper preserves they were! Only eight of the sixty-three were shielded from logging and twenty-three of them already had logging plans ready to go.[25] While running the Indian Forest Service for Harold Ickes in the Department of the Interior, Robert Marshall learned that the Forest Service wanted to build roads in Primitive Areas using New Deal funds from the Public Works Administration in Interior. Marshall talked to his friend Ickes to make sure the money wasn't available. This led the new Chief, Ferdinand Silcox, to ask regional foresters to take better care of the Primitive Areas.[26]

In May 1936, Silcox asked Bob Marshall to come back to work for the Forest Service as head of recreation where he would oversee the Primitive Areas. In his short time at that job (he died way too young in 1939), he worked to name new Primitive Areas—such as standouts Selway-Bitterroot, Sawtooth, and Three Sisters—and put together the U-1 and U-2 regulations, signed by Chief Silcox in September 1939. Under these regulations, the Secretary of Agriculture, with Forest Service recommendations, could set aside Wilderness Areas of 100,000 acres or more and Wild Areas of 5,000 to 100,000 acres. At that time, there were seventy-three Primitive Areas, 13 million acres in all. All were

24 Miles, *Wilderness in National Parks*, 39.
25 Miles, *Wilderness in National Parks*, 82.
26 Miles, *Wilderness in National Parks*, 83.

in the West, but for the Boundary Waters Canoe Area in Minnesota. (Nevada and Alaska had none.)[27] The U regs directed the National Forests to study the Primitive Areas each had and then to recommend them as Wilderness or Wild in line with their size, after more careful boundaries had been drawn and public hearings held. Wilderness and Wild Areas were administratively protected from logging, roads, resorts, summer homes, motorboats, and airplane landings.[28] (Fifteen more Primitive Areas with one million acres in all were set aside by the Forest Service before the 1964 Wilderness Act.)[29]

We'll later see how the Forest Service after World War Two worked to chop up the Marshall/Silcox wilderness system, and how that raid led to conservationists asking for and gaining congressional protection of Wilderness Areas. After World War Two and before the 1964 Wilderness Act wilderness folks were busy as bees keeping Primitive Areas from being cut back by the Forest Service.[30]

As of 2014, the fifty-year anniversary of the passage of the Wilderness Act, there are 758 Wilderness Areas with 109,511,038 acres. Of this, more than half, 57 million acres, are in Alaska. Some states, led by New York (1,170,312 acres), Alaska (922,700 acres), and California (466,320 acres), have Wilderness Area systems more or less following the federal Wilderness Act. A few Indian tribes, such as Taos Pueblo in New Mexico and the Flathead Reservation in Montana, have named Wilderness Areas on their lands.

The National Wild and Scenic Rivers System

Four years after the Wilderness Act, President Johnson signed the National Wild and Scenic Rivers Act on October 2, 1968: "It is hereby

---

27   *Search for Solitude: Our Wilderness Heritage* (USDA Forest Service, Washington, D.C., June 1970).

28   Frome, *Battle for the Wilderness,* 117-126.

29   *Search for Solitude.*

30   *The Living Wilderness* magazine, published by The Wilderness Society, has the blow-by-blow history of those fights.

declared to be the policy of the United States that certain selected rivers of the Nation which, with their immediate environments, possess outstandingly remarkable scenic, recreational, geologic, fish and wildlife, historic, cultural or other similar values, shall be preserved in free-flowing condition, and that they and their immediate environments shall be protected for the benefit and enjoyment of present and future generations."

The Wild Rivers Act came during the heat of America's frenzy to dam the last free rivers for hydropower, irrigation, flood control, and motorboat recreation. Many saw that without protection in law, few rivers would stay free-flowing and not be choked by dams. Olaus Murie had earlier called for protecting wild rivers. The Craighead brothers, John and Frank, were well-known grizzly bear researchers, river runners, adventurers, and authors of a WWII military survival guide and a field guide to wildflowers. They were the leading spokesmen for the wild rivers campaign. Frank Church and Walter Mondale pushed the bill in the Senate. The river runners and conservationists behind the bill wanted to insure that some American rivers would be off limits to dams and other building that would wreck a river's free-flowing soul.

The Act set up three classes of rivers: Wild, Scenic, and Recreational, with different qualifying standards and different management guidelines for each. Wild Rivers could be designated in Wilderness Areas for added protection (a compromise in the Wilderness Act allowed the President to authorize dam construction in Wilderness Areas under special circumstances). The boundaries of a Wild and Scenic River corridor take in one-quarter of a mile on either side of a river's banks. As with Wilderness Areas, Wild & Scenic Rivers can be managed by whichever of the federal agencies has it on their land; when a designated stretch of river is on lands managed by two or more agencies, one of them takes the lead. Where there is little or no federal land along a designated river (as in the East), the federal government may condemn land if an owner is unwilling to sell. But where at least 50 percent of the river corridor is federal land, the government has no condemnation power—this is a critical point since foes of river protection holler like goosed buffaloes about the evil feds coming in and confiscating land and throwing people out of their homes. (Notwithstanding such hollering by foes of protection, governments far more often exercise the power of eminent domain to develop land—as for roads, bridges, dams, and pipelines— than to conserve it.)

In 1995, the Forest Service, Park Service, Fish & Wildlife Service, and Bureau of Land Management signed the Interagency Wild & Scenic Rivers Coordinating Council Charter. The goal of the charter is better cooperation between the agencies on river management, looking at likely additions to the system, and working with states. States can also manage such rivers if there is little federal land along the river. Moreover, many states have established their own rivers systems modeled more or less on the federal.

As with Wilderness Areas, agencies or citizens study rivers, make proposals, and work to get Congress to pass legislation to study or immediately designate rivers. State rivers can be added upon request of the governor of the state. Sadly, the National Wild and Scenic Rivers System (NWSRS) has not gotten the attention from conservationists that Wilderness has. The NWSRS has 12,508 river miles on 203 rivers in thirty-eight states and Puerto Rico—less than one-quarter of one percent of America's river mileage. Conservationists need to put more energy into designating Wild Rivers. For more information about the NWSRS and the history of the fight for free-flowing rivers, see the books by Tim Palmer.[31]

31   Tim Palmer, *The Wild and Scenic Rivers of America* (Island Press, Washington, DC, 1993); *Endangered Rivers and the Conservation Movement* (University of California Press, Berkeley, 1986); and other books.

THE NATIONAL LANDSCAPE CONSERVATION SYSTEM

After President Clinton wielded the Antiquities Act to withdraw and designate some big National Monuments on BLM land in the last years of his administration, the BLM worked to get a handle on coordinating management. In 2000, they set up the National Landscape Conservation System (NLCS) to include all National Monuments, Wilderness Areas, Wilderness Study Areas, Wild & Scenic Rivers, and other protected areas on BLM lands. In the 2009 Omnibus Public Land Management Act, the NLCS was congressionally established. Within the NLCS, BLM now cares for twenty National Monuments (5.6 million acres), 221 Wilderness Areas (8.7 million acres), 528 Wilderness Study Areas (12.8 million acres), and 69 Wild & Scenic Rivers (2,423 miles), among other classifications.

A PROPOSED NATIONAL OCEAN CONSERVATION SYSTEM

I led you slightly astray in the last chapter by looking only at the U.S. Forest Service, National Park Service, U.S. Fish and Wildlife Service, and Bureau of Land Management. For there is another federal land managing agency even less known than the BLM. Moreover, it administers more acres than does the BLM, indeed, more acres than all four of the other agencies put together.

The agency is NOAA—the National Oceanic and Atmospheric Administration, best known for being the parent agency of the National Weather Service. The reason we don't think of it as a sibling to the other agencies at which we've looked is because all of its land is underwater— under the Atlantic, Pacific, and Arctic oceans, and under the Great Lakes. They oversee the water, too. The acreage under NOAA comes to about 2.6 billion. No typo there. NOAA has 2.6 *billion acres*—almost the size of the land area of the lower 48 states.

The Law of the Sea treaty, which the US signed and follows (but which has not yet passed the Senate thanks to a few nutty GOP Senators who think it would give the United Nations control over us), recognizes that every seaside nation has an Exclusive Economic Zone (EEZ) 200 miles out from its coasts or to the halfway mark to a nearby neighbor. NOAA has authority over our EEZ. The EEZ of the United States isn't just around Alaska and off our Pacific, Atlantic, and Gulf of Mexico coastlines. It is also a 400-mile-wide swath along the Hawaiian Island chain, and 200 miles around all US territories—islands in the Caribbean Sea and Pacific Ocean. This, by the way, puts a lot of coral reefs under NOAA.

Within these 2.6 billion acres are a few National Marine Sanctuaries, which too often are rather toothless for protected areas (or not). But above all, are two actions taken by President George W. Bush through the Antiquities Act to establish stunningly big National Monuments within our EEZ in the northwestern Hawaiian Islands and around a batch of island territories in the tropical Pacific. The two Monuments come to nearly *220 million acres!* It is amazing that Bush, otherwise no friend to conservation, set aside under strict protection a total acreage larger than California, Oregon, and Washington together. Notwithstanding his otherwise rotten conservation record, Bush's Pacific Ocean National Monuments are a mindboggling legacy. As I write this, rumors fly that President Obama plans even bigger protected areas around US island territories in the tropical Pacific. What makes Marine Protected Areas worth the paper on which they are authorized is "no take" or no fishing whatsoever.

Ten years ago, Bradley Barr and James Lindholm, both with NOAA's National Marine Sanctuary System, proposed in *Wild Earth* and other journals that NOAA become a full-fledged land/water administrator on the level of the USFS, NPS, USFWS, and BLM for the 2.6 billion acres in our EEZ. Since there are major shipping lanes, commercial fisheries, transportation corridors for undersea cables, and other industrial impacts in and through our EEZ, they called for a system that would span the range of the four land-managing agencies.

Barr also called for NOAA to be able to recommend areas for the National Wilderness Preservation System.[32]

As FLPMA was for BLM, NOAA needs an organic act to establish a National Ocean Conservation System that would have the mandate to recommend areas for Wilderness designation. This is one of the greatest opportunities conservationists have been offered. Making our EEZ comparable to our other public lands is a great campaign for the 21st Century.

32   Bradley Barr and James Lindholm, "Conserving the Sea Using Lessons from the Land," *Wild Earth*, Winter 2002-2003, 54-61.

CHAPTER 13

The Arrogance of Resourcism

THE ARROGANCE OF RESOURCISM

Humanism is the secular religion of the modern and postmodern world ... and of its last phase—the Anthropocene world.[1] In his no-false-gods book, *The Arrogance Of Humanism*, ecologist David Ehrenfeld sees humanism as "a supreme faith in human reason—its ability to confront and solve the many problems that humans face."[2] Likewise, philosopher Max Oelschlaeger writes that modernism is the hope "to transform a base and worthless wilderness into industrialized, democratic civilization" and that it "underlies the emergence of a profound homocentrism... which may be characterized as *the ideology of man infinite* or the rise of *Lord Man.*"[3] Humanism makes Man the measure of all things, the

---

1   I say the Anthropocene is the last phase of Humanism because it is the thorough conquest of Earth by Man. I'll deal further with this in my next book, *True Wilderness*.

2   David Ehrenfeld, *The Arrogance Of Humanism* (Oxford University Press, New York, 1981), 5.

3   Max Oelschlaeger, *The Idea Of Wilderness* (Yale University Press, New Haven, CT, 1991), 68-69.

vessel of all values. Humanism is engineering—of machines, society, individuals, and Nature. Resourcism is Humanism put to Nature (or "natural resources," in the argot of resourcism). When Gifford Pinchot said there were only two things in the world: Man and natural resources, he cut the philosophy of resourcism/humanism down to the bare bones. It is the Weltanschauung of the world establishment in a nutshell. The latest fads of sustainable development, wilderness deconstruction, and the "Anthropocene" are nothing but Pinchot's resourcism warmed over for today.

THE RESOURCE ELITE

Conservation and the Gospel of Efficiency: The Progressive Conservation Movement 1890-1920 by historian Samuel P. Hays is the best start for understanding the beginning and beliefs of what he calls the Progressive Conservation Movement and what some of us call Resourcism.[4] Hays writes, "Its essence was rational planning to promote efficient development and use of all natural resources. The idea of efficiency drew these federal scientists from one resource task to another, from specific programs to comprehensive concepts."[5]

Hays shows how these resource scientists in Theodore Roosevelt's administration believed that upcoming science and technology were opening up "unlimited opportunities for human achievement" and thus they were filled "with intense optimism." They thereby bought into the technological zeitgeist of the time. While they worried some about likely resource shortages later, "They emphasized expansion, not retrenchment; possibilities, not limitations." These professional men who called themselves conservationists did not believe in locking up

---

4   Hays is a great conservation historian and one of my key teachers. Much of what follows in this chapter is drawn from his trailblazing study, though with my own slant.

5   Samuel P. Hays, *Conservation and the Gospel of Efficiency: The Progressive Conservation Movement 1890-1920* (Atheneum, New York, 1979 (1959)), 2.

the land. "In fact, they bitterly opposed those who sought to withdraw resources from commercial development."[6]

So much for one conservation movement fighting the myth of superabundance, so much for a feeling of humility before the workings of Nature, so much for letting some land keep its own will. From 1900 on there has been a deep gulch between resourcism and conservation notwithstanding how some have worked to bridge the gap. These two schools have shared two stands: being against landscalping and being for public lands. Otherwise they've been at odds, sometimes hot and sometimes cool. Those who think the two are one have failed to see that what each holds dear is not the same.

A professional, scientific resource manager elite was deeply rooted in the resourcism movement. Hays wrote that this elite believed, "Since resource matters were basically technical in nature … technicians, rather than legislators should deal with them." And, "Conflicts between competing resource users … should not be dealt with" by the political process, but rather by professional resource managers coolly making "rational and scientific decisions." They had a dream of a school of resource management "guided by the ideal of efficiency and dominated by technicians."[7]

The resource managers were bent toward the reductionist, engineering side of science—how to manhandle Nature. In his enlightening book on the history of natural science, *Nature's Economy: A History of Ecological Ideas,* Donald Worster sees "two ways of reasoning, two moral allegiances." One is "Arcadian" science, which works to understand the world about us; the other is "imperialist" science, which is the "drive for the domination of nature."[8] Resourcism was and

6   Hays, *Gospel of Efficiency,* 2.
7   Hays, *Gospel of Efficiency,* 3.
8   Donald Worster, *Nature's Economy: A History of Ecological Ideas* (Cambridge University Press, New York, 1992), xi. *Nature's Economy* is a good way to fully understand the split between conservation and resourcism. The Nature Conservancy and some other rich

is steadfastly in the imperialist school. Landscalping also spurs to lord over Nature, but there is nothing scientific or rational about it. Like the pirates of yore, or the cattlemen of West Texas one hundred and fifteen years ago, landscalpers want only to get as much as they can get while the getting's good. Or to take on the big outside with the feckless glee of their kind of "recreation."

Hays writes that the early resource elite "maintained close contact with the four major engineering societies"—Civil, Mechanical, Electrical, and Mining.[9] Indeed, the resource managers set up their own professional societies, after those of the engineers. The Society of American Foresters and the Society for Range Management were and are professional associations more for engineers than for scientists. Even the Wildlife Society is torn between wildlife biologists and wildlife engineers. Alas, now the Society for Conservation Biology, birthed nearly thirty years ago as a mission-driven, ethically grounded science society to stop the extinction crisis, seems to be slipping into being another resource-manager/engineer professional society. Indeed, it now calls itself "The International Organization of Conservation Professionals." The Nature Conservancy, now shorn of its greatness and wild-loving trustworthiness, would be better named The Nature Business. And its top executives, now recruited from Wall Street and big corporations, would be better named The Nature Engineers.

Gifford Pinchot and the other resource engineers sought not only professionalism in managing "resources," but also a new social order, "based on cooperation instead of monopoly, on sharing instead of grasping, and that mutual helpfulness will replace the law of the jungle."[10] "Law of the jungle" shows the loathing held by the resourcists for self-willed land, methinks. Aldo Leopold biographer Curt Meine

"conservation" outfits have mostly shifted from Arcadian to Imperialistic Science since 1990.

9   Hays, *Gospel of Efficiency*, 123.
10   Gifford Pinchot, *Breaking New Ground* (Island Press, Washington, D.C., 1987 (1947)), 509.

writes about Pinchot's thinking: "Nature unmanaged was rule by unbridled red-in-tooth-and-claw competition. It was a world, in the end, of constant struggle for existence, *a wild world that should and would be civilized* through the application of human managerial skill."[11] (My italics.) In other words, resourcism could tame landscalping, but the goal would still be the same: to squeeze as much wealth out of the land as could be done. To tame the land. Pinchot went so far as to call for opening up the Adirondack "Forever Wild" State Park to logging.[12]

Let's revisit a quotation I ran in the Introduction: A Bureau of Reclamation cheerleader from Utah wonderfully set out the innermost belief of hard resourcism when the heyday of dam-building was getting underway: "The destiny of man is to possess the whole earth, and the destiny of the earth is to be subject to man. There can be no full conquest of the earth, and no real satisfaction to humanity, if large portions of the earth remain beyond his highest control."[13] This was no extremist statement, however. Pinchot, himself, wrote in 1910, "The first duty of the human race is to control the Earth it lives upon." The man Pinchot thought the "brains" of early resourcism, W. J. McGee, said that the duty of government resourcists was to "progressively artificialize the earth with its life and growth for the benefit of man and nations."[14] This would be the motto of the Anthropoceniacs if they knew conservation

11   Curt D. Meine, "The Oldest Task in Human History," in Richard L. Knight and Sarah F. Bates, eds., *A New Century for Natural Resources Management* (Island Press, Washington, D.C., 1994), 23.

12   Paul W. Hirt, *A Conspiracy of Optimism: Management of the National Forests since World War Two* (University of Nebraska Press, Lincoln, 1994), 32.

13   J. Widtsoe, *Success on Irrigation Projects* (New York, 1928), 138. Quoted in Donald Worster, *Rivers of Empire: Water, Aridity & The Growth of The American West* (Pantheon, New York, 1985), 188.

14   Hirt, *Conspiracy of Optimism*, 34. McGee was a wide-ranging anthropologist, geologist, and philosopher, and highly influential theorist and big-picture thinker about waterway management and development during the Roosevelt Administration. See Hays, *Gospel of Efficiency*, 102-107.

history better. Pinchot held up a new Platonic society. Instead of a philosopher king, he put forward an engineer king.[15]

THE PROFESSIONAL RESOURCE MANAGERS

Pinchot seems the shaper and sparkplug of the resource engineering movement, and the United States Forest Service seems the outstanding bureaucratic child of it. Pinchot was indeed a smart, bigger than life, politically sharp man, and a truehearted Republican progressive, but he was also one of the great self-promoters in American history (of which there have been more than a few). Although Pinchot saw himself as the father and leader of the resource conservation movement and was the high lord in the government resource agencies, we have seen how both wild (Nature) conservation and resourcism began earlier with the uprising by sportsmen to stop the slaughter of wildlife.

Also before Pinchot came John Wesley Powell, the one-armed Civil War major who lost his arm in battle, and who led two long, harrowing expeditions down the mostly unknown Green and Colorado rivers in 1869 and 1872. Powell is widely, and rightly, hailed as a hero, the last great explorer of the West, and the great-granddaddy of river runners today. But Powell also stakes a strong claim to coming up with resourcism before Pinchot, as libertarian resource economist and truehearted wildlover Karl Hess, Jr., shows in his idol-shattering "Wising Up to the Wise Use Movement."[16] Powell begat the resourcist wing of the stewardship current birthed by George Perkins Marsh.

After his explorations, Powell became head of the Geological Survey in the Department of Interior from 1881 to 1894. Although

---

15   I am not knocking engineering or even resource management as thoroughly bad ways to do some things. Nor am I putting down engineers. I am, however, slamming engineering as a Weltanschauung or guiding frame for civilization.

16   Karl Hess Jr., "Wising Up to the Wise Use Movement," in Philip D. Brick and R. McGreggor Cawley, eds., *A Wolf In The Garden: The Land Rights Movement And The New Environmental Debate* (Rowman & Littlefield Publishers, Inc., Lanham, MD, 1996), 161-183.

he was a booster for dams and irrigation in the West, he became hated by the boomers when he told the second International Irrigation Congress in Los Angeles in 1893, "I tell you gentlemen you are piling up a heritage of conflict and litigation over water rights for there is not sufficient water to supply the land."[17] (The chickens Powell talked about in 1893 have truly come home to roost today.) Irrigators didn't want to hear about limits then; they don't want to hear about limits now. The boomers in Los Angeles, Phoenix, Las Vegas, and other cities built on now-drying-up reservoirs want to hear about limits even less. The Los Angeles International Irrigation Congress was an early clash between prudent and no-limits resource engineers.[18]

However, as Hess shows, Powell was hot for irrigation. He told the 1889 Montana constitutional convention to go for irrigated agriculture: "It means that no drop of water falling within the area of the state shall flow beyond the boundaries of the state. It means that all the waters falling within the state will be utilized upon its lands for agriculture."[19] Nor did Powell see the mountains and forests of the West as wilderness to be kept—they were good only for collecting irrigation water. He said that "the best thing to do for the Rocky Mountain forests was to burn them down."[20] So much for Powell as anything but a die-hard resourcist.

In 1902, Congress passed the Reclamation Act, setting up the Bureau of Reclamation (BuRec) to build irrigation projects in the dry West. At first the agency was for the family farmer; "subsidized federal water was to irrigate no more than 160 acres owned by any one person."

17 Donald Worster, *Rivers of Empire*, 132.
18 In today's time of great drought in the Southwest, Powell's ghost stalks the land on rainless, hot days when reservoirs evaporate to puddles in the sun and irrigation ditches dwindle to trickles, wailing in the bone-dry wind, "I told you so." Today's irrigation farmers from pioneer families should curse their great-granddaddies for not listening to Powell way back then.
19 Hess, "Wising Up," 172.
20 Hess, "Wising Up," 173.

Bern Shanks tells how BuRec came to work for big agribusiness: "This 160-acre limitation was soon circumvented by large landowners and by the blatantly dishonest Bureau. By the 1960s thousands of acres on some corporate farms were flushed with cheap federal water."[21] BuRec early on showed the slippery slope from resourcism into landscalping when corporate sway becomes strong. (The Forest Service started slipping down the same slide after World War Two.)

Pinchot and the other resource professionals believed that if science could steer the engineering of forests and rivers to build civilization, so could it steer livestock grazing. Pinchot worked to open the forest reserves to commercial livestock grazing. He believed grazing on the public lands, like other uses, should be run as "a limited permit, [with] prompt use, and a user fee," and "should not exceed the carrying capacity of the land."[22] Notwithstanding the mettle and best hopes of scientific resource management, cattlegrowers were a lawless bunch and bristled at any oversight by the government. Standard gear for forest rangers was a .45 pistol. More than one shoot-out between rangers and ranchers happened before permits and fees were yielded to with a whiny snarl. (Such childish shirking of paying for grazing public lands goes on yet today; witness the Bundy Rebellion comic opera in Nevada.) By 1910, range management had become a "science" taught at cow colleges and researched by the Forest Service.[23]

Pinchot's bluster about the carrying capacity of the land, notwithstanding, the early Forest Service knowingly played with overgrazing by sheep and cattle to chew off the grass understory in forests so that wildfire would not spread. Cows and sheep were the first Forest Service fire crews. After the great, gruesome fire year of 1910, fighting forest fires became job one for the Forest Service.

21   Bernard Shanks, *This Land Is Your Land: The Struggle to Save America's Public Lands* (Sierra Club Books, San Francisco, 1984), 136.
22   Hays, *Conservation and the Gospel of Efficiency*, 71.
23   Hess, "The Oldest Task in Human History," 16.

Scientific management of the wildlife "resource" came late. Aldo Leopold wrote the first textbook, *Game Management,* in 1933, and was the first professor of wildlife management (at the University of Wisconsin). He wrote, "The central thesis of game management is this: game can be restored by the *creative use* of the same tools which have heretofore destroyed it—axe, plow, cow, fire, and gun."[24] Alas, game management soon went to game farming of a few "good" species (deer, pheasants, brook trout, and the like) by state game and fish agencies— but with a scientific gloss. Leopold continued to grow in wisdom, understanding, and insight—far beyond *Game Management.* Thank goodness, or we never would have gotten *A Sand County Almanac.* Two anthologies of Leopold's articles show well his growth as a thinker.[25]

NATIONAL PARK RESOURCISM

Gifford Pinchot was a bitter, stubborn foe of National Parks or any lands withdrawn from his kind of resource "harvest." He even fought the "forever wild" provision in the New York State Constitution for state lands in the Adirondack Mountains. He wanted the Adirondacks logged.[26] But the late Northwest conservationist Carsten Lien calls Pinchot "the father of the National Park Service" because his attacks on National Parks built public support for them.[27]

Although Pinchot's resource managers were foes of the National Parks and sneered at the "preservationist" feelings behind them, the early leaders of the National Park Service, Stephen Mather and Horace

24 Aldo Leopold, *Game Management* (University of Wisconsin Press, Madison, 1986), xxxi.
25 David E. Brown and Neil B. Carmony, eds., *Aldo Leopold's Southwest* (University of New Mexico Press, Albuquerque, 1995) and Susan L. Flader and J. Baird Callicott, eds., *The River of the Mother of God and Other Essays by Aldo Leopold* (University of Wisconsin Press, Madison, 1991).
26 Hays, *Conservation and the Gospel of Efficiency,* 191-192.
27 John C. Miles, *Wilderness in National Parks: Playground or Preserve* (University of Washington Press, Seattle, 2009), 21.

Albright, believed in getting as many folks as they could into these "public pleasuring grounds." Under their leadership, roads and grand hotels became hallmarks of the National Parks—along with such abominations as Yosemite's Fire Fall (where rangers pushed a bonfire off Sentinel Point for the delight of campers) and Yellowstone setting up bleachers for tourists at the open garbage dump where dozens of bears came to feed every night. Later leaders of the Park Service also worked for development, not seeing the harm it did to wild things. National Park Service historian Richard Sellars has shown that the NPS was a "multiple-use" agency from the start.[28] Engineers led the National Park Service, as they did the other resource agencies. Even before setting up the National Park Service in 1916, government backers were calling for engineers to run the agency.[29] The first director of the NPS, Steven Mather, hired engineers as superintendents for many of the early Parks.[30] Sellars's 1997 book, *Preserving Nature in the National Parks: A History*, is the best work for understanding the Park Service, and shows how the NPS has been run by engineers, landscape architects, foresters, and (lately) law enforcement officers, not by scientists or naturalists. Sellars writes that "national park management with its emphasis on tourism and use has largely reflected the values and assumptions of the Service's utilitarian-minded leadership culture."[31] This leadership has almost always been against wildeors and self-willed land in the Parks and has scorned science. A leading NPS forester said in 1935, "Nature goes to extremes if left alone."[32]

From almost the beginning, there was broad backing for roads and tourist development in the Parks so Americans would visit and fall in love with them. At a 1912 National Park Conference, automobiles were

28   Richard West Sellars, *Preserving Nature in the National Parks: A History* (Yale University Press, New Haven, CT, 1997), 205.
29   Sellars, *Preserving Nature in the National Parks*, 34.
30   Sellars, *Preserving Nature in the National Parks*, 55.
31   Sellars, *Preserving Nature in the National Parks*, 285.
32   Sellars, *Preserving Nature in the National Parks*, 129.

brought up. The Sierra Club's representative, William Colby, said, "[W]
e think the automobile adds a great zest to travel and we are principally
interested in the increase of travel to these parks."[33] As John Miles puts
it, "Mather had aggressively promoted the parks to auto clubs, and
his success meant demand for better roads."[34] Mather's vision for the
National Parks went so far that, writes Miles, "He wanted to position the
national parks and the Park Service at the center of the emerging auto-
driven tourism."[35] One can see the shift in how to visit National Parks
as a snapshot of American transportation history. For the first Parks,
railroad executives were the main Park boosters talking to Congress,
since they saw themselves filling the lucrative role of getting tourists to
the Parks. The motorcar, though, brought the National Parks to the less
wealthy. It also made National Park tourism much more individualistic.

As we shall see, this push for motorcar roads in the National Parks
led to a break between conservationists and the National Park Service
and it led to the true coming together of the wilderness movement
and establishment of The Wilderness Society. Others have made the
argument, however, that auto-based tourism built the love of Americans
for National Parks, thereby shielding them from those who wanted to
grub out the raw goods in them. It also led to public backing for adding
to the National Park System.[36]

INTERNATIONAL RESOURCISM

By no means was the ideology of resourcism a North American
oddity. It has been a key strand of modernism around the world. In
1905, Sir Charles Eliot, Commissioner of the East Africa Protectorate
(British Empire), wrote, "Marshes must be drained, forests skillfully
thinned, rivers be taught to run in ordered course and not to afflict
the land with drought or flood at their caprice; a way must be made

33   Miles, *Wilderness in National Parks*, 24-25.
34   Miles, *Wilderness in National Parks*, 31.
35   Miles, *Wilderness in National Parks*, 37.
36   Miles, *Wilderness in National Parks*, 36-37.

across deserts and jungles, war must be waged against fevers and other diseases whose physical causes are now mostly known." Historian John MacKenzie writes, "It is a fascinating statement. ... he applies the language of discipline and training to nature in the same way in which it was invariably used of indigenous peoples. Natural forces, like people, were to be acculturated to the modern world."[37] The will of the engineer had to take over from the will of the land. Wild things had to be broken to civilization just as "natives" had to be. This is the same belief being brought to bear today, albeit in politically correct and anticolonialist words, by the social and land engineers of "sustainable development," which has now been taken to its furthest end by the Anthropoceniacs.

I cannot gainsay, however, that resourcism has often been high-minded. Its stalwarts believed they were making the world better and lifting up the lot of Mankind. As with so many true beliefs, sadly, the road to hell is paved with good intentions.

THE IDEOLOGY OF RESOURCISM

Resourcism had its roots in the sky's-the-limit bliss that came with the first blossoming of modern science, engineering, and technology. It also had roots in Prussia where scientific forestry was born. Pinchot built his Forest Service on a military model—uniforms, a hierarchy, bureaucratic forms, standardized operations, discipline, unit cohesiveness, and organizational loyalty. If you got with the program, you had a home. One hundred years later, it is the same: the Forest Service and other land and wildlife managing agencies are homes for their folks as much as are any institutions in society—so long as their folks are true to the Weltanschauung. There was a can-do outlook and a Dudley Do-Right kind of fresh-scrubbed righteousness within the first brood of forest rangers. They were our Mounties. Yet, the Forest

37   John M. MacKenzie, "Empire and the ecological apocalypse: the historiography of the imperial environment," in Tom Griffiths and Libby Robin, eds., *Ecology and Empire: Environmental History of Settler Societies* (Melbourne University Press, 1997), 217.

Service was something more, writes David Clary, former chief historian for the agency. "[O]ther bureaucracies... operate on a body of policy that continually adjusts to conditions in the world. The Forest Service, however, has something more like a religion."[38]

The ideology of resourcism was made up of linked beliefs that have held up amazing well throughout the Public Lands Century. I would carve them up as follows:

1) Professionalism—Trained experts are most fit to handle natural resources and public lands.

2) Progressivism/Optimism—Progress as a secular religion of material, informational, moral, and organizational advances is key to resourcism, as is an earnestly optimistic belief in the good that wise management will bring.[39]

3) Engineering—The science behind resourcism is Imperial: manipulative and controlling—not pure science, but rather technology and engineering.[40]

4) Resources for people—Resource management is to be done democratically with good for everyone.

5) Multiple Use—Properly managed public lands can produce multiple uses of timber, minerals, forage, water, wildlife, and recreation, often on the same acre.

6) Sustained Yield—Lands are to be managed for the maximum they can produce on a sustained basis without harming the future productivity of the land.

7) Utilitarianism—Resources and the land are here to be used to produce goods and services for Men now living.

38   David A. Clary, *Timber and the Forest Service* (University Press of Kansas, Lawrence, 1986), xi.

39   For the influence of optimism, see Hirt, *A Conspiracy Of Optimism.*

40   Donald Worster, *Nature's Economy: A History of Ecological Ideas* (Cambridge University Press, New York, 1977).

An enlightening tale of this Weltanschauung came from the president of the American Society of Civil Engineers in 1908 when he told an engineering convention a tale about Lord Kelvin. The great physicist had been asked how the natural beauty of Niagara Falls would be harmed by waterpower development. "His reply was that of a true engineer: 'What has that got to do with it? I consider it almost an international crime that so much energy has been allowed to go to waste.'"[41] In a pamphlet done for the Bicentennial of the United States Constitution, the Bureau of Land Management set out the same feeling in a more easy-going way: "Your lands are not idle lands. They are bountiful as well as beautiful. Each year, they produce a steady stream of goods and products that enrich the lives of all Americans."[42] In other words, self-willed land is idle. The human will of resource management will stand it at attention and get it working. Pinchot said it most pithily when he wrote, "Forestry is Tree Farming."[43] No room there for self-willed land. No room, indeed, for anything but the Will of Man.[44] Pinchot also made clear what his conservation was about with "The first principle of conservation is development."[45]

41   Hays, *Conservation and the Gospel of Efficiency*, 127.

42   "Public Lands, USA: The Story of America's Public Lands," GPO: 1987 0 173-639.

43   Pinchot, *Breaking New Ground*, 31.

44   This slur that wildland is idle land comes through today in the blather about "working forests" in New England. Ecologist Steve Trombulak of Middlebury College in Vermont took the wrecking ball to this idle lands hogwash in "Wild Forests ARE Working Forests: Some Thoughts on the Language of Despoilment," *Wild Earth*, Fall 1998, 73-76. The Nature Conservancy has long been wedded to this careless "working lands" balderdash. I take "working lands" to the woodshed in my earlier book, *Take Back Conservation*.

45   Gifford Pinchot, *The Fight for Conservation* (Harcourt Brace, Garden City, NY, 1910).

Hays underscores this mind-set:

As early as the 1920s, the dendrology textbooks and courses in forestry schools that described forest species and their distribution became restricted to commercial types. The texts explained that foresters need not know all forest species—foresters were not botanists—but only those that were useful for wood production. This narrowed their conception of a forest considerably.[46]

Likewise, in 1953, Paul Herbert, forester for the National Wildlife Federation, noted that of twenty-seven forestry schools then operating, in only one was a course in water conservation needed to graduate, and in only three a course in recreation.[47]

Ecology is not rocket science. It is much more complex and tangled. Rocket science is just engineering. Ecology needs wisdom and humility.

---

46 Samuel Hays, *Beauty, Health, and Permanence: Environmental Politics in the United States, 1955-1985* (Cambridge University Press, New York, 1987), 396.

47 Clary, *Timber and the Forest Service*, 152.

CHAPTER 14

Clashes Between Resourcism and the Wild, 1890-1945

MUIR AND PINCHOT

Look at the photographs, over one hundred years old now. Muir with the wind-blown, bedraggled beard and hair, eyes agleam. Pinchot with his tight smile and dapper mustache, feelings well spiled. The two mighty men of the early "conservation movement."

John Muir, reared on a hardscrabble frontier farm in Wisconsin by a Calvinist-thug of a father, came to California in 1868 and the next summer headed to the Sierra Nevada mountain range—the "range of light" he called it for its sheer, shimmering granite crags and rock-rimmed lakes. For the next twenty-some years, he tramped through this sprawling, up-and-down wilderness, being the first to climb many of the peaks, picking through blossoms to learn what to call them, worrying out the wonder of glaciers, and dropping into Yosemite Valley now and then to woo winsome lassies. Muir also wandered around the West and then up into Alaska. By the 1890s, he was one of America's most-loved writers and the best-known flag bearer for National Parks.

In 1892, he founded and became president of the Sierra Club in San Francisco.[1]

Gifford Pinchot was the chip off the block of a wealthy, patrician family. He was schooled as a forester in Prussia and France and became first Chief of the United States Forest Service. Politically go-getting, Pinchot became one of Theodore Roosevelt's insiders and was later elected governor of Pennsylvania as one of the last Bull Moose Republicans. He was a mainstay of the Progressive Movement within the Republican Party.

Muir and his friends and Pinchot and his saw themselves together in the fight against landscalping in the 1890s, but split over what to do with the National Forests. The crack deepened into a gulch when Muir fought a dam in Yosemite National Park that Pinchot backed.

With that background, let us now get down in the duff to look at the key clashes in the war over wild things between conservationists and resourcists before 1945:

USFS ORGANIC ACT OF 1897

The 1891 law "merely established reserves; it did not provide for their management," writes Samuel Hays. Lovers of wild things from Muir to the sportsmen of the Boone and Crockett Club hoped to keep logging, livestock grazing, and other commercial uses out of the forest reserves. They wanted the reserves held for their wildlife, watershed, and "picturesque" settings. Gifford Pinchot, however, called for "management" that would bring logging, livestock grazing, and dam building.[2] To Pinchot, anything else was "sentimental nonsense." In those days, engineers and other practical men had no worse put-down than "sentimental"—a feminine weakness that true men did not suffer.

---

1   Michael P. Cohen, *The Pathless Way: John Muir And American Wilderness* (The University of Wisconsin Press, Madison, 1984). Cohen's is the deepest study of Muir.

2   Samuel P. Hays, *Conservation and the Gospel of Efficiency: The Progressive Conservation Movement 1890-1920* (Athenum, New York, 1979), 36.

In 1896, with a $25,000 appropriation from Congress, Secretary of the Interior Hoke Smith set up an advisory commission to put forward management choices for the forest reserves. Harvard botanist Charles Sprague Sargent and John Muir called for shielding forests as wilderness, but Gifford Pinchot and Arnold Hague of the U.S. Geological Survey thought their job was to "get ready for practical forestry." The commission deadlocked. Sargent and Muir seemed to win when President Grover Cleveland withdrew another 21,000,000 acres of new forest reserves on February 22, 1897. Then on June 4, 1897, Congress passed the Forest Management Act, which opened the reserves to the kind of heavy management and commercial exploitation Pinchot wanted.[3] By that time, William McKinley, a Republican and champion of business, had taken office as President, and signed the bill.

The forest reserves were put under the General Land Office in Interior; Pinchot lobbied to have them shifted to his Bureau of Forestry in the Department of Agriculture, and at last got his way in 1905. To get backing from the western establishment for this shift, he called for opening the reserves to cattle and sheep grazing. For this, the American National Livestock Association hailed Pinchot in 1901. Letting great flocks of sheep and herds of cattle into the forest reserves was more than a political ploy by Pinchot to gain backing for the transfer. Hays wrote that "Pinchot felt that his major problem was to restrain the influence of those who wished to leave [the forest reserves] in their natural state, untouched by lumberman or stockman."[4] Underline this, please. Pinchot saw as his main foe not the landscalpers, but the landkeepers, not Two-Gun Desmond, but John Muir.

The split between Muir and Pinchot was such that one of Muir's dearest friends, Robert Underwood Johnson, an editor of the leading literary magazine of the day, *Century,* came to call Pinchot

---

3   Roderick Nash, *Wilderness and the American Mind* (Yale University Press, New Haven, CT, 1967), 135-137.

4   Hays, *Conservation and the Gospel of Efficiency,* 41.

a "de-conservationist." And, wrote Roderick Nash, Pinchot, as organizer of the 1908 Governors' Conference on the Conservation of Natural Resources, "carefully kept Muir, Johnson, and most other preservationists off the invitation list." Nash also wrote that Muir, after seeing that Pinchot had the forest reserves under his thumb, switched his work to the National Parks—federal lands that could be warded from logging and livestock grazing.[5] Indeed, the next big fight between Resourcism (Pinchot) and Conservation (Muir) came over National Parks.

HETCH HETCHY

After the city-wrecking 1906 San Francisco earthquake and fire, the city, as part of its rebuilding, resent an application to the Department of the Interior to build a municipal water supply reservoir in Hetch Hetchy Valley on the west side of the Sierra Nevada. The Secretary of the Interior signed off on the application in 1908. All hell broke loose. Not only was Hetch Hetchy one of the loveliest wilderness valleys in California (and the world), it was in Yosemite National Park, meant to be a hands-off acreage—and the marrow of John Muir's world.

Muir spurred the Sierra Club and their national friends, such as the Appalachian Mountain Club, American Civic Association, and *Century* magazine, into the greatest public conservation fight to that time. Muir roared, "These temple destroyers, devotees of ravaging commercialism, seem to have a perfect contempt for Nature, and instead of lifting their eyes to the God of the Mountains, lift them to the Almighty Dollar."

And what did Pinchot say? "As to my attitude regarding the proposed use of Hetch Hetchy by the city of San Francisco…I am fully persuaded that…the injury…by substituting a lake for the present swampy floor of the valley…is altogether unimportant compared with the benefits to be derived from its use as a reservoir."[6]

---

5   Nash, *Wilderness and the American Mind*, 138-139.
6   Nash, *Wilderness and the American Mind*, 160.

Thus, resourcism and Nature conservation came head to head in a bloody clash. For the first time, the nation heeded a conservation fight; for the first time, conservationists well stood against development. Muir and his friends held off the damming of Yosemite National Park until December 19, 1913, when President Woodrow Wilson signed the bill to build the dam.[7] Muir died soon thereafter.

Hetch Hetchy was lost, but brought out strong backing for wilderness among the public. One dam backer, Senator James A. Reed of Missouri, was thunderstruck that over wilderness "the Senate goes into profound debate, the country is thrown into a condition of hysteria."[8]

Most Republicans in the Senate voted against Hetch Hetchy Dam. Many of the backers of the dam believed in it on the grounds that it was a public water and hydroelectric project (to be owned by the City of San Francisco) and therefore undercut greedy and hated private water and power companies. Republicans were leery of such government ownership, so the Senate vote can't be taken as an up-or-down on wilderness.[9]

NATIONAL PARK ROADS

Although Muir held National Parks over National Forests and although the Parks were mostly shielded from commercial logging and grazing, the Park Service by no means thought to leave them alone. Richard Sellars writes, "Areas selected for intensive public use in the national parks took on the appearance of resorts, and effectively served that purpose."[10] Mather may not have wanted "the parks 'gridironed'

7　Wilson was one of the most anticonservation presidents. Republicans Coolidge and Hoover were better friends of wild things than was Wilson. Barack Obama is much like Wilson on conservation, it would seem.

8　Nash, *Wilderness and the American Mind*, 180.

9　My understanding of the first big dam fight comes mostly from Roderick Nash's chapter on Hetch Hetchy in *Wilderness and the American Mind*, 161-181.

10　Richard West Sellars, *Preserving Nature in the National Parks: A History*

with roads," but he built main roads that sliced through some of the Parks' best wilderness, in Glacier (Going to the Sun Highway), Mt. McKinley (Wonder Lake Road), Rocky Mountain (Trail Ridge Road), and other National Parks, thereby cleaving some of the biggest wildernesses in half.[11]

With the New Deal struggle against the Great Depression came the Civilian Conservation Corps and lots of busywork in the National Parks, such as "Skyline Drives." The National Park Service went bully for roads. In August of 1934, Bob Marshall went to a forestry conference in Knoxville, Tennessee. The founder of the Appalachian Trail, Benton MacKaye, and some of his wilderness friends were also there. The Park Service was ballyhooing skyline drives along the Appalachians, even in the wildest chunk of Great Smokies National Park. After talking with each other at the conference, Marshall, MacKaye, and some others came together to set up The Wilderness Society to fight the National Park Service over roads in the Parks.[12] Wilderness folks were so upset by this road-building and resort-development hustle, that The Wilderness Society, Redwoods League, and even the National Parks Association hedged on making Kings Canyon National Park out of National Forest land in California's Sierra Nevada. They felt the Forest Service

(Yale University Press, New Haven, CT, 1997), 17. Sellars is the retired chief historian of the NPS and his book is the best for understanding the National Parks. Now it has been joined by John C. Miles, *Wilderness in National Parks* (University of Washington Press, Seattle, 2009). Miles goes into detail on the early automobile promotion by the NPS.

11   Sellars, *Preserving Nature in the National Parks,* 61.

12   Michael Frome, *Battle for the Wilderness* Revised Edition (University of Utah Press, Salt Lake City, 1997) 123. Paul S. Sutter, *Driven Wild: How the Fight against the Automobile Launched the Modern Wilderness Movement* (University of Washington Press, Seattle, 2002) strongly shows how fear over road-building drove the setting-up of The Wilderness Society. Stephen Fox also goes into the founding of The Wilderness Society in his matchless *The American Conservation Movement: John Muir and His Legacy* (University of Wisconsin Press, Madison, 1985). Also see Miles, *Wilderness in National Parks.*

could do a better job of taking care of this breathtaking wilderness. The Redwoods League even backed away from a Redwood National Park over fears that the National Park Service would overdevelop it.[13] Instead, they worked for California state parks to shelter the mighty trees. Wilderness Society founders Bob Marshall and Aldo Leopold also were in no way cheerleaders for the National Park Service.

Robert Sterling Yard, once the publicity chief for the Park Service but who grew more and more upset with roads and other building in the Parks, became a charter member of The Wilderness Society and edited its first issue of *The Living Wilderness* magazine. Yard wrote, "The Wilderness Society is born of an emergency in conservation which admits no delay." A big part of that emergency was the chopping up of wilderness in National Parks by the Park Service's road binge. Yard slammed the "craze" to "build all the highways possible everywhere while billions may yet be borrowed from the unlucky future. The fashion is to barber and manicure wild America as smartly as the modern girl. Our duty is clear."[14] In 1938, Park Service biologist Lowell Sumner wrote about his fears that the NPS building spree would soon shatter true wilderness in the Parks and that the NPS "had been more at fault than many other agencies" in taming the wild.[15]

Just as Pinchot's resourcism slew wilderness with logging, livestock grazing, and dams, the resourcism of the Park Service marred wilderness with roads and industrial tourism. The Park Service also worked to kill off wolves, mountain lions, and other wild hunters, and to thoroughly tame wildfire—both chores coming from the mindset

13   Sellars, *Preserving Nature in the National Parks*, 143.

14   Dyan Zaslowsky and T. H. Watkins, *These American Lands* (Island Press, Washington, DC, 1994), 204-205.

15   Sellars, *Preserving Nature in the National Parks*, 105. Sumner was the first to warn about the harm recreation could do to wilderness, and was among those who got Arctic National Wildlife Refuge in Alaska set up. After retiring from the NPS, he lived in Glenwood, NM, where I had the great, good luck to be his neighbor in the 1970s. He is owed far more acknowledgement than he has gotten.

of breaking will-of-the-land and hobbling it with will-of-Man. The NPS campaign to slaughter predators may take the cake as the most gruesome tale of taming "protected" public lands. Alack, it goes on yet today in many of our public lands. Even in designated Wilderness Areas—the throwback Idaho Game & Fish Department recently funded a trapper to wipe out two wolf packs in the middle of the River of No Return Wilderness Area. The U.S. Forest Service, to its eternal shame, opened an administrative cabin deep within the Wilderness for the assassin to use.

Predator "Control" and Game Farming

Early on, high-minded conservationists, even those of a wilderness bent, such as Aldo Leopold, William Hornaday, and Teddy Roosevelt, beat the drum for killing off wolves, mountain lions, bears, hawks, and other predators. It was believed that by getting rid of predators, populations of "beneficial" animals such as deer, elk, and grouse would climb. Even the early Audubon societies backed killing hawks and owls so as to shield "good" birds.[16] At heart, this was a war to wipe out wildeors—and will-of-the-land. As we'll see, these conservationists soon came about to see the good in predators, though the resource agencies did not. Indeed, the war against wolves, coyotes, mountain lions, and others by resourcists has gone on to today.

The Park Service trapped, shot, and poisoned wildhunters in the National Parks. It wasn't stockmen who cleaned the wolves out of Yellowstone Park—it was the Park Service. Richard Sellars writes, "To protect popular wildlife species, predators such as mountain lions, wolves, and coyotes were systematically slaughtered. Naturally occurring forest fires were suppressed to protect green landscapes; and to please anglers, millions of fish—native and non-native—were

16   Thomas R. Dunlap, *Saving America's Wildlife* (Princeton University Press, Princeton, NJ, 1988), 15.

released in lakes and streams."[17] Years before Uncle Walt opened Disneyland, the Park Service worked to make Disneylands of the first great Parks. Forest fire control, exterminating predators, and the introduction of exotic game fish were done to snuff out the will of the land and to stamp in Man's will. Even before the Park Service was set up in 1916, full-throated war on wolves, cats, bears, and other meateaters was underway in Yellowstone, Mount Rainier, Yosemite, and Sequoia National Parks.[18]

Horace Albright, superintendent of Yellowstone from 1919 to 1929 and Director of the NPS from 1929 to 1933, was wedded to snuffing predators. Although he left the NPS in 1933 to run after a buck-making line in the mining industry, as a held-high elder from the birth of the National Park Service, he loudly spoke against science and ecological thinking in the Parks well into the 1980s. When he ran Yellowstone, rangers were sent out to crush pelican eggs and kill river otters because pelicans and otters ate trout (including nonnatives), which were for fishermen. I do not make this up as if for an article in *The Onion*. When National Audubon Society reformer Rosalie Edge lay bare the pelican slaughter in 1932, Director Albright outright lied that "no pelicans have been killed in Yellowstone National Park."[19] Albright had earlier been untruthful in answering an Ecological Society of America resolution in 1921 against putting non-native fish in National Parks.[20] Besides killing mountain lions and wolves, the Park Service targeted coyotes, lynx, bobcats, foxes, badgers, mink, weasels, fishers, otters, and pine martens! If it had sharp teeth, kill it seemed to be the rule. By 1924, wolves and

---

17 Richard West Sellars, "Science or Tradition?" *National Parks*, January-February 1998, 39. In his landmark book, *Preserving Nature in the National Parks*, he fully lays out this Park Service war on wild things.

18 Sellars, *Preserving Nature in the National Parks*, 24.

19 Carsten Lien, *Olympic Battleground: The Power Politics of Timber Preservation* (Sierra Club Books, San Francisco, 1991), 110. Sorry, I can't sugarcoat it; the man lied.

20 Sellars, *Preserving Nature in the National Parks*, 81.

mountain lions were functionally extinct in Glacier, Yellowstone, and Rocky Mountain National Parks.[21] By 1931, "wolves and cougars had been virtually eradicated from all national parks in the forty-eight states."[22]

Now, I'm well known as a sweet, forgiving old softie, but I can't help but dislike Albright. For all the coming sins by Park Service Directors I name in this book, I pin the blame on Albright for hammering together the frame.

The Park Service pogrom had a skilled, willing friend in another Interior Department agency. The Biological Survey, now the U.S. Fish and Wildlife Service, had a core program called PARC—the Predatory Animal and Rodent Control division. With the hotheartedness of today's ethnic cleansers in the Middle East, PARC set out to slay all wolves, lions, bears, bobcats, coyotes, and other "pests" in the United States. Retired Arizona Game and Fish Department manager David Brown tells the sad story of how PARC *thoughtfully* and thoroughly killed off wolves and grizzly bears in the Southwest in his books, *The Wolf in the Southwest* and *The Grizzly in the Southwest*.[23] By far the most in-depth look at federal wolf killing is Michael Robinson's *Predatory Bureaucracy*.[24] Thomas Dunlap's *Saving America's Wildlife* is the best overview of the federal war on predators.

State game and fish agencies also went hog-wild over killing wildhunters. Their job was game farming—growing a "crop" of white-

21   Sellars, *Preserving Nature in the National Parks*, 72-73.
22   Sellars, *Preserving Nature in the National Parks*, 119.
23   David E. Brown, *The Wolf in the Southwest: The Making of an Endangered Species* (University of Arizona Press, Tucson, 1984); *The Grizzly in the Southwest* (University of Oklahoma Press, Norman, 1985).
24   Michael J. Robinson, *Predatory Bureaucracy: The Extermination of Wolves and the Transformation of the West* (University Press of Colorado, Boulder, 2005). Robinson, of the Center for Biological Diversity, has written a thoroughly researched work of science and history—but with the dash of a Wild West tale.

tailed deer or exotic ring-necked pheasants for hunters. Because these game species do well in disturbed habitats, the "wildlifers" also liked logging and disliked Wilderness Areas more often than not.

As early as the 1920s, though, field biologists began to understand the overriding good of wildhunters both in keeping populations of game animals healthy and in caretaking habitat. E. A. Goldman of PARC tried to brush away such thoughts of his fellows in the American Society of Mammalogists, saying:

Large predatory mammals, destructive to livestock and game, no longer have a place in our advancing civilization."[25]

The whole meaning of that stand is a thoroughgoing casting out of wild things, even wildness itself, in our "advancing civilization." Such a "civilization" (if we can call it that) stood for taming everything and killing everything we could not tame. (Goldman was not university trained; he had gotten his "education" in the field with the "gopher-chokers" of PARC.) Today's Anthropoceniacs follow Goldman, whether they know of him or not.

Half-brothers Olaus and Adolph Murie of the Biological Survey had done fieldwork on wolves, bears, and coyotes in Alaska and in Yellowstone, and knew what they were talking about on predators better than did anyone else. They were among the first to speak out against predator control scams. Aldo Leopold came around thanks to the Muries after having beaten the drum for killing wolves and cougars as head of the New Mexico Game Protective Association and editor of their newsletter *The Pine Cone*. I earlier wrote about the leadership of Victor Shelford and the Ecological Society of America in gainsaying the killing of big meateaters in 1932.[26] In 1931, the American Society

---

25   Dunlap, *Saving America's Wildlife,* 51.
26   Victor E. Shelford, "The Preservation of Natural Biotic Communities," *Ecology,* April 1933.

of Mammalogists also took a stand against PARC's predator slaughter.[27] The Boone and Crockett Club and the New York Zoological Society stood up to say "no" to the slaughter of wolves, cats, and such in the National Parks. Park Service biologists, led by George Wright, fought predator control in the Parks. Ade Murie, who had gone to work for the NPS, was so outspoken that top bosses wanted to fire him.[28]

Those who cared about wild things at last stopped the wholesale killing in the National Parks in the 1930s, alas too late for wolves outside of Alaska but good for everything else. Sadly, outside the National Parks, the lynch mob against wildhunters still rides high—very high in Alaska where the dirty deed is done from helicopter and airplane. Airplane gunning is now coming back in Idaho and other benighted states. The gunners work for livestockmen and those like resigned governor Sarah Palin who dirty the name "hunter." Conservationists who fight today against the mindless killing of wolves, mountains lions, and other meateaters should take heart from the little-known victory for predators in the 1930s.

These early set-tos between Nature conservationists and resource managers give a feeling for the bloodier fights after World War Two.

27 Dunlap, *Saving America's Wildlife*, 53-61.
28 Sellars, *Preserving Nature in the National Parks*, 119-123.

CHAPTER 15

The Forest Service Against The Wilderness After World War Two

BEFORE AND AFTER WWII

Right before World War Two, conservation and resourcism were friendlier than they had been since the 1890s. With Harold Ickes as Secretary of the Interior, Ferdinand Silcox as Chief of the Forest Service, Bob Marshall as Head of Recreation for the Forest Service, and Ding Darling as Director of the Bureau of Sport Fisheries and Wildlife, conservation groups like The Wilderness Society, National Parks Association, National Audubon Society, and Sierra Club were pretty chummy with the agencies—although they kept being watchdogs. Once the Forest Service felt it was here to stay after World War One, many forest supervisors and district rangers settled into a custodial easy chair. There was little call for National Forest timber; in fact, many timber companies were against Forest Service timber sales because they would undercut the more gainful logging of privately owned forests. Since the "Big Blowup" in 1910 that burned 3 million acres in the Northern Rockies, the Forest Service had become foremost a wildfire-fighting agency, busy with building fire lookout towers and stringing crude telephone lines to the lookouts whether in roadless backcountry or Primitive Areas or reachable by rough "truck trails."[1] Throwing a diamond hitch and handling mules were needed skills for working in the Forest Service—as well as knowing how to wield ax, crosscut saw, and shovel. Many packtrails for fire fighting were built, some carefully engineered. These trails are still the trail network on National Forests, though many have become roads while thousands of miles have become overgrown and lost.

After World War Two, however, conservationists and resource agencies found themselves at odds, as resource managers started an all-out onslaught against America's last wilderness. The United States Forest Service, National Park Service, and later the Bureau of Land Management worked tirelessly to bring their backcountry to heel. Land that yet sneered at the will of Man upset the engineering pride of the resource managers as a job yet undone. Roadless areas were seen as lands that hadn't yet had roads chopped through them. The Bureau of Reclamation, Army Corps of Engineers, and Tennessee Valley Authority targeted the wildest, loveliest canyons and rivers for flooding behind dams for irrigation, hydropower, flood control, and powerboat recreation. The Fish & Wildlife Service kept to its chosen road of slaughtering "bad" wildlife such as predators and prairie dogs for the welfare of ranchers and farmers—and because wolves and cougars no longer had a place in our "advancing civilization."

State game and fish departments went after wild things as well, taming state hunting and fishing areas with a heavy hand (such as clear-cut logging, spraying herbicides, and killing unwanted "pests" and predators) for the highest yield of white-tailed deer, pheasant, and other wildlife "crops" that do well in human-disturbed habitats. State "wildlifers" threatened—even sometimes snuffed—native fish as they stocked rivers, streams, lakes, and reservoirs with exotics like brown

---

1   In my early backpacking days fifty years ago, I often saw old insulators nailed to trees and broken telephone wire along trails to high spots.

trout, brook trout, lake trout, bass, and other "put-and-take" fish raised in government hatcheries.[2] Wild fish stocks also were weakened with such hatchery breeding. The yardstick state game and fish folks held up was how many fish caught and how many deer bagged—not the health of wildlife and their homes. To be sure, there were good and steadfast professionals and conservationists in these agencies, federal and state, but the overall path and leadership of each since 1945 has been to tame wilderness, to overthrow will-o'-the-land by the will o' Man.

Although conservationists have fought against landscalping by timber companies, miners, lousy ranchers, the recreation industry, developers, irrigators, and slob hunters, most of the work of wilderfolk since 1945 has been to thwart federal and state resource agencies and their taming of wilderness. This truth is key for understanding the history of conservation in the last half of the twentieth century. The war to tame wilderness spurred conservation clubs to become less likely to go along and more likely to stand up and say "No."

Young turks back from World War Two, such as Dave Brower, began to steer the stuffy old Sierra Club onto more of a grassroots path and geared up to fight against as well as work with the agencies. Dr. Edgar Wayburn was the grand old man of the Sierra Club, still going strong in his nineties when he wrote his memoirs in 2004; he was given the Presidential Medal of Freedom in 1999.[3] Ed died in 2010 at the age of 103. Whenever I got the chance to talk to him, I went after his memories and wisdom like a mosquito after a shirtless hiker on the tundra. He told me that in 1951 he set out to remake the Federation of Western

2   European brown trout are exotic to all of North America. Brook trout, lake trout, and bass are native to some of North America, but have been stocked in streams and rivers where they are not native, such as in the western United States.

3   See "Doctor Ed's" memoir for much of the raw history of conservation since the 1930s. Edgar Wayburn with Allison Alsup, *Your Land And Mine: Evolution of a Conservationist* (Sierra Club Books, San Francisco, 2004).

Outdoor Clubs from a bunch of mountaineering clubs, such as the Sierra Club (San Francisco), Mazamas (Portland), and Mountaineers (Seattle), into a conservation team. By 1952, he said the Sierra Club had made up its mind to work throughout the United States instead of mostly in California so as to better deal with national threats—such as Forest Service axe jobs on Primitive Areas. It was these strikes against wilderness that led conservationists to call for congressional shielding of Wilderness Areas through a Wilderness Act, gained at last in 1964.

The late Phil Berry, one of the Sierra Club leaders in the generation after Wayburn and Brower, started working as a teenager with the Club in the 1950s. When we served together on the Sierra Club Board in the 1990s, he told me that the struggle over a dam in Dinosaur National Monument (more on this later) goosed the Sierra Club in two main ways: one, to grow beyond California; and, two, to drop its policy of not tongue-lashing government agencies.

These were big shifts in the Sierra Club, which had softened its bearing and style after Muir's death. Until the 1950s, the Club leadership was anything but bold. To wit, on November 12, 1949, the Sierra Club Board of Directors gave thumbs-up to a weak-kneed resolution backing the building of a Bridge Canyon Dam in the Grand Canyon.[4] After Brower was hired as part-time executive director of the Club in 1952 and Ed Wayburn and Richard Leonard stepped into volunteer leadership, things shifted.[5] Brower had flipped his recreational way of thinking about wilderness into an ecological outlook after reading Aldo Leopold's *A Sand County Almanac* in 1950.[6] In 1988, Michael

4   Brower, David R., "Let the river run through it," *The Albuquerque Tribune,* September 17, 1997. Even Brower voted for the dam, he once told me, shaking his head.
5   Knowing these three old gunfighters was both a thrill and deep learning seminar, though I never really saw them together. Sadly, Ed and Dick had fallen out with Dave by the late 1960s and were leaders in firing him as Sierra Club executive director.
6   Michael P. Cohen, *A History Of The Sierra Club: 1892-1970* (Sierra Club Books, San Francisco, 1988), 117. Cohen's book does a great

McCloskey wrote of that time and later, "Environmentalists feel a massive sense of betrayal with respect to America's national forests."[7] Key to the makeover of the Sierra Club and to a more forthright stand by conservationists as a whole were the Biennial Wilderness Conferences cosponsored by the Sierra Club and Wilderness Society from 1949 to 1973. Many of today's thoughts about wilderness were worked out at these national meetings.[8] I was lucky enough to go to the last one in Boulder, Colorado, in 1973. It was a mistake to end them. Thanks to Polly Dyer and other old timers with great help from Vicky Hoover, wilderness conferences of a kind have started up again. And, thanks to the Wild Foundation and its hard-working chairman Vance Martin, international wilderness conferences have been going on since 1977.[9]

For the rest of *The Great Conservation Divide*, I'll highlight the fights and wrangles that show how resourcism, as ideology and practice, has been the foremost threat to America's dwindling stock of self-willed land, and has cut ecological wounds that bleed the land yet. My tale is not thorough; it spotlights those clashes over wilderness and wildeors that

job of showing how the Sierra Club went from being an upper-crust mountaineering club into being a hard-hitting conservation group. Harold Bradley, a Club leader and friend of Leopold, gave Brower a copy of Leopold's book. Bradley's son Charles, by the way, married Leopold's daughter Nina. Nina and Charley still lived near the Leopold "Shack" in Wisconsin and were great conservationists and beacons to many others and me until their deaths. Nina died in 2011 at the age of 93.

7   Paul W. Hirt, *A Conspiracy of Optimism: Management of the National Forests since World War Two* (University of Nebraska Press, Lincoln, 1994), xxvi.

8   Cohen, *History of Sierra Club*, 121-134. The modern Wilderness Area Idea, along with policies, management, and strategy, was hammered out at these biennial Wilderness Conferences. Folks heard not only from wilderness leaders such as Brower and Zahniser but also from agency heads, scientists, writers, and others who knew about wilderness. The Sierra Club published books with key talks and such for most of the conferences. These books are essential sources for understanding how the Wilderness Act came to be and how the National Wilderness Preservation System created by it was first put together.

9   http://www.wild.org

best show the bedrock gap between conservation and resourcism over wild things. For one, I don't go into the late-1970s history-setting battle for one hundred million acres of new National Parks, Wildlife Refuges, Wilderness Areas, and Wild Rivers in Alaska. Why? The campaign for the Alaska National Interest Lands Conservation Act likely was the best cooperative effort between federal agencies (the National Park Service and Fish & Wildlife Service most of all) and conservation groups in the twentieth century.[10] (Though conservationists and the Forest Service had a knockdown brawl over the Tongass National Forest in Southeast Alaska at the time.)

TIMBER AND ROADS

With after-war giddiness, the United States was on the road again—and resource agencies were ready at last to manage "their" lands. First to feel this hurry were the timberlands of the National Forests—foresters had been waiting forty years for this glad day. David Clary, the retired chief historian of the Forest Service, laid out in flint-sharp thoroughness the growing overlordship of timber extraction in the National Forests in his book, *Timber and the Forest Service*. He wrote, "Before World War II the national forests were mostly custodial institutions,"[11] but after the war the call for National Forest timber became louder thanks to how logging companies had scalped their private lands and had little left to be cut. Since soldiers home from the war were marrying, starting families, and wanting homes, the Forest Service was ready—nay, eager—to build new roads and get out the cut for the Baby Boom. In 1940, the Forest Service sold 1.371 billion board feet (bbf) of timber, in 1946, 2.470

---

10 Two good treatments of the Alaska Lands Campaign are: John C. Miles, *Wilderness in National Parks: Playground or Preserve* (University of Washington Press, Seattle, 2009) and James Morton Turner, *The Promise of Wilderness: American Environmental Politics Since 1964* (University of Washington Press, Seattle, 2012).

11 David A. Clary, *Timber and the Forest Service* (University Press of Kansas, Lawrence, 1986), 119.

billion board feet, and in 1952, 4.516 billion board feet.[12] To cut this much timber from the back-of-beyond, old-growth wildwood of the West, roads had to be built—often up, over, and down rugged slopes. This rough, tough chore was an engineer's dream and St. George against the dragon for the bulldozer jockeys. The Forest Service loudly asked for more money from Congress, and with it bulldozed timber haul roads throughout the National Forests, splitting up big roadless areas as if splitting logs for kindling. In 1946 the Forest Service came up with "a $260-million program, extending over thirteen years, to provide for a total of 26,000 miles of roads."[13] This request was soon overtaken as the Forest Service, with backing from sawlog senators and representatives, needed more money for more roads to cut more timber to bring lots of money to rural counties in the West. Thus began the "Iron Triangle" of the Forest Service, big timber corporations, and their pet members of Congress.

The clash was on. The long goal was to log all old-growth forests and road all roadless areas (outside of the piddling handful of Wilderness, Wild, and Primitive Areas) so as to bring self-willed forests and the backcountry under the steady hand of the Forest Service's professional, managerial will. Paul Hirt writes that the Forest Service "saw their mission as one of overcoming limits, not establishing them. A consciously disseminated 'can-do' technocratic optimism imbued the Forest Service with a sense of mission and excitement."[14] The goal of arrogant resourcism was to make over the western wilderness into neat, garden-like timber plantations—to take the wild tangle of millions of years of evolution and in no more time than the career of

---

12   Clary, *Timber and the Forest Service*, 111 & 125. A board foot (bf) is a piece of lumber one foot wide, one foot long, and one inch thick. A twelve-foot-long two by four, then, works out to 8 bf.

13   Clary, *Timber and the Forest Service*, 117. Since that year of my birth, the Forest Service has built more than tenfold the miles of roads it first offered.

14   Hirt, *Conspiracy of Optimism*, xxii.

a professional forester smooth it out into a well-behaved tree farm. Over the last sixty years, as we shall see, the Forest Service has almost done it—and darned well would have done it if not for hikers, climbers, birders, hunters, anglers, paddlers, horse packers, and other wilderfolk standing in the road athwart "progress" and shouting "No!" "Hell, no!" Nor have the mountains of the West meekly let themselves become so tamed as flatland Kansas field squares.

Let me give a snapshot of the growth in National Forest timber cutting. In 1950, 3.5 billion board feet (bbf) were cut. By 1962, yearly "harvest" was up to 9.0 bbf, where it stayed in that range for thirty years. In the early 1990s the yearly cut dropped from 10.5 in 1990 to 3.7 in 1996—back to the cut level in 1950. High points were 1966 (12.1 bbf) and 1987 (12.7 bbf).[15] Those thirty years must have felt like heaven to Forest Service timber beasts.

Nearly all Forest Service Chiefs have been slavering-at-the-mouth timber beasts. But Ed Cliff in the 1950s may have been the worst—the most single-minded on "getting the cut out." In 1957, he told a congressional committee that "by the year 2000 the national forests should annually produce 24 billion board feet of timber...."[16] Wow. Talk about a conspiracy of optimism! What planet were Cliff and his fellow foresters living on? The National Forest cut in 2000—ta da *drum roll*—was 2,542,427,000.[17] One-tenth of what Cliff called for. Less than the cut in 1944. Only sixty years ago the Forest Service could not see where their cutting practices and land stewardship were heading. To ruin.

---

15   Hirt, *Conspiracy of Optimism*, xliv. Hirt's book is just one of many listings for USFS official timber sale figures, both in print and on the web. The books by Hirt and Clary are the key works for understanding National Forest logging in the fifty years from the mid-1940s to mid-1990s.

16   Clary, *Timber and the Forest Service*, 158.

17   www.fs.fed.us/forestmanagement/reports/sold-harvest/ documents/1905-2008_Natl_Sold_Harvest_Summary.pdf

I put "harvest" in quotation marks because Forest Service timber cutting is not a harvest at all. As the first in my family born off the farm, I learned from my grandmother that you harvested what you planted and tended. What the Forest Service was doing was *mining*—the one-time liquidation of sprawling, deep, dark ancient forests with big trees hundreds of years old. After the timber mining, old wildwood became a barren hillside bleeding soil and life into once-upon-a-time shady, cold streams, now warm ditches running through torn-up dirt and baked by the sun. In their arrogance of optimism, the forest engineers (c'mon, they weren't rangers), believed they were replacing a "decadent, overmature" forest that was a "biological desert" with better trees that would quickly grow and be ready for harvest in as little as sixty years.[18]

As for the growth in Forest Development Roads (whose main reason for being was for logging), there were some 160,000 miles in 1950. The engineers and bulldozers went to work slicing through roadless backcountry so that by 1975 there were over 200,000 miles and by 1985 some 350,000 miles—mostly paid for by taxpayers.[19]

On top of the crazed rush to blade roads and wipe out "decadent" ancient forests, the Forest Service went overboard in spraying DDT to "control" insects. From 1950 to 1960 aerial spraying jumped to over one million acres a year—a 300% increase.[20] The wilderness was becoming a cornfield in Indiana. Wildlife also worked into multiple-use. Deer populations jumped with logging. Hunters were happy. Loggers were happy. And to the timber beasts in the Forest Service, deer came to mean "wildlife."[21]

---

18 I take the "arrogance of optimism" term from Paul Hirt's *A Conspiracy of Optimism*.

19 There are many sources for these figures, which are not in question. I got mine from a draft 1998 Forest Service report on the National Forest Road System and Use.

20 Hirt, *Conspiracy of Optimism*, 235.

21 Clary, *Timber and the Forest Service*, 167.

Selective cutting had long been thought the way to cut trees on the National Forests, but in the 1950s clearcutting, which is as bad as it sounds, became the method of "harvesting" many forest types. Besides its ugliness, clearcutting on steep slopes led to unforeseen (but not unforeseeable) woes: mass wasting of soil on steep slopes; blown-out streams and rivers as a flood of logging debris, dirt, and heavy runoff came down from bare slopes when it rained; regeneration failure; and washed-out roads. In two states, citizens rose up in anger. In Montana, terracing steep mountainsides for clearcutting became the chosen path for the Forest Service. Upset hunters, hikers, homeowners, and others were aghast at the butchered vistas. Arnold Bolle, head of the Montana Forestry School, was asked by Senator Lee Metcalf to give him a report on what was going on. Bolle and the rest of his panel were not against logging, but they were rocked by what they found. In their November 1970 report, they called the Forest Service practices *timber mining* and wrote, "Multiple use management, in fact, does not exist as a governing principle."[22]

The other big hit on clearcutting came from turkey hunters in West Virginia. By 1973, they saw turkey populations dropping with clearcutting. They protested to Chief Cliff without getting anywhere; they then, with help of the Izaak Walton League and National Wildlife Federation, filed a federal lawsuit saying clearcutting violated the 1897 National Forest organic act. They said the 1897 law, which was the only legal basis for NF logging, made two points, which clearcutting violated. First, that trees to be harvested were to be "marked." Second, that only "dead, mature, or large" timber could be cut. Clearcutting did not mark individual trees for cutting and it cut everything of whatever size or age class. The federal court enjoined the Forest Service from clearcutting on the Monongahela National Forest in West Virginia and, in 1975, the Fourth Circuit Court of Appeals upheld the decision throughout the Fourth Circuit.[23]

---

22 Clary, *Timber and the Forest Service*, 186.
23 Clary, *Timber and the Forest Service*, 190-191.

Bolle's report and the Monongahela decision led to two big pieces of legislation: the 1974 Forest and Rangelands Renewable Resources Planning Act (RPA) and the 1976 National Forest Management Act (NFMA). RPA bid the Forest Service to do a national planning process with budget to implement it, updated every five years. NFMA, after the Monongahela case, legalized clearcutting, to much gnashing of teeth by conservationists, but also tossed us a few bones—mandating the agency to keep viable populations of wildlife and to maintain natural vegetative diversity.[24] These two have been the basis for many lawsuits filed over the years by EarthJustice (successor to the Sierra Club Legal Defense Fund), Center for Biological Diversity, and other "sue-the-bastards" conservation teams. NFMA also called for individual National Forest Plans. Hear that Giant Sucking Sound? That's the work conservationists have put into these forest plans and their irregular updates. These two laws came with trumpets blaring like the Second Coming, but they changed very little on the ground.

By the nineties, even some within the Forest Service were rebelling against the "Cut it all!" path of the leaders. The *Economist* in London quoted a forestry professor who said my "former students call up to say 'we're raping the forest.'"[25]

Paul Hirt sums up this era:

Continuing the trend that had begun among some conservation groups in the 1950s, the leaders of the environmental movement of the 1960s and 1970s abandoned the traditional alliance between their groups and the Forest Service. Both the new environmentalists and the Forest Service lost respect for each other, and antagonism escalated.[26]

24   Hirt, *Conspiracy of Optimism*, 243-244.
25   Hirt, *Conspiracy of Optimism*, xvi.
26   Hirt, *Conspiracy of Optimism*, 217.

NATIONAL FOREST WILDERNESS AREAS

In the 1930s, forest supervisors and district rangers of the custodial bent put up and backed most of the Primitive Areas named by the Forest Service. Theirs was the Forest Service of creaking saddle leather, mule trains coughing in trail-dust, canvas wall tents, and Dutch ovens. They liked to hunt and fish in wilderness. A long pack trip took them back to their early days in the new Forest Service. This was not acknowledgement of wilderness for its own sake but a love of pioneer travel and skills. Such foresters could have a strong bond to their chosen Primitive Areas and yet be against locking up "too much" of the backcountry.

The Forest Service's studies of Primitive Areas were put on hold by the war. After the war, conservationists thought the studies would go on as though Bob Marshall were still there to shepherd them. The Primitive Areas, whatever their acreage, were most often rugged, scenic mountain ranges within a much bigger acreage of wild, roadless backcountry. The part of the bigger roadless area not designated as a Primitive Area was likely flatter, smoother, and cloaked in bigger trees. Conservationists thought the Forest Service, after study, would ask the Secretary of Agriculture to make new Wilderness Areas of all of each Primitive Area along with much of the roadless acreage around each. Instead, the Forest Service more often than not called for shrinking Primitive Areas, bringing into the new Wildernesses little if any of the other roadless acreage—so that they could then road and log the unprotected roadless lands *and* what was cut out of the old Primitive Areas shielded by Marshall. What the Forest Service put forward as the new Wilderness Areas had little to no saw-log timber. If this was not enough to warn wilderfolks about the Forest Service and Wilderness, well, in 1948, the Forest Service said it did not plan to set aside more Wilderness.[27]

---

27   Miles, *Wilderness in National Parks*, 139.

The Gila Wilderness in New Mexico tells the tale. Recall that this was the first Wilderness/Primitive Area and that it was Aldo Leopold's baby. In 1924 at birth, it weighed in at 750,000 acres.[28] But after Leopold left the Southwest, new leaders at the Gila National Forest hacked the "North Star Road" through the Wilderness, leaving a Gila Primitive Area to the west and a Black Range Primitive Area to the east (following the terminology of the L-20 regulations). Another road was driven like a stake into the heart of the Gila Primitive Area from the south to the Gila Cliff Dwellings National Monument and private inholdings where the forks of the Gila River came together. Ranchers, with the backing of the Forest Service, dammed mostly dry streams with mule-drawn fresnos and even bulldozers for "stock tanks" deep within the Primitive Area and on its edges.[29] The Gila Primitive Area was 563,000 acres when the U Regs were made before World War Two, and was one of the first of the Primitive Areas to be looked at for permanent Wilderness classification after the War.

In 1952, Southwest Regional Forester C. Otto Lindh called for reclassifying 375,000 acres of the Gila Primitive Area as the Gila Wilderness and dropping 188,000 acres of the Primitive Area from any kind of protection—75,000 acres of old-growth ponderosa pine and Douglas-fir on Iron Creek Mesa to the north and over 100,000 acres to the east between the North Star Road and the road to the Gila Cliff Dwellings. One-third of the Gila Primitive Area would lose all protection. The Forest Service wanted to log Iron Creek Mesa and believed that the other land was too flat to be kept from Jeeps and trucks—in truth it did not meet their belief of what a "Wilderness Area" should look like. The Sierra Club's Weldon Heald wrote, "[T]he Forest Service proposed to get rid of the headache by cutting off the head."

---

28 However, Bob Marshall mapped over 1.3 million acres of roadless lands in the Gila in 1927.

29 For you youngsters, a "fresno" is pretty much a mule-drawn bulldozer blade.

The Wilderness Society and Sierra Club were against chopping up the Gila; amazingly (to conservationists today, leastways), so were the folks in nearby Silver City.[30] Heald, who lived not far away in the Chiricahua Mountains of Arizona, wrote about the August 7, 1952, public hearing in Silver City for *The Living Wilderness*:

> *For more than four hours a steady procession marched to the lectern and spoke against eliminating one square inch of the Gila Wilderness Area. The American Legion, chambers of commerce, sportsmen's' associations, service clubs, women's clubs, garden clubs, VFW, and every organization in four counties had representatives who spoke or read statements vigorously opposed to any reduction whatsoever. Not one organization in the whole region favored the changes.*[31]

Taken aback, but not beaten, the Forest Service shuffled their proposal a little. On January 15, 1953, the Secretary of Agriculture announced a new Gila Wilderness—410,000 acres keeping Iron Creek Mesa in. One hundred and forty-eight thousand acres, mostly the East Side but also in scattered acreages around the Wilderness, remained of the old Primitive Area and was kept as the Gila Primitive Area for study at a later time. When it was restudied in 1972, the Forest Service worked again to cut out most of the Primitive Area, but conservationists got Congress to put nearly all of the Primitive Area in the Gila Wilderness in 1980.

---

30 In those days, hunters expected to go into the backcountry on foot or by horse—not by motors and roads. At first, The Wilderness Society was conned by the Forest Service's phony line and went along with the boundary shift. Naysaying by locals led TWS to look again and then to fight shrinking the Wilderness.

31 Weldon F. Heald, "Report from the Gila," *The Living Wilderness*, Autumn 1952, 27. *The Living Wilderness* is the key primary source for such wilderness fights.

In 1953, the Forest Service got away with taking an ax to the Three Sisters Primitive Area in the Oregon Cascades. Fifty-three thousand acres of lordly, lower-elevation old-growth forest were dropped from protection and opened up for clear-cut logging. The Regional Forester told the Sierra Club "that harvesting some of its 1.5 billion board feet of timber would help to prevent the closing of more mills in the area."[32] The other acreage, mostly high-elevation volcanoes, rock, and subalpine forest, was redesignated as the Three Sisters Wilderness Area.

Even after the Wilderness Act was being worked on in Congress, the Forest Service still hacked away at Primitive Areas. The Yolla Bolly in northern California was halved. The sprawling Selway-Bitterroot Primitive Area in Idaho and Montana (1,875,306 acres[33]) was reclassified as a 1,240,605 acre Selway-Bitterroot Wilderness Area and a 216,870 acre Salmon River Breaks Primitive Area. A gravel road was built between the two and 446,906 well-forested acres—nearly half-a-million acres—were dropped from protection.[34] Michael Frome tells the tale of other Primitive Areas taken to the slaughterhouse in *Battle for the Wilderness*.[35] Conservationists quickly learned that instead of a growing network of National Forest Wilderness Areas, they were being given half the loaf they thought they already had—never mind what they thought they would get.

This onslaught against the old Primitive Areas for the sake of clearcutting ancient forest is what truly drove The Wilderness Society,

32 Dennis M. Roth, *The Wilderness Movement and the National Forests: 1964-1980* (Forest Service History Series FS 391, Washington, D.C., December 1984), 49. Roth's 70-page booklet is an outstanding guide to the wilderness battles after the Wilderness Act. Douglas W. Scott, *A Wilderness-Forever Future: A Short History of the National Wilderness Preservation System* (Pew Wilderness Center, Washington, DC, 2001) is also top-notch.

33 *The Living Wilderness*, Autumn-Winter 1960-61, 50.

34 *The Living Wilderness*, Winter-Spring 1962-63, 25.

35 Michael Frome, *Battle for the Wilderness*, Revised Edition (University of Utah Press, Salt Lake City, UT, 1997 (1974)), 134-138.

Sierra Club, other wildlovers, and many members of Congress to work hard for a congressional Wilderness Act—one that would take away the Forest Service's lordship over Wilderness Areas. This is key. One could say that for Howard Zahniser of The Wilderness Society and main author of the Wilderness Act, at least, this was the real goal of the Wilderness Act. He seems to have mostly wanted to stop the Forest Service from paring back its Primitive Areas. How else to explain his statement to the Society of American Foresters in 1968 that he "*would be satisfied with only 14 million acres of wilderness.*"[36]

36   Hirt, *Conspiracy of Optimism*, 180.

CHAPTER 16

Parks, Dams, and
The Wilderness Act

GOING BACK TO THE FIRST LEADERS of the National Park Service—Stephen Mather and Horace Albright—the NPS boasted of its wilderness but said there was no need to worry about it or to carefully map it. Albright said, "[O]nly the outstanding [features of the parks], which were the prime reason for creation of the park, would be considered for development. The remainder, usually seventy-five percent or more of the total, were to be preserved as wilderness areas."[1] Notwithstanding such soothing words, as conservationists watched more roads and development elbow into what had been Park wilderness, they felt more and more strongly that the National Park Service could not be left with the stewardship of wilderness. Happenings in the 1940s and 1950s only worsened the worry of wilderfolks.

LOGGING THE NATIONAL PARKS

The hot potato of our great National Parks was Olympic in the

1   John C. Miles, *Wilderness in National Parks: Playground or Preserve* (University of Washington Press, Seattle, 2009), 35.

state of Washington—thanks to the mind-boggling forests in the lowland valleys of the Hoh, Quinault, and Bogachiel Rivers, where Douglas-fir and other conifers rise to over 250 feet in height. After years of dogged work, conservationists won an Olympic National Park in 1938. Those who had fought the Park over the big trees kept up their struggles. These foes were the timber companies of Washington, the Seattle business establishment, the Forest Service, then-Congressman Henry Jackson—and the National Park Service. With the backing of the Park Service, steps were soon taken to cut out the mighty woods from the Park. Newton Drury, Director of the National Park Service, worked in the shadows to rid his Park of the big trees. Former Secretary of the Interior Harold Ickes, who had been the might in the Roosevelt Administration to set up Olympic National Park, said later, "I am responsible for the naming of a gutless pygmy" (Drury) as Director of the National Park Service.[2] Carsten Lien, a former president of the Seattle Mountaineers, set out the whole shameful tale in his book, *Olympic Battleground,* and it is the well-marked path for my tale here.

The Park Service backed legislation to redraw the Park edge so that the big trees in the river bottoms were no longer in the Park. When that failed, they ran commercial timber sales *within Olympic National Park* through the 1940s and 1950s. Lien wrote:

> *For the staff at Olympic National Park, the team of Wirth* [the new Director of the Park Service, Conrad Wirth] *and Overly* [the new Superintendent of Olympic, Fred Overly] *meant only one thing—logs would flow from the park to the mills. By 1952, so much timber had begun to flow from Olympic National Park that Washington State's timber harvest statistical records could not accurately account for the quantity produced. For the first time, a special category had to be added to the state's timber*

2   Carsten Lien, *Olympic Battleground: The Power Politics of Timber Preservation* (Sierra Club Books, San Francisco, 1991), 243.

harvest report—National Park Timber Harvested—Western
Washington 1952."[3]

Olympic's logging was said to be of windblown trees, which
threatened visitors, but Overly let timber companies log millions of
board feet—much of which was from sound, healthy, standing trees.
In 1953, timber companies took 14.6 million board feet out of the
National Park, some trees so big that you could lay three yardsticks end
to end across the stump.[4]

As Overly cranked up commercial logging in the Park, the
seasonal naturalists working for Olympic NP rose up against logging
in 1956. The ringleader was Paul Shepard, who had gotten his Ph.D.
in ecology with Paul Sears at Yale in 1954. Shepard also happened to
be conservation chairman of the National Council of State Garden
Clubs, with 250,000 members. Shepard's work with the garden
clubs and national conservation organizations was the shove needed
for Wirth to at last halt the logging. Overly was sent to Great Smoky
Mountains National Park in 1958. He should have gone to Alcatraz.
Although Wirth buckled to the conservationists, he kept lying about
the logging, even saying that photographs of the logging that ran in *The
Living Wilderness* were from outside the Park, when he knew good and
well they weren't. Shepard, who later went on to be one of the deepest
ecological thinkers and author of books such as *Thinking Animals* and
The Others, was forever banned from working for the National Park
Service.[5] There have been a few black-hatted knaves who worked for
the National Park Service, with Wirth and Overly at the top.

No less than 100 million board feet were cut out of Olympic
National Park. Lien writes, "Even though the illusion of virgin forest is

---

3   Lien, *Olympic Battleground,* 271.
4   Lien, *Olympic Battleground,* 277-278, 280, 288.
5   Lien, *Olympic Battleground,* 285-298; see also Richard West Sellars,
     Preserving Nature in the National Parks: A History (Yale University Press,
     New Haven, CT, 1997), 153-154.

present for the visitor today, the Park Service achieved the destruction of the largest and most magnificent of Olympic Park's trees in the face of an absolutely clear mandate from society to preserve them."[6]

Olympic was not the only National Park threatened by Park Service foresters. Early on, the Park Service chose to hire foresters, who shared the taming-the-wild mindset of the Forest Service, to care for the forests of the National Parks against forest fires, insects, and diseases. Botanists and plant biologists were not hired. Keep this in mind—it helps to show how antiscience the Park Service brass was. The Civilian Conservation Corps (CCC) cut down snags, green trees, and underbrush along Park roads in the 1930s for fire control and "to improve the appearance of the immediate landscape."[7] In other words, to open up "scenic vistas" along roads. NPS biologists such as George Wright and Adolph Murie loudly fought it, but Park Service foresters logged twelve square miles of Glacier National Park that had burned.[8] Early salvage logging.

To kill bark beetles and other insects that NPS foresters thought threatened National Park forests, Wirth had tens of thousands of acres of Yosemite, Yellowstone, and other Parks sprayed with DDT, notwithstanding fish kills afterward and warnings from NPS biologists such as Lowell Sumner. The Park Service went all out to fight wildfires in the Parks, without heed for ecological upsets.[9] By the 1950s, many foresters, like Overly, had become park superintendents and chief rangers. In 1957, the former chief biologist of the NPS, Victor Cahalane, said the forestry group "pretends to know everything about ecology, but actually has no competence in that field," and warned, "they can work havoc."[10] Which is what they did throughout the Parks.

6   Lien, *Olympic Battleground*, 298.
7   Sellars, *Preserving Nature in the National Parks*, 127.
8   Sellars, *Preserving Nature in the National Parks*, 128-130.
9   *Sellars, Preserving Nature in the National Parks*, 162-163.
10   Sellars, *Preserving Nature in the National Parks*, 171-172.

MISSION 66

Conrad (Connie) Wirth became the director of the National Park Service in 1952. As we have seen, he winked at unlawful commercial logging in Olympic National Park. Even worse, in cahoots with the American Automobile Association, in 1956 he came out with "Mission 66"—an overweening ten-year swagger to build roads, visitor centers, and resorts in some of the wildest spots of the National Parks. Wirth also led the Park Service against the Wilderness Act on the grounds that the Park Service was already taking care of wilderness and did not need outside meddling or oversight.[11] Mission 66 and the logging of Olympic steeled conservationists to be steadfast in putting National Park lands in the Wilderness Act, whether Wirth liked it or not.

Sellars writes that with Wirth, "recreational tourism, culminating in the Mission 66 emphasis on intensive public use, would become more than ever the driving force within the National Park Service. It was the antithesis of the scientific approach to park management."[12] At a 1956 event cosponsored by the American Automobile Association, Wirth hoorayed Mission 66. Conservationists not only disliked the wave of development targeted for the Parks, but also the mood. Gone was the woodsy look of Old Faithful Lodge. New developments were modern, urbanized—and ugly. Conservationists sneered that the bulldozer was the fitting symbol for Mission 66, given that Mission 66 built 2,700 miles of new or upgraded roads through the Parks.[13]

BIG DAMS

Although damming Western rivers became a secular religion of the holy-roller kind among the region's politicians and boomers in the twentieth century, it was only the federal government that had the wherewithal to build such bust-the-bank hulks as Boulder, Glen

11   Miles, *Wilderness in National Parks* is the best source for NPS opposition to the Wilderness Act.

12   Sellars, *Preserving Nature in the National Parks,* 173.

13   Sellars, *Preserving Nature in the National Parks,* 180-191.

Canyon, Grand Coulee, Shasta, Fort Peck, and other big dams on almost all the rivers of the West. (Of the big to middling Western rivers, only the Yampa, Yellowstone, and Smith are without big dams. The Smith River with all its tributaries in northern California is a National Wild & Scenic River with no dams from the headwaters to the Pacific Ocean.) The federal government—in the duds of the Bureau of Reclamation— was the most hallelujahing preacher of this socialistic faith, though the amen corner was made up of government-hating Republicans as much as New Deal Democrats. In the South, the Tennessee Valley Authority (TVA) of the federal government hustled dams. Throughout the country, the U.S. Army Corps of Engineers, like beavers on cocaine, channelized rivers, built locks and canals, and choked rivers with mighty dams. While private interests were a head-over-heels love-struck lobby for dams, it was the federal agencies that not only built them, but also were the most hopped-up boosters for the authorization and funding to do so. Pork-barrel politicians loved the federal dammers.

Taming and lording over rivers is the soul of resourcism. Indeed, stamping human will on rivers was the first big-scale resource management, and may be what beget early civilizations with their hierarchical and ruthless framework seven to eight thousand years ago. Karl Wittfogel, a scholar of early irrigation-bedded societies in southwestern Asia, believed that an elite bureaucratic class came to rule because of the need to oversee water. Lording over rivers led to lording over people—"Oriental Despotism."[14] The first cities, such as Sumer between the Tigris and Euphrates Rivers in what is now Iraq, could be built only after the rivers were fettered to water wheat fields.

Many of the framing fights in the western United States between conservation and resourcism came over dams. We have seen how

---

14   Donald Worster, *Rivers of Empire: Water, Aridity & The Growth of The American West* (Pantheon Books, NY, 1985), 22-30; Karl A. Wittfogel, "The Hydraulic Civilizations," in William L. Thomas Jr., ed., *Man's Role In Changing The Face Of The Earth* (The University of Chicago Press, 1956), 152-164.

the Hetch Hetchy fight was the first conservation struggle to gain widespread heed. Echo Park was the next big fight in the open. In 1950 a billion dollars was a lot of money. It would build ten dams for the Colorado River Storage Project. One of those dams was set for Echo Park at the confluence of the Green and Yampa rivers in Dinosaur National Monument on the border of Colorado and Utah. Again, National Park land was threatened by high and mighty plumbing. Moreover, Echo Park, where the Green and Yampa rivers flow together and brawny sandstone walls rise over the slapping waves is one of the most awestriking spots in America. The fight against Echo Park Dam from 1950 to 1956 made the modern conservation movement, with hitherto unthought-of fund-raising, public education, coordination among groups, and congressional lobbying.[15] In 1956, Congress authorized the Colorado River Storage Project, but without Echo Park Dam, and stating that no dam or reservoir would go into any National Park or Monument.[16] For the first time, wilderfolk had gone toe-to-toe against resourcism and won.[17]

Ten years later, though, the most overweening, fulsome dam-dream of all stormed into Congress with trumpets blaring like Moroni come down from the steeple of the temple in Salt Lake City. Two dams for the Grand Canyon! crowed the Bureau of Wreck-the-nation.

---

15   Wallace Stegner, ed., *This Is Dinosaur: Echo Park Country and Its Magic Rivers* (Alfred A. Knopf, 1955) is the wonderful little book by conservationists that was a key publicity tool in the history-making campaign.

16   Roderick Nash, *Wilderness and the American Mind* (Yale University Press, New Haven, CT, 1967), 209-219.

17   Although conservationists won a hard fight on Echo Park over the line-in-the-sand stand of no dams in National Park units, they lost the fight to keep wilderness. The Colorado River Storage Act authorized Glen Canyon Dam on the Colorado, which drowned 180 miles of a matchless redrock-canyon wilderness. See Eleanor Inskip, *The Colorado River through Glen Canyon Before Lake Powell: Historic Photo Journal 1872 to 1964* (Inskip Ink, Moab, UT, 1995). Nash, *Wilderness and the American Mind*; Worster, *Rivers of Empire*; and other books give the history of our loss on Glen Canyon Dam.

The Grand Canyon, the Sierra Club roared back. Marble Gorge and Bridge Canyon dams were cash cows. Their only good was hydroelectric power. In an Earth-shaking struggle, the Sierra Club led the fight against the dams, using full-page ads in *The New York Times* and other papers, and crunching the numbers better than did the Bureau of Reclamation. The Grand Canyon dams were killed. The dam lobby hotheartedly roared that the dams were stopped because of David Brower's lies. Lies? The Sierra Club rightly said that the dams would be in the Grand Canyon. Floyd Dominy, head of BuRec, shot back that they would have been built outside of Grand Canyon *National Park*. While the two dams would have flooded much of the geographical Grand Canyon, the chunk of the Grand Canyon within the artificial boundaries of Grand Canyon National Park would not have been flooded. So mad were the dam-builders in the Department of the Interior and in Congress, that the Internal Revenue Service yanked the Sierra Club's tax-exempt status.[18] This is but a short, swift overview of the dam wars and leaves much out, but it gives a taste of how differently resourcists and conservationists saw flowing water.

THE WILDERNESS ACT

By the early 1950s, conservation clubs at last realized that they could not trust the Forest Service and Park Service to keep their wilderness whole. With the Forest Service's road-building and logging madness reaching deep into the National Forest backcountry and with the National Park Service seeming to pave the Parks for industrial tourism, The Wilderness Society and Sierra Club called for a Wilderness Act to give Congress authority for Wilderness Areas. Senator Hubert Humphrey (D-Minnesota) and Representative John Saylor (R-Pennsylvania) dropped the first Wilderness bills in the hoppers of their Houses of Congress in 1956. After sixty-six rewrites

---

18   Marc Reisner, *Cadillac Desert: The American West And Its Disappearing Water* (Penguin Books, New York, 1987), 283-300.

(mostly by Howard Zahniser of The Wilderness Society), eighteen public hearings, 6,000 pages of testimony, and a well-led campaign by Zahniser, Congress voted yes with strong bipartisan majorities in each house and President Johnson signed the Wilderness Act in 1964 with a public ceremony at the White House. Standing behind the President were Alice Zahniser and Mardy Murie, widows of the executive director and president of The Wilderness Society, both of whom had died before passage.[19]

From the first whisper of a Wilderness Act to the signing at the end, the Forest Service and Park Service fought the bill tooth and nail. The agency bosses disliked it on sundry grounds:

- They felt legislation would squeeze their freedom of management.
- They didn't like a public hand in the wilderness review.
- They said legislation was not needed since they were taking care of wilderness anyway.
- At the bottom, they were against keeping much wilderness and were for resource exploitation and developed recreation.
- The Park Service feared being in a system with the Forest Service would weaken protection for National Parks.

In a 1964 booklet, *Highlights in the History of Forest Conservation*, the Forest Service let slip that shielding Wilderness was not high in their world of forest "conservation." In listing over one hundred forest conservation highlights from 1626 to 1962, the Forest Service never breathed the word wilderness, not even its own administrative work to set up Primitive Areas and then Wilderness and Wild Areas.[20]

19 Douglas W. Scott, *A Wilderness-Forever Future: A Short History of the National Wilderness Preservation System* (Pew Wilderness Center, Washington, DC, 2001) is the best overview of the campaign for the Wilderness Act. Scott also discusses implementation of the Wilderness Act from 1964 to 2001.

20 *Highlights in the History of Forest Conservation*, Forest Service, U.S. Department of Agriculture, Agriculture Information Bulletin, No. 83, Washington, DC, January 1964.

Sellars writes that "the wilderness bill represented the antithesis of developmental programs such as Mission 66—and it got a cool reception from Park Service leadership."[21] He also writes that "the Wilderness Act was intended to prohibit the very kinds of alterations of natural conditions then being wrought by Mission 66."[22] No wonder Conrad Wirth bristled at it. It would be easy to see The Wilderness Act as a witting slap at Wirth and his beloved Mission 66. Early in 1956, Zahniser, with David Brower of the Sierra Club and Charles Woodbury of the National Parks Association, met with Wirth to discuss the draft Wilderness bill Zahniser had sent him. Wirth later wrote Zahniser to say National Park wilderness was better protected as it was than it would be in a National Wilderness Act.[23] After John F. Kennedy became President in 1961, he endorsed the Wilderness bill before Congress. His Secretary of the Interior Stewart Udall stoutly called for Congress to pass the bill. With their boss at Interior now working for the Wilderness bill, Wirth and the Park Service could no longer openly work against it.[24] Notwithstanding Interior's stand, Wirth and the NPS brass still did their best to undercut the bill behind the scenes.

Dig-and-cut businesses—loggers, miners, drillers, irrigators, some ranchers—and the highway lobby fought the Wilderness Act, too. Their man in Congress, Representative Wayne Aspinal, a Democrat from western Colorado and iron-fisted chairman of the House Interior Committee, held off passage for many years until he got weakening words put in.

I went through the four definitions and yardsticks of wilderness in the Wilderness Act in Chapter Two. Since Stewart Brandborg wrote the first Wilderness Act Handbook for The Wilderness Society soon after the act became law, The Wilderness Society has kept a handbook in print. These handbooks in whatever edition give the full text of the Act,

---

21 Sellars, *Preserving Nature in the National Parks,* 191.
22 Sellars, *Preserving Nature in the National Parks,* 194.
23 Miles, *Wilderness in National Parks,* 139-140.
24 Miles, *Wilderness in National Parks,* 152.

a thorough explanation of it, and other needed and helpful information for wilderfolk working to add new lands to the National Wilderness Preservation System.[25] Anyone working to add new landscapes to the National Wilderness Preservation System *must* have a copy.

25   Jay Watson and Ben Beach, eds., *The Wilderness Act Handbook* Fourth Edition (revised) (The Wilderness Society, Washington, August 2000).

CHAPTER 17

Chopping Down the Wilderness Act

Wayne Aspinall, the iron-fisted Chairman of the House Interior Committee and leading foe of the Wilderness Act in Congress, surprisingly made the best change to the bill before it became law. His amendment called for the agencies to have public hearings on their Wilderness proposals before finalizing them. These hearings would become the biggest opening for public participation in the federal government. Aspinall's amendment led to at least three great steps forward for conservationists.

First, we had to work together before hearings to cobble out our own Wilderness proposals to be offered at the hearings to better the agencies' recommendations. This meant conservationists—locals and nationals—had to work together to field check wilderness suitability of areas and to draw the best boundaries for Wilderness Areas. Then we had to sit down with each other and agree to one proposal. The Wilderness Society then sent out notices of each hearing to conservation group members in that particular state or region for every one of the "mandate areas." These notices, besides information on when and where the hearing(s) would be held, also had a map of the joint conservationists' proposal, reasons why it was better than the agency proposal, where and by when to send comments, and a list of all the groups backing the joint proposal.[1]

Second, this heavy public participation led Stewart Brandborg, executive director of The Wilderness Society (after Zahniser died), Clif Merritt, western director, and Ernie Dickerman, eastern director, to recast The Wilderness Society as the spark for organizing grassroots wilderness clubs. Not, mind you, to organize chapters of The Wilderness Society, but fully independent state and local wilderness clubs that would work with The Wilderness Society. Wilderness Society staff, both field representatives in western states and staff in the DC and Denver offices, served such groups. When locals came to Washington to visit their congressfolks or to testify at a hearing, TWS provided working space, phones, copy machines, and so on. Moreover, TWS offered weeklong training sessions in Washington at no cost for a dozen or so local leaders at a time. Folks got to meet with agency heads and key members of Congress as part of the training. All of this made TWS the key organizer in the conservation movement up until it was effectively destroyed and remade as something else in 1979. There's been nothing like it since. And that has weakened the conservation network as nothing else has.

Third, it gave *organizers* a job and status in the conservation movement until about 1980. James Turner lays all this out in his top-notch book on the wilderness movement since the 1964 Wilderness Act. I'm not going to rehash his good work since *The Great Conservation Divide* is a book about the struggle between wilderness conservation and

---

1   I have copies of nearly every one of these mandate area mailers. Today's conservationists could learn much from studying the style of these.

resource conservation, not about the wilderness movement itself and its infighting and factions. Therefore, read *The Promise of Wilderness*.[2]

After the Wilderness Act became the law of the land, the Forest Service and Park Service still saw it as a mistake overall and did what they could to undercut it and to keep as much of their land as they could out of Wilderness (although at times darned good staffers sat behind the wilderness desks of the three agencies under the Wilderness Act). The Fish & Wildlife Service was more friendly to Wilderness Area designation and overall offered good boundary recommendations. One reason for the FWS being friendly to wilderness was Harry Crandell. Harry had been refuge manager of Cabeza Prieta NWR on the Mexican border in Arizona—Cabeza (as desert rats call it) is the biggest and wildest refuge in the lower 48 States. Harry became chief of wilderness for the FWS in Washington and insured that good recommendations in keeping with the Wilderness Act would come from the service.[3] He later was hired by The Wilderness Society and then as head staffer for the House Public Lands Committee by its Chair, Rep. John Seiberling, where he guided many Wilderness bills through Congress.

The Wilderness Act at once named all National Forest Wilderness and Wild Areas as Wilderness Areas in the congressionally overseen National Wilderness Preservation System (NWPS). The Act bade the Forest Service to get the studies done on its last Primitive Areas and send recommendations to Congress by 1974. The Park Service and Fish & Wildlife Service were told to study all roadless areas on their lands of 5,000 acres or more (or "of a size practicable for management") and send designation recommendations to Congress by 1974. Under the Wilderness Act, now only Congress could add or drop areas from the Wilderness System.

2   James Morton Turner, *The Promise of Wilderness: American Environmental Politics Since 1964* (University of Washington Press, Seattle, 2012). The dumbfounding flip in the personality and work of The Wilderness Society in 1979-1980 is richly laid out in *Promise*.

3   Turner, *The Promise of Wilderness*, 52-53.

Conservation clubs, led by The Wilderness Society with help from the Sierra Club, organized across the fifty states to implement the Act. Clif Merritt, Ernie Dickerman, and Stewart Brandborg of TWS were bulldogs for grassroots organizing, while Harry Crandell was a bloodhound at smelling out what the agencies and Congress were up to. It is through their foresight that a mighty wilderness tide came in by the 1970s. Until 1979, the leaders of The Wilderness Society were fully bound to finding, training, and empowering *independent* grassroots wilderness clubs and activists. Brandborg and the others believed wholeheartedly that such a path was the right way to go, although Michael McCloskey and some other leaders of the Sierra Club did their best to undercut Brandborg and TWS to push their own top-down, insider way. [4]

SAME OLD TALE FOR USFS PRIMITIVE AREAS

All agencies got off to a slow start in their studies. The Forest Service brushed off the wilderness network's backing for big Wildernesses, and kept at their game of offering chopped-away Primitive Areas for Wilderness. [5] Overall, lands with trees were shunned and "rocks and ice" got the nod for Wilderness in USFS recommendations. [6] Moreover,

4   After he was named executive director of the Sierra Club in 1969, Michael McCloskey worked behind the scenes against Brandborg and The Wilderness Society's grassroots strategy, even though many Sierra Club leaders backed TWS. He believed that an insider, more accommodating strategy would get the job done quicker, and that conservation clubs had become outmoded and needed to get with the new environmental movement. See Turner, *The Promise Of Wilderness,* 101-103, 120-121. Turner's book truly blazes a new trail for understanding the infighting within and between conservation clubs from 1970 on. Also see Dave Foreman, *Take Back Conservation* (Raven's Eye Press, Durango, CO, 2012), 54-55, for how McCloskey worked to push conservationists into environmentalism.

5   Montana-based wilderness guide and outfitter Howie Wolke slams the Forest Service's wrecking of wilderness in *Wilderness on the Rocks* (Ned Ludd Books, Tucson, 1991).

6   I write this after having read all the USFS Primitive Area reclassification

the Forest Service came out with timber sales for bid and built logging roads along the edges of Primitive Areas so as to keep neighboring roadless lands (*de facto* wilderness, in the words of conservationists[7]) from being added to new Wilderness Areas. This was a witting sham in the Forest Service's grab bag of tricks to narrow National Forest acres Congress could designate as Wilderness.

East Meadow Creek next to the Gore Range-Eagles Nest Primitive Area north of Vail, Colorado, was the poster child for this underhanded scam. In the 1960s, White River National Forest timber beasts drew up blueprints to log the old-growth fir, spruce, and lodgepole pine of East Meadow Creek.[8] Wilderfolk in Vail were against the timber sale and wanted that acreage in the upcoming Eagles Nest Wilderness Area, which otherwise was jagged and icy high country. They talked to Clif Merritt, Western Regional Director of The Wilderness Society in Denver. Clif, a soft-spoken but steadfast fighter for Wilderness, far-sighted strategist, and matchless organizer, got young lawyer and wilderness lover Tony Ruckel on the job.[9] In April of 1969, going against legal orthodoxy that "the United States cannot be sued without its consent," Ruckel, with Merritt's backing, sued on the grounds that the Forest Service's logging next to the Primitive Area would violate the Wilderness Act's provision allowing the President to recommend "the addition of any contiguous area of national forest lands predominantly of wilderness value."

Federal Judge William E. Doyle first let the conservationists sue the government and then enjoined the timber sale. Forest Service

studies. I have copies of all of them, along with copies of nearly all the Park Service and Wildlife Refuge Wilderness studies in my library.

7　*De facto* means "in fact." *De jure* Wilderness is legally protected Wilderness, or "Big W" Wilderness. *De facto* wilderness is wilderness in fact, but not in law. It's also called "little w" wilderness.

8　"Timber beast" was the name Forest Service foresters smilingly gave themselves.

9　Ruckel went on to help start the Sierra Club Legal Defense Fund. It was my good luck to serve with him on the Sierra Club National Board in the mid-1990s.

historian Dennis Roth wrote that Doyle "interpreted the language of the Wilderness Act to mean that the Forest Service must refrain from developing a contiguous area which was potentially of wilderness value until the President and Congress had acted on the agency's recommendations."[10] This "Parker Case" was the first judicial decision to shield wilderness.

Grounding their boundary lines and acreages on careful fieldwork, conservation clubs in the ten years after 1964 asked for Wilderness Area designation of nearly all the acreage in the 34 Primitive Areas (5.5 million acres) and for much of the neighboring roadless lands.[11] Congress, more often than not, designated Wilderness Areas nearer to the conservationists' map lines than to the Forest Service's.[12]

NATIONAL PARK "DO-NUT HOLES"

Referring to the Wilderness Act, professor emeritus John Miles of Western Washington University writes, "Never before in its history had the Park Service suffered a loss like this." Park Service leaders feared they would lose "managerial control of part of their domain."[13]

10 Dennis M. Roth, *The Wilderness Movement and the National Forests: 1964-1980* (FS 391, USDA Forest Service, Washington, 1984), 19-22.

11 However, conservationists often missed big acreages of roadless lands next to their Wilderness proposals. The New Mexico Wilderness Study Committee overlooked more than 150,000 roadless acres in drafting their Aldo Leopold Wilderness proposal, and the Sierra Club and others in Arizona somehow didn't notice roughly 250,000 acres of roadless lands next to their Blue Range Wilderness. Some of us who came into the game after these early Primitive Areas were studied updated the conservationists' proposals by tacking on all the roadless land. It was the same in other states. Idaho conservationists kissed off one million acres of contiguous roadless lands in their proposal for a River of No Return Wilderness. Dave Foreman and Howie Wolke, *The Big Outside* Second Edition (Harmony Books, Crown Publishers, New York, 1992).

12 Turner, *Promise of Wilderness*.

13 John C. Miles, *Wilderness in National Parks: Playground or Preserve* (University of Washington Press, Seattle, 2009), 159.

The Park Service halfheartedly made Wilderness proposals, but at first the maps looked like Swiss cheese. In their early Wilderness Area proposals for Yellowstone, North Cascades, and Yosemite, the NPS had 1/8-mile-wide non-wilderness buffers all along the Park edge unless National Forest Wilderness Areas were next door (where roadless NF land neighbored, however, the nonwilderness buffers were kept, on no grounds at all), and non-wilderness "do-nut holes" were dotted all over the backcountry for sundry little things such as fire tool caches in boxes not much bigger than a footlocker. In my neck of the woods, the Wilderness proposal for Bandelier National Monument had the same buffer zone and do-nut holes—one such nonwilderness exclusion was so the NPS could build a little roof over the Stone Lions Shrine to keep the rain from further eroding the two side-by-side mountain lion stone carvings. New Mexico conservationists scoffed at this and said there would be nothing wrong with building such a little roof in a Wilderness Area.[14] In Guadalupe Mountains National Park in West Texas along the New Mexico border, the NPS Wilderness proposal deleted lands for a "high-standard" foot trail "corridor" to the escarpment of the high country. Even worse was an 1100-acre cutout for a tramway from the flatlands to the top of Texas's highest mountain Guadalupe Peak![15]

After an outcry by The Wilderness Society through Senator Frank Church, Nathaniel Reed, the Assistant Secretary of Interior, who oversaw the Park Service and Fish and Wildlife Service, wrote to both services that such nonwilderness holes and buffers would be taken out of all Department of Interior Wilderness Area proposals.[16]

14 A good Bandelier Wilderness Area became law in 1976, but the roof has never been built.

15 *Wilderness Recommendation Guadalupe Mountains National Park, Texas* (DOI National Park Service, August 1972), 13-14. We waged a good fight to kill the tramway and got a good Wilderness Area in Guadalupe in 1978.

16 June 24, 1972 memo from Assistant Secretary for Fish and Wildlife and Parks to Director, Bureau of Sport Fisheries and Wildlife, and Director, National Park Service, Guidelines for Wilderness Proposals—Reference

In his long-awaited study of the National Park Service and Wilderness, *Wilderness in National Parks,* John Miles goes into enlightening detail on the lousy National Park Wilderness recommendations and how conservationists worked to get their own much-better Wilderness proposals adopted by Interior and then passed by Congress. I will not try to match that here. Read his book.

Unlike the Park Service and Forest Service, the Fish & Wildlife Service was happy with the Wilderness Act and did a good job with their Wilderness studies. Indeed, sometimes National Wildlife Refuge managers proposed more Wilderness than did local conservationists. For example, in New Mexico, Bosque del Apache National Wildlife Refuge Manager Dick Rigby recommended three Wilderness Areas in the uplands of the Refuge. Clif Merritt at The Wilderness Society's Denver office (with my help) had to come down hard on leaders of the New Mexico Wilderness Study Committee not to *oppose* Wilderness in Bosque del Apache. They thought it looked like "cow pasture." In the end, they agreed to say nothing, while I testified for a Bosque del Apache Wilderness on behalf of TWS before Congress in Washington, DC. The Wilderness Areas were designated in 1976.

DE FACTO WILDERNESS

The United States Forest Service did not like the Wilderness Act. It did not like being told what to do—even by Congress and the President. It did not like outsiders coming in and redefining Wilderness. After all the Forest Service proudly boasted that they had invented Wilderness Area protection and, damnit, they knew better than anyone else what was and was not Wilderness. So, in the fall and winter of 1964-1965, a Forest Service wilderness task force came together to

Secretarial Order No. 2920. For The Wilderness Society role, see Roth, *The Wilderness Movement and the National Forests: 1964-1980,* 8-9. Nathaniel Reed, a Nixon appointee and Republican stalwart from Florida, has been by far the best conservationist to hold that key job. Also see Miles, *Wilderness in National Parks,* 196-201.

see if the Service's and the Wilderness Act's ideas of wilderness were compatible. They were not, the Forest Service experts found. So, the Forest Service decided to stick with their idea—the one they had been using to butcher Primitive Areas—that "only the most pristine forest lands in the American West" should be designated. Dick Costley, the Forest Service's wilderness honcho, said that "the only practical—and supportable—wilderness management stance which the Forest Service can defend is a 'pure' one."[17]

The Wilderness Act did not tell the Forest Service to inventory all its roadless areas, as it told the Park Service and Fish & Wildlife Service. The fifty-four areas already named by the USFS as Wild, Wilderness, or Canoe Areas, with 9.1 million acres in all, were right away put into the new National Wilderness Preservation System by the Wilderness Act. The Forest Service had only to wind up the studies and recommendations for the thirty-four still-to-do Primitive Areas, 5.5 million acres in all, as called for in the U Regulations twenty-five years earlier. Hunters, hikers, horse packers, and naturalists, however, knew there were many millions of acres of *de facto* wilderness in the National Forests beyond the Primitive Areas. From the research Howie Wolke and I did for *The Big Outside*,[18] I would say that in 1964, at least 120 million acres of the then-187 million-acre National Forest system met the yardstick for Wilderness Area designation.[19]

---

17   Turner, *The Promise of Wilderness*, 54-55.

18   Dave Foreman and Howie Wolke, *The Big Outside* (Harmony Books, Crown Publishers, New York, 1992).

19   At the beginning of RARE II in 1977, there were likely still 100 million acres of roadless areas and Wilderness in the National Forests (14.6 million acres of the 1964 Wilderness, Wild, and Primitive Areas, at least 82 million acres of RARE II areas and other roadless areas not included for sundry grounds, and new areas already added to the NWPS by Congress). In the thirteen years between 1964 and 1977, the Forest Service wiped out millions of acres of roadless area through timber sales and road building. They also continued their job of splitting up big roadless areas. If anything, my 120 million-acre figure is low.

But the Forest Service was bent on keeping National Forest Wilderness below twenty or twenty-five million acres. With fifteen million acres already named Wilderness or Primitive, this meant not more than another five or ten million acres for new Wilderness, which would leave more than 100 million acres of roadless land open for logging and road-building. Moreover, the Forest Service brass was steadfast that little marketable timber would be "locked up" in the new Wilderness acreage. What little else the Forest Service was willing to recommend was called "rocks and ice" by world-weary conservationists who had been jacked around by the Forest Service before. Deputy Chief Art Greeley told regional foresters in 1964, "It seems we have the choice—Maybe 16-18 million acres of pure wilderness—or 2 or 3 times as much half-baked wilderness, all with an encumbrance on truly multiple-use management." Multiple-use management meant logging.[20] "Pure" and "purity" were words used by the USFS along with "quality" to mean lands that met their self-serving standards.

Between 1926 and 1961, the Forest Service had broken up most of the big roadless areas in the Western mountains with roads, even though the acreage of roadless and undeveloped land was still high overall. In 1926, there were seventy-four roadless areas bigger than 230,400 acres (fifty-five million acres in all); a study by the University of California in 1961 found only nineteen areas of that size (seventeen million acres in all).[21] These numbers do not say that the USFS developed thirty-

20   Roth, *The Wilderness Movement and the National Forests: 1964-1980*, 6. Note Greeley's use of the word "pure" for wilderness. *Purity* was the FS word for untouched by Man.

21   Foreman and Wolke, *The Big Outside*, 4-5. However, Wolke and I found more 230,500-acre roadless areas in 1992. Also see Michael Frome, *Battle for the Wilderness* Revised Edition (University of Utah Press, Salt Lake City), 20. By the way, the odd acreage of 230,400 comes from using the section and township-surveying frame. A township is thirty-six sections (square miles) or a square six by six miles. A square mile (section) is 640 acres; a township then comes out to 23,040 acres. Aha! Do you see where we got 230,400 acres? Ten townships. The Ordinance of 1785 still rules; see Chapter 4.

eight million acres of roadless areas; they say mainly that the Forest Service split up the big roadless areas into many smaller roadless areas by cutting roads through them. In the words of today's conservation biology, they *fragmented* National Forest lands. Michael Soulé, the father of conservation biology, would say that a 5 million-acre roadless area has more worth as habitat than five 1 million-acre roadless areas split from one another by roads.

In 1926, Bob Marshall mapped the biggest FS roadless area left at that time: 7,668,480 acres in central Idaho. The way the Forest Service sliced up the Clearwater-Selway-Salmon area over the years tells the tale.[22] In 1935 (only nine years after Marshall's inventory), retired Lolo NF Supervisor Elers Koch wrote:

> *Only a few years ago the great Clearwater wilderness stretched from the Bitterroot to the Kooskia; from the Cedar Creek mines to the Salmon River and beyond. No road and no permanent human habitation marred its primitive nature....*
>
> *The Forest Service sounded the note of progress. It opened up the wilderness with roads and telephone lines, and airplane landing fields....*
>
> *Has all this effort and expenditure of millions of dollars added anything to human good? Is it possible that it was all a ghastly mistake like plowing up the good buffalo grass sod of the dry prairies?*[23]

In the late 1960s when conservationists asked the Forest Service to think about Wilderness recommendations for roadless areas that had never been Primitive Areas, they got the cold shoulder—Forest

---

22   Foreman and Wolke, *The Big Outside*, 470.

23   Elers Koch, *Journal of Forestry*, February, 1935, quoted in *The Living Wilderness*, September 1935, 9. Koch wrote in the middle years of the Dust Bowl—caused in part by plowing up the "good buffalo grass sod of the dry prairies."

Service Director of Recreation Dick Costley sneered at such "wildcat wilderness proposals."[24] The first of the wildcats to claw the Forest Service was the Lincoln-Scapegoat area in Montana, next to the Forest Service's flagship Wilderness Area—the Bob Marshall. In truth, it was not *next* to the Bob, it was part of one roadless area with the Bob and other de facto wilderness—over two million acres in all. The Lincoln-Scapegoat wasn't knock-your-boots-off breathtaking; it was just milk-and-honey country for pack trips, hiking, and big game hunting. Local redneck shopkeeper Cecil Garland and The Wilderness Society's Western Regional Director, Clif Merritt (Montana born and bred), put together and led a grassroots citizens' campaign against Forest Service wishes to log the area. Montana's Republican congressman, "Big Jim" Battin introduced a 240,500-acre Lincoln-Scapegoat Wilderness Area bill in 1965, which threw the brass of the Forest Service into a tizzy. Tellingly, this was the first Wilderness bill in Congress after the passage of the Wilderness Act.[25] The Lincoln-Scapegoat bill came before bills for any "mandate areas" (FS Primitive Areas, and NPS and FWS roadless areas). That a wildcat would be looked at by Congress before anything put up by professional land managers was a chicken bone on which the ol' Forest Service hound dog almost choked to death. It was an unspeakable rudeness, but, thanks to it, the Scapegoat Wilderness Area, the first "citizen Wilderness," is a big player and game-changer in the Wilderness saga.

Although the Lincoln-Scapegoat bill did not become law until 1972, it spurred other wilderfolk to go over the Forest Service right to members of Congress. The Forest Service saw this as a threat that could lead to too much "half-baked" Wilderness, and also as breaking the way things should be done in their reading of the Wilderness Act: the Forest

24 Roth, *The Wilderness Movement and the National Forests: 1964-1980*, 7.
25 Montana's Democratic senators Lee Metcalf and Mike Mansfield had written a smaller Lincoln-Scapegoat bill before Battin's, but backed his after it was introduced. Roth, *The Wilderness Movement and the National Forests: 1964-1980*, 24-35.

Service would study an area and send a professional recommendation for or against Wilderness to the Secretary of Agriculture who would send it on the president. The president would then send it to Congress. (Though seldom done, both the Secretary and the President could make changes). There would be steps along this path for citizens to speak on the Forest Service proposal, but it was not kosher for citizens to come up with their own proposals and take them straight to Congress. And then Congress would ask the Forest Service to comment on what citizens proposed! This was a ghastly ass-over-teakettle slap at the United States Forest Service's professional honor.

Right away, the Forest Service's worst fears came alive. In 1969, climbers and hunters in New Mexico came together as the New Mexico Wilderness Study Committee and began to ask for new National Forest Wilderness Areas that were not Primitive Areas being studied by the Forest Service.[26] Hikers in the East, where the Forest Service swore there were no lands of Wilderness Area quality, were finding rewilded ridges and hollows. Big trees were growing on what had once been fields and the wildwood was hiding stonewalls and crumbled-down chimneys. And these hikers had the cheek to say such spots should be set aside by Congress as Wilderness Areas even though the Forest Service *knew* nothing in the East met the yardstick for Wilderness. After all, the Forest Service had thought up Wilderness Areas. By god, they were the experts on what qualified for Wilderness designation. Nonetheless, by July 1971, Wilderness bills had been introduced in Congress for *de facto* Forest Service areas in Montana, Washington, Wyoming, Idaho, Oregon, Colorado, California, West Virginia, and North Carolina.[27]

26   Milo Conrad, "New Mexico Wilderness Fact Sheet" and letter "To Proponents of Wilderness in New Mexico," September 24, 1969.
27   Stewart M. Brandborg, "The Wilderness Society Memo to Conservation Cooperators," July 2, 1971. James Turner goes into satisfying detail on this "wildcat" wilderness uprising in *The Promise of Wilderness.*

President Nixon's Council on Environmental Quality (CEQ), which had been set up by the National Environmental Policy Act (NEPA) in 1970, drafted, with Nixon's knowledge, an Executive Order to agencies to leave alone candidate Wilderness Areas until Congress could act, and bidding the Forest Service to inventory all *de facto* roadless areas and *to protect them from impairment* until Congress weighed them for Wilderness designation. Needless to say, the Forest Service did everything it could to keep the Executive Order from being signed.[28] Earl Butz, the Secretary of Agriculture, in whose department the Forest Service sat, had clout with Nixon and he used every bit of it to kill the Executive Order. Had Nixon signed it, conservation history would have taken another path.

QUALITY AND PURITY

In one of their slickest games, the Forest Service brass wrapped themselves in the lore of Bob Marshall and Aldo Leopold to buck up the "quality and purity" of America's Wilderness Areas as a way to block more Wilderness Areas asked for by conservationists. Forest Service leaders were both slippery and guileless in being against "lesser areas" as Wilderness. BLM leaders later followed the Forest Service's trail on quality and purity. Some agency bosses saw Wilderness designation as an award akin to the Nobel Prize or Congressional Medal of Honor. They honored the symbol of Wilderness more than the wild neighborhoods. Also, to the Forest Service, Park Service, and BLM brass, Wilderness Areas were recreational resources, not ecological havens. The "quality" of Wilderness came from meeting classic standards of landscape loveliness, drawn from a medieval Alpine aesthetic.

"Purity" was whether "signs of man" were "noticeable" or not. Such purity standards, though, were grounded in a shallow way of looking. A faint truck trail where a rock or two had once been kicked out of a rut

---

28   Undated alert from the Montana Group of the Sierra Club and the
       Montana Wilderness Association.

was more of a work of Man than a highly engineered, well-built trail for pack stock. A few sawn stumps from eighty or so years ago were worse than a dog-hair thicket from wildfire control. Aldo Leopold warned that "One of the penalties of an ecological education is that one lives alone in a world of wounds."[29] The agency purity stewards showed none of that ecological education. The wounds that beset their eyes were shallow traces on the ground done long ago that would now be outlawed if the area were Wilderness.

Some agency folks truly believed in these quality and purity yardsticks. Others wielded them to keep lands from being "locked up" from logging, road building, and other development.

High-minded words from the Forest Service about upholding the soundness of the National Wilderness Preservation System, notwithstanding, members of Congress have time and again shown that they do not share the "purist" thinking of the agency. During the 1973 Senate Subcommittee on Public Lands hearings on the Eastern Wilderness Areas bill, both Democratic and Republican senators tossed out the Forest Service doctrine of purity. Senator James Buckley (R-NY) had sound thoughts on what qualified for Wilderness designation:

The "untrammeled by man" criteria, in my view, reflects an overly literal and narrow interpretation of the term "wilderness." It ignores the elucidative phrases which also appear in Section 2(c) of the Wilderness Act, defining candidate areas as those which are "without permanent improvements" and "with the imprint of man's work substantially unnoticeable." [30]

29 Aldo Leopold, *Round River* (Oxford University Press, New York, 1953), 165.

30 James L. Buckley, "Statement," Hearing Before The Subcommittee On Public Lands Of The Committee On Interior And Insular Affairs United States Senate On S. 316, February 21, 1973, U.S. Government Printing Office, Washington: 1973, 36. For more on the purity dustup, see Doug Scott, *The Enduring Wilderness* (Fulcrum Publishing, Golden, CO, 2004) and Dave Foreman, *Rewilding North America* (Island Press, Washington, 2004), 191-201.

The fight to come would be over the Forest Service's Roadless Area Review and Evaluation (RARE) and the conservationists' Eastern Wilderness Areas Act, with which I deal in the next chapter.

CHAPTER 18

RARE and Its Aftermath

THE FIRST FOREST SERVICE PRIMITIVE AREA to come up for study was the San Rafael in the mountains above Santa Barbara, California. It set the stage for other Primitive Area recommendations and hearings, with unified conservation groups showing up in crowds wanting more Wilderness than the Forest Service offered. One thing that upset the Forest Service was that conservationists often knew the areas on the ground better than did anyone with the Forest Service. I found this time and time again in the 1970s.[1]

RARE

So. The Forest Service's professional pride took three heavy blows between 1965 and 1971: 1) a federal judge forbidding the FS from logging or road-building in roadless areas next to Primitive Areas; 2) conservationists going over the Forest Service's head to Congress and

---

1   James Morton Turner, *The Promise of Wilderness* (University of Washington Press, Seattle, 2012), 54-58. Turner does a good job covering the Primitive Area battles as does Roth (see below).

asking for new Wilderness Areas that had not been Primitive Areas; and 3) Congress making bigger Wilderness Areas than the Forest Service had wanted. Forest Service Chief Edward P. Cliff gruffly whined, "Every time we made a move into a roadless area we ran into opposition which generally materialized in the form of a lawsuit or a wilderness proposal by a congressman."[2] The Forest Service took these setbacks as the biggest and most frightening threats since its beginning in 1905. These blows were mighty ax swings at the hallowed timber and road-building program and at the Forest Service's wish to stamp its managerial will over the whole National Forest System.[3] That wish of taming unruly, wasteful wilderness in the National Forests with professional management had been a holy goal for the Forest Service from its birth. Some gung-ho foresters acted as though Gifford Pinchot had come down from a mountain with such inscribed on a stone tablet.

Nonetheless, in 1971, the United States Forest Service said that it would inventory all roadless areas on the National Forests and evaluate their suitability for Wilderness designation. That was the official line, anyway. But I believe the truth was that the Roadless Area Review and Evaluation (RARE) was a carefully drawn-up stealthy strike by the USFS brass to undercut the calls—from citizens and members of Congress alike—for new Wilderness Areas, foremost those with trees. The inventory was quick, fickle, uneven, sloppy, and underhanded; the evaluation was set up to recommend the fewest areas and the smallest acreage. The goal was to stop dead in their tracks "wildcat" Wilderness Area proposals from tying up the Forest Service's logging program and managerial freedom to bring wildlands to heel.

This is by no means my belief alone. David Clary, retired chief historian of the Forest Service, writes, "The decision to undertake a comprehensive completion of the wilderness system was not only an effort to define what ought to be wilderness; it was also an attempt to

2   Dennis M. Roth, *The Wilderness Movement and the National Forests: 1964-1980* (FS 391, USDA Forest Service, Washington, 1984), 36.
3   Most of the Forest Service brass were road engineers or foresters.

prevent wilderness from interfering with timber and development and to end the question once and for all."[4]

A smoking chainsaw to back up my belief is that the Forest Service had been slyly laying the groundwork for such a review as early as May 1969: "New Study Areas. By June 30, *-1972,-* Regional Foresters will identify and submit a brief report on unclassified areas which seem to warrant further and more intensive study."[5]

On August 11, 1971, Forest Service Chief Cliff told all National Forests "to inventory all roadless areas and to make recommendations by June 30, 1972 on areas that should later be studied intensively for possible wilderness designation." However, the Sierra Club warned, "Few conservationists even learned of the expanded scope of studies until mid-November 1971."[6] The way this stealth inventory came out—after eighteen months undercover—hampered conservationists doing their own field studies. Jerry Mallett of The Wilderness Society wrote that "there is not time for [conservationists] to do groundwork of their own, and make good informed comments on the areas involved. They have only a matter of weeks in the dead of winter to study over a hundred areas in Colorado alone."[7] Mind you, forty years ago most of the National Forest roadless areas were yet unknown to conservationists. Moreover, most of them were in the high country. How do you check on boundaries and "signs of man" when the landscape is under feet of snow? In New Mexico, I roped in over thirty University of New Mexico students to run whirlwind field studies of roadless areas in the name of the UNM Wilderness Committee, while scientists at Sandia and Los Alamos labs, gathered as the New Mexico Wilderness Study Committee, did likewise.

---

4   David A. Clary, *Timber and the Forest Service* (University Press of Kansas, Lawrence, 1986), 175.

5   Forest Service Manual. Amendment No. 35. May 1969. (Odd punctuation in original.)

6   Sierra Club Bulletin, March 1972.

7   Jerry Mallett, The Wilderness Society, undated alert.

The Forest Service studies were tilted against Wilderness. In the Southwest Region (New Mexico and Arizona), roadless areas had to be "truly unroaded." The Regional Forester wrote to his forest supervisors, "Exclude all areas where parallel wheel tracks or rut roads remain plainly visible the season following their occurrence."[8] In other words, if an elk hunter drove into a wet meadow right before snowfall, and his tracks could be seen in spring after the melt, a whole roadless area would be kicked from the inventory. Or, if a daredevil jeeper drove through a rough, back-of-beyond canyon and some of his tracks were left above the snowmelt flood line, the canyon was no longer a roadless area. (Under a sounder yardstick, the Forest Service inventoried three times the roadless acreage in New Mexico and Arizona in 1977-79, thanks to Assistant Secretary of Agriculture Rupert Cutler and Forest Service staff such as George Davis.)

The Evaluation came after the Inventory. Each roadless area was weighed on a handful of scales; though some were dropped for sundry reasons during the evaluation (marked with *).

- Quality Index
- Size
- Opportunity Cost
- Public Views
- Regional Foresters' Picks
- More Wilderness Near Cities*
- Ecological Diversity*

RARE was only for the National Forests in the West, by the way. National Grasslands were not included and only two roadless areas were found in the East (one was in Puerto Rico). The Forest Service's love for alpine peaks and lakes and horse-based recreation came through in the Quality Index used to numerically rate roadless areas on three factors:

---

8   Roadless Inventory procedure, Southwestern Region, Forest Service, 1971.

- Scenic Quality
- Isolation and likely dispersion of visitors within an area to minimize contacts
- Variety of wilderness experiences and activities available in the area

These three ratings made up the Wilderness Quality of a roadless area.[9] Note that they were all about recreation. Worksheets listed characteristics with a range of quality for each. A number was awarded for the "quality" of an area for each characteristic. Totals were then added up for each rating category. The total points for Scenic were multiplied by 4, while those for Isolation and Variety by 3. Possible scores for the Quality Index ranged between 0 and 200 for each roadless area. Some typical criteria were: An area with "numerous lakes" got a 6, while an area with "no lakes and few streams" was hit with a 1. An area with lots of campsites got a 4, while an area with few campsites: 1. "Numerous access points and trails" rated a 3, while only a few trails were slapped with zero.[10]

Areas were also given points for size. However, the Forest Service stacked the deck against timbered areas by chopping up big roadless areas into a few smaller inventory units—and then giving each unit lower marks for its smaller size! To wit, the Nezperce NF in Idaho cleaved the 300,000-acre Gospel Hump roadless area into nine roadless areas and rated each on its own, now smaller acreage.[11]

Another telling yardstick for picking New Wilderness Study Areas was the "opportunity cost"—"the estimated dollar loss if the area was designated as Wilderness." If, say, the local forest supervisor made a high guess that a roadless area could crank out two million dollars of

9   *Roadless and Undeveloped Areas (Final Environmental Impact Statement),* (USDA Forest Service, Washington, DC, October 1973), 26.
10   Scenic Quality Rating Criteria worksheets, U.S. Forest Service.
11   Roth, *The Wilderness Movement and the National Forests: 1964-1980,* 51-52.

timber yearly, then the opportunity cost would be two million dollars. But the Forest Service guesstimated only a high *gross* opportunity cost, not a *net,* which would have been "the values of the timber minus road construction and maintenance, construction and maintenance of developed campgrounds, fire protection, reforestation, etc."[12] Also not reckoned in any way was how much an area might be worth in dollars if designated as Wilderness—recreation, wildlife, watershed, and so on. But added to the negative side of the ledger were costs if an area became Wilderness: price of buying inholdings, costs of doing Wilderness studies, and so on. Talk about juggling the books! But this was the cockeyed, shady way the Forest Service had been working since World War Two.

Notwithstanding the short time to organize, wilderfolk showed up in droves at public hearings, although most were held in small towns in the Western sticks, not in cities. We also flooded the Forest Service with letters. The Forest Service acknowledged in their RARE Final Environmental Impact Statement that most public input was *for* more Wilderness Areas. Up to that time, RARE was the largest public involvement process ever undertaken by the federal government.

More than a year after the close for comments, in October 1973, the Forest Service made known its "New Wilderness Study Areas" (NWSAs), which would be managed and studied just as if they were Primitive Areas. Picked as NWSAs were 274 areas with 12.3 million

---

12 Dick Gale, Untitled memo on how to respond to USFS EIS on Roadless Area Inventory, in author's files. Other conservationists also wrote thorough critiques of RARE. In my files, I have an anonymous memo "Analysis of Selection Methodology Used for Roadless Areas Inventory," "A Short Review of RARE," by Colorado State University forestry student Henry Carey, and an analysis from Colorado wilderness outfitter Bill Mounsey. That unpaid grassroots folks wrote these reviews of RARE on their own tells us much about how things have shifted in the conservation network. Moreover, I think they were as good as anything professional analysts at The Wilderness Society or other outfits would do today.

acres out of 1,449 roadless areas making up 55.9 million acres. Even the 12.3 million-acre NWSA figure was fudged. Forty-six of the areas making up 4.4 million acres were already under study for Wilderness recommendation by the Forest Service because they were next to Primitive Areas or "had already been officially committed to study by prior Forest Service decisions or Congressional action."[13] So in truth only 238 areas with 7.9 million acres in all were picked for new study. The areas dubbed as NWSAs were mostly "rocks and ice." Lots of alpine lakes and peaks above timberline. Darn little wildwood. The Forest Service claimed they had bent over backward to make wilderfolk happy. Well, they hadn't. We were steamed.

The Sierra Club Legal Defense Fund went to court in June 1972 arguing that RARE failed as an Environmental Impact Statement under the National Environmental Policy Act (NEPA). The Club's grounds were that the Forest Service gave too little time for public comment and lacked enough information to make their decision. A federal judge issued a preliminary injunction that stopped timber sales in all roadless areas. The timber industry freaked out and the Forest Service settled out of court with the Club. There would be no timber sales in roadless areas during 1973; after that, Environmental Impact Statements would have to be done for road-building, logging, and other development in each roadless area.[14]

EASTERN WILDERNESS AREAS ACT

But for Minnesota's Boundary Waters Canoe Area—a world-class wilderness of Northwoods lakes and portages (and the only one at that time in the lower 48 that still had wolves)—the 1964 Wilderness Act shielded only three little National Forest Wild Areas east of the Rockies.[15] Many in the Forest Service still grumbled that the

13   CI Report No. 11, "New Wilderness Study Areas," Forest Service USDA, October 1973.
14   Turner, *Promise of Wilderness*, 115.
15   Linville Gorge, 7,575 acres, and Shining Rocks, 13,350 acres, both in

designation of these areas as Wilderness was a mistake. Nevertheless, citizen conservationists in West Virginia and Alabama had gotten Wilderness bills dropped into the Congressional hopper by 1970; and wilderfolk in other Eastern states had drafted Wilderness proposals. The Forest Service came down flatly that there was no true Wilderness in the East: "To include [Eastern areas] would dilute the significance of the entire Wilderness System," snarled a 1971 position paper from the Forest Service's Division of Recreation in Washington, D.C. That summer, the Regional Foresters in Atlanta and Milwaukee came up with a separate and lesser Wildwood Heritage System for hiking areas in the Eastern National Forests.[16] The Roadless Area Inventory had only found three Eastern areas, one each in North Carolina, Florida, and Puerto Rico.[17]

Spurred on by The Wilderness Society's Appalachian-loving Ernie Dickerman, who cut his teeth bushwhacking in the Smokies, conservationists in Eastern states did their fieldwork on National Forest roadless areas of which they knew or had gone out and found. With Ernie's leadership they then put together an Eastern Wilderness Areas Bill. The Forest Service did its best to undercut The Wilderness Society and for a while even had some Sierra Club leaders thinking that a new stand-alone, lesser Eastern system would be better. We in TWS undertook a heavy-handed lobbying campaign with Sierra Club members to get them to gainsay the Forest Service's sleight-of-hand on Wilderness Areas. Dickerman hammered home that Easterners, such as Howard Zahniser of New York and Harvey Broome of Tennessee, wrote the definition of Wilderness in the Wilderness Act. "None of us who helped draft that definition were about to exclude the wildlands of the Appalachian Range from qualifying for the protection of the

North Carolina, and Great Gulf, 5,552 acres, in New Hampshire. *Search for Solitude* (USDA Forest Service, June 1970).

16   Roth, *The Wilderness Movement and the National Forests: 1964-1980*, 39.

17   Final Environmental Impact Statement Roadless and Undeveloped Areas (USDA Forest Service, October 1973).

Wilderness Act," Ernie stormed.[18]   Had the Sierra Club not come around, we were ready to go to war with our long-time partner.[19]

Senator James Buckley, Republican-Conservative of New York (William F. Buckley's brother), sponsored the Eastern Wilderness Areas Act with Senate Interior Committee Chairman Henry (Scoop) Jackson (D-WA) in January 1973.[20] When a Senate hearing was held in Washington, 150 grassroots conservationists showed up to speak for Wilderness. The mainstay for the 1964 Wilderness Act, Representative John Saylor of Pennsylvania (another Republican), introduced the bill in the House. President Ford signed the Act on January 3, 1975. It designated fifteen Wilderness Areas and seventeen Wilderness Study Areas in the Eastern National Forests.[21] Congress and the people had spoken—telling the Forest Service that the Wilderness Act was written for rewilded spots in the National Forests of the East, too. Like it or not, the Forest Service had been given a more sweeping yardstick for Wilderness.

18   Roth, *The Wilderness Movement and the National Forests: 1964-1980*, 43.
19   Dave Brower was gone from the Club by then and there was a strong "wilderness purist" clique of Sierrans. There was also much overlap between the Society and the Club—I worked for The Wilderness Society and was wilderness chair and on the executive committee of the Rio Grande Chapter of the Sierra Club. See James Morton Turner, *The Promise of Wilderness* (University of Washington Press, Seattle, 2012), for a top-flight exploration of the Sierra Club purists and the struggle between the two groups over what to do for Eastern wilderness.
20   Many folks wrongly call the legislation the Eastern Wilderness Act. It is not a new Wilderness Act in any way. See Wilderness Society memo, February 7, 1977, from Raye-Page, "RE: There is NO Eastern Wilderness Act."
21   Roth, *The Wilderness Movement and the National Forests: 1964-1980*, 36-46. Roth goes into the infighting between The Wilderness Society and weak-kneed Sierra Club very well, and shows how Ernie Dickerman and others at TWS finally got the other conservation clubs on board. See also *The Promise of Wilderness*. Jay Turner's digging through Wilderness Society archives at the Denver Conservation Library hit pay-dirt, which he shares in his often eye-opening book.

ENDANGERED AMERICAN WILDERNESS ACT

"We was robbed." In the West, conservationists rightly believed that RARE had been an underhanded play by the Forest Service to keep more Wilderness Areas from being set aside. Citizens geared up to fight timber sales in their most-loved roadless areas. Grassroots clubs asked their members of Congress to write Wilderness bills for areas not backed by the Forest Service. Senator Bob Packwood of Oregon, Senator Pete Domenici of New Mexico, and Representative Manuel Lujan Jr. of New Mexico—all Republicans—introduced conservationists' bills.

Doug Scott, Northwest Representative of the Sierra Club, hatched the "Endangered American Wilderness Act," which folded-in western roadless areas that had not been picked by the Forest Service as New Wilderness Study Areas (NWSAs) in RARE. This bill was a big organizing tool for The Wilderness Society, Sierra Club, and state wilderness groups, and a means for teaching Congress about the downsides of RARE and the need for more Wilderness Areas. In New Mexico, Domenici and Lujan had sponsored stand-alone bills for the Sandia Mountains, Manzano Mountains, and Chama River Canyon.

The Sandias and Chama helped tell the tale of what was wrong with RARE. Though the Sandia Mountains had nearly 40,000 acres of roadless land and was believed to be wilderness by Albuquerque hikers and climbers, the Forest Service was aghast at the thought of a Sandia Wilderness Area because it was so close to Albuquerque. They earnestly said the Sandias were disqualified because one could "experience" the sights and sounds of New Mexico's biggest city from nearly anywhere in the mountains. As for the 50,000-acre Chama Canyon, the Forest Service hadn't even inventoried it in RARE. They had utterly overlooked it. It was our foremost exhibit for the sloppiness of RARE. The New Mexico Wilderness Study Committee got hundreds of letters into New Mexico congressmen and some 300 Sandia Wilderness boosters to a hearing in Albuquerque called by Domenici and Lujan. With their backing, the Sandia Mountains and Chama Canyon, along with the

Manzanos, which the Forest Service okayed, went into the Endangered American Wilderness bill.

The bill was introduced in 1976 and passed in January 1978. It did three good things: It locked up some key Wilderness Areas that the Forest Service didn't want, shoved the Forest Service into doing another roadless areas inventory (RARE II), and helped build a strong citizen network for Wilderness, which would come into its own for RARE II, the Alaska Lands Act, and the new Bureau of Land Management wilderness review—all happening in the last few years of the 1970s. Whew. We were busy.

CHAPTER 19

RARE II

THE BEGINNING OF RARE II

After becoming President in January 1977, Jimmy Carter nominated Dr. Rupert Cutler for Assistant Secretary of Agriculture to oversee the Forest Service. The timber industry whined because Cutler had been a top staffer at The Wilderness Society (TWS) in the 1960s before joining the resource management faculty at Michigan State University. To smooth over grumbles to his appointment, Cutler met with timber industry leaders early in 1977. The roadless areas from RARE were still in limbo, thanks to the Sierra Club lawsuit, and would be until being dealt out by forest plans for each National Forest. Therefore, big timber was unhappy that they didn't know which roadless areas might be open for logging. This lack of knowledge kept them from reckoning later log flows and work needs.

After his meeting with the timber industry bigwigs, Cutler came back to Washington to tell the Forest Service brass how worried the industry was over the "uncertainty" of what National Forest timber would be available for sale and cutting. Cutler thereupon asked the Forest Service to do a new roadless area review and evaluation—RARE II.[1] Cutler thought a new roadless area review would be able to quickly decide for the most part what Forest Service roadless areas would be recommended for Wilderness Areas and which would be available for logging and other development ("dewilding," as I call it) right away. Not only did Cutler want the Forest Service to do a better job of inventorying roadless areas, "he wanted as much as possible to resolve the 'uncertainty' by recommending some areas for wilderness designation and 'releasing' others." These would be unknown waters for the Forest Service to sail into, and the Forest Service was worried about whether such a program could pass NEPA muster in the courts. They also doubted it would "resolve the wilderness issue." And they worried about more work for field staff already buried in fulfilling the mandate of the Resource Planning Act by 1980.[2] Roth writes, "Thus, the Forest Service leadership was not enthusiastic about Cutler's proposal and would not have done it 'if left to its own devices.'"[3] At first, the timber industry was also unsettled about RARE II.

After his meetings with timber executives and the Forest Service leadership, Cutler testified in April 1977 at congressional hearings to say that the Carter Administration backed the Endangered American Wilderness Act and asked Congress to pass it. This was a real turnaround, since the previous Ford Administration had followed Forest Service opposition to the Endangered American Wilderness Act. Now the Forest Service had to go along with it—even Wilderness designation for places such as the Sandia Mountains which gave them such heartburn. "Purity" was taking a big hit.

1 Dennis M. Roth, *The Wilderness Movement and the National Forests: 1964-1980* (USDA Forest Service, FS 391, December 1984), 53-55. Cutler truly wanted a good, full review done that would do a better job of picking new Wilderness Areas. He's someone I hold high.

2 Roth, *The Wilderness Movement and the National Forests*, 54-55.

3 Roth, *The Wilderness Movement and the National Forests*, 55.

We conservationists were thrilled. But we were blindsided and upset by the rest of Cutler's testimony when he announced the new roadless area inventory and study—RARE II. Most of us were unhappy because we felt as Tim Mahoney of TWS did that the timber industry could well organize its minions against "a perceived threat." However, Doug Scott of the Sierra Club thought it "a great opportunity."[4] Whether or not it was good, we all knew that it would mean a hell of a lot of work for the wilderness movement and a resetting of our priorities. I was The Wilderness Society staffer for New Mexico and Arizona and chair of the New Mexico Wilderness Study Committee (NMWSC) and recall the grassroots being damned irked about RARE II. In New Mexico, we felt that Sen. Pete Domenici and Rep. Manuel Lujan, Jr., were working well with us to introduce bills for our proposals (both Republicans were cosponsors of the Endangered American Wilderness Act). RARE II kicked over our merrily perking coffee pot and drenched the campfire. We would have to build a new campfire.

On the other hand, I don't think the grousing of the timber industry and Forest Service timber beasts was on the up-and-up. Either from the beginning or soon thereafter, I believe they saw how they could make RARE II serve their purposes. With a rising tide of worry and wrath among traditional users of public lands brought on mostly by the Bureau of Land Management's growing oversight of their lands after FLPMA along with much greater involvement by conservationists in BLM doings, the so-called "Sagebrush Rebellion" had sprung up.[5] The timber industry milked the Sagebrush "Whining" for all it was worth and made timber workers fear for their jobs. They spun RARE II as a federal takeover of the rural West with urban environmentalists calling the shots. It worked. Goddamn, it worked.

4   Roth, *The Wilderness Movement and the National Forests*, 55.
5   I'll go into the Sagebrush Rebellion and other anti-public lands and anticonservation campaigns of the 20th Century in my forthcoming book *The Nature Haters*.

After their early carping, I think timber beasts in the Forest Service saw it as their last, great hope to befog, flummox, and sidetrack everyone (except for their timber industry pals) while gaining their twofold goal: (1) to keep lands with operable timber and other development possibilities from being locked-up in Wilderness Areas and (2) to limit the Forest Service part of the National Wilderness Preservation System to a few more million acres of "pure" Wilderness. They snookered conservationists (and Cutler, too, I think) with their "technical" (incomprehensibly tangled) RARE II process. Their decision-making "black box" would let them come up with what they wanted—a recommendation on roadless areas that was for the most part predetermined. Moreover, they could jigger how public opinion would be weighed to claim that the antiwilderness side overwhelmed the prowilderness side. And we, we dewy-eyed believers in reform liberalism (even after the RARE I shell game), came around to play the RARE II game the way the Forest Service told us it was to be played.[6] Only late did we realize that they switched the rules on us.

THE INVENTORY

At first, the RARE II inventory seemed much more thorough and aboveboard than that of RARE I. Foremost, roadless areas in eastern National Forests and in National Grasslands were fully brought in. In Arizona and New Mexico, the Southwest Region of the Forest Service found *threefold* the roadless acreage they had in RARE I. (However, conservationists in timber-rich Oregon believed the Forest Service was blind to another million acres or so of roadless areas not inventoried.) Also, the maps were much more thorough—blueprints of National Forest Class A maps with a half inch to the mile scale. It was easy to

---

6   For how conservationists before 1980 believed in reform liberalism, see James Morton Turner, *The Promise of Wilderness* (University of Washington Press, Seattle, 2012).

see where Forest Service boundaries were.[7]   Moreover, the USFS offered a seemingly fair process for us to challenge their roadless area boundaries if our fieldwork found mistakes. It was great busy work for conservationists to field check the USFS maps, find where they had left out qualifying acres or had drawn the boundaries too tightly, and then fill out the challenge forms and send them in to Doug Scott who coordinated getting them to the Forest Service.[8] Often we would find that our challenges had been accepted and the roadless boundaries shifted. This gave us a feeling that RARE II was more trustworthy and open than was RARE I. RARE II ended up looking at 62 million acres in 2,919 areas in 38 states and Puerto Rico. We felt better about the whole process and cooled our wariness. Also by being busy with fieldwork we weren't closely watching what else was going on with RARE II— which, I think, is what the USFS had hoped. We later learned that the other side paid little heed to such on-the-ground details and just said, "No!" They said even more than "no" when industry and freelance agitators began to flash the RARE II maps around rural counties saying that the roadless areas were a done deal and everything on the map was going to be shut down to local folks and locked up for elite urban "environmeddlers." Rural counties with National Forests would die.

The mood in Catron County where I lived in the midst of the Gila National Forest grew unfriendly. When I came home early in 1979 after a year in Washington, my town of Glenwood was no longer the

---

7   There also were great state maps at 1:1,000,000 for the West and
     1:500,000 for the East showing in color existing Wilderness Areas,
     administratively endorsed Wilderness proposals for all agencies, RARE
     II roadless areas, Congressionally designated Wilderness Study Areas,
     and so on. There was also a US map in color with the same information.
     These maps were by far the best layout of existing and potential Wilder-
     ness Areas in the United States thus far. Indeed, there had never been
     anything like them before.

8   I write "great busy work" because, although it helped us to know the
     land better than the Forest Service, it distracted us from watchdogging
     how the Forest Service wasn't playing on the up-and-up.

same. I was a thoroughly disliked man. The same jump from frostiness to downright hate was happening elsewhere. The timber industry and other rabble-rousers were making the most of hick fears.

EVALUATION

The Forest Service cobbled together a much more technical evaluation process for RARE II than for RARE I but its goal was the same: to limit new Wilderness Areas on the National Forest and to keep timber from being locked up. Among the yardsticks were a Wilderness Attribute Rating System (WARS), the Development Opportunity Rating System (DORS), and the Economic Impact Analysis (EIA). Ecosystem targets based on the Bailey-Kuchler Ecosystem map of the United States and landform representation targets also would help pick areas for a representative National Wilderness System.[9] Conservationists overall were taken in with this and thought we would get more Wilderness recommended from such targets. Other things were in the mix, too.

In truth, though, much of this was for the sake of appearances and to help make the selection process unfathomable.[10] The old RARE I biases came in front and center. WARS highlighted recreational and scenic values. DORS made highly optimistic forecasts of the value of timber and other raw goods that would be foregone if the area was made Wilderness—and, once again, negative costs, such as road construction, watershed damage, loss of habitat, and so on, were not subtracted from the optimistic value figure. Moreover, there were no positive economic values given for Wilderness designation. DORS

9   A national color map of Bailey-Kuchler ecosystems was also part of the map package.

10   The Forest Service ecosystem-targets team led by George Davis was not in on how the Forest Service brass would jack all this around for a low Wilderness recommendation. Davis was a truehearted, visionary conservationist and went on after the Forest Service to outstanding conservation work in Siberia and New York's Adirondack State Park. No one was better on the Forest Service RARE II team.

was as one-sided and dishonest as RARE I had been. The EIA mostly left out cities and overstated negative impacts on rural counties from Wilderness designation. Looking at my notes on the New Mexico Supplement to the RARE II Draft EIS, I see at the end of my list of nineteen objections, "This is more an economic impact statement than an environmental impact statement."[11] Economics (in the Forest Service's twisted, one-sided game where there are no costs of doing business) was the deciding factor.

ALTERNATIVES

But it was the Forest Service's span of ten alternatives A to J, supposedly derived from weighing the different evaluation criteria in sundry ways, that led conservationists to howl. All but the "All Wilderness Alternative J" (required by NEPA) allocated piddling percentages of roadless areas to Wilderness. The Alternatives were grounded in varying the calculation of targets for resource availability and Wilderness quality and ecosystem representation (to boil it down to something understandable), and unashamedly stacked against Wilderness. Other than J, the alternatives ranged from 6 to 33 percent or 3.4 million to 20.6 million acres of the 62 million roadless acres to Wilderness.[12]

A team of us from The Wilderness Society and Sierra Club worked with state and local wilderness groups and our own state and regional field staff on Wilderness recommendations for each state. Though we encouraged some consistency, the states had their own agendas, so the percentage of roadless areas proposed for Wilderness varied among the states. Our national RARE II team then pulled all the state proposals

---

11 *RARE II New Mexico Supplement to Draft Environmental Statement Road-less Area Review and Evaluation* (USDA Forest Service, June 1978). Each western state and regions east of the Rockies had their own supplements.

12 *Draft Environmental Statement Roadless Area Review and Evaluation,* USDA Forest Service, June 1978.

together into a national proposal we called Alternative W.[13] We were still good little boys and girls believing in reform liberalism. Did we ask for everything? Oh, no. Moderation was the safe path. We asked for only about half of the roadless area acreage—35 million acres— and kissed off the rest. We truly thought that, by offering a moderate proposal that left much timbered land available for logging, Alternative W was something the Carter Administration, if not the Forest Service, could back. Were we ever mistaken. I admit that I was one of the makers of this moderate strategy, as Turner rightly says in *The Promise of Wilderness.*

THE PUBLIC SPEAKS

The Wilderness Society and Sierra Club worked with our partners nationally, regionally, and especially at state and local levels to get as many wilderness backers as we could to field hearings and to write letters. From the beginning, the Forest Service told us it wasn't interested in letters, form letters, and petitions that were just for or against Wilderness on individual areas or overall. What they were looking for were knowledgeable, specific comments on the technical aspects of RARE II and on individual areas. We believed them and our experts on the ground sent detailed letters on each area in Alternative W. The local groups sent detailed letters on their statewide proposals. The national groups sent detailed letters on the process and on why our Alternative W was the best one. Our national mailing had two pieces. One was the national overview with key points to make in one's letter. The other was a flyer for the recipient's state with state-specific points and an annotated list of areas recommended for Wilderness. We encouraged folks to support Alternative W for their state and nationally, and to write specifically about areas they knew and why they should be

13   This was a rather different team than the so-called "Gang of Four" from the Sierra Club and Wilderness Society that coordinated legislative strategy after RARE II.

recommended for Wilderness. We turned out a strong response from wilderfolk.

The No-Wilderness side, led by the timber industry, took another tack. For hearings in timber country, buses took workers from the mills (a paid day off) to the hearings; and convoys of timber trucks drove around hearing towns blaring horns. In some towns conservationists were threatened. Some were so intimidated they didn't go into the hearing. The message from the loggers and their allies wasn't detailed and specific, it was just "No Wilderness!" Likewise, for written comments the No-Wilderness crowd relied on petitions and simple form letters and postcards needing only a signature. "No Wilderness!" Such was the bulk of the comment from the antiwilderness side. Of course, there were some letters on certain roadless areas arguing why they did not qualify or should not be Wilderness.

The Forest Service had told us that they were not seeking a vote or a numbers game but wanted factual content. We believed them. Individual letters in favor of Alternative W outweighed antiwilderness letters. But. But. They snookered us. The way the Forest Service analyzed comments was 264,000 replies with a total of 360,000 signatures—3 to 1 against Wilderness. So much for playing by what we thought were the rules of the game.

THE DECISION

On January 4, 1979, the Forest Service drew back the blinds to show its decision. Of 62 million acres of National Forest land weighed (there were in truth some 80 million acres of roadless areas, but on sundry grounds the Forest Service didn't look at all of them), 36,151,558 acres of roadless areas were allocated to "timber and mineral production, intensive recreation, etc.," 15,088,838 acres were recommended to Congress for Wilderness Area designation, and 10,796,508 acres were put in the "further planning" category.[14] One-third of the Wilderness recommendation was in the Tongass National Forest of Alaska—5 million acres.[15] More than 80 percent of the roadless acreage was decided. Truly dreadful were the recommendations for the big timber states of Washington and Oregon where only 637,007 acres of high-elevation mountains were recommended for Wilderness, 4,240,613 acres for Nonwilderness, and 618,913 for Further Planning. Oregon Sierra Club leader Holway Jones told Cutler about the reaction from conservationists: "Most of them feel downright cheated—in fact, angry."[16]

After the recommendations were announced came another kick to wilderfolks' teeth: "[T]he administration declared that all nonwilderness lands would be 'released' for other uses under the first cycle of forest plans...."[17]

The mainstream Citizens for America's Endangered Wilderness summed up the reaction of conservationists as James Turner reports: "In their view, WARS and DORS were unintelligible 'black boxes' which used 'suspect data, out-of-date resource evaluations, and misinterpreted public input results' to make faulty recommendations."[18]

Conservation groups telegrammed President Carter, underlining their "extreme disappointment" in the Forest Service recommendations and asking him to "intervene and improve the acreage recommended for wilderness."[19] Alas, Carter came up with only some 300,000 acres

---

14   Bob Bergland, Secretary of Agriculture, "Record of Decision: Roadless Area Review and Evaluation RARE II," January 4, 1979, Washington, D.C.

15   Much of the recommended Tongass NF Wilderness was in the National Monuments (Admiralty Island and Misty Fjords) that Carter had withdrawn under the Antiquities Act because Congress had not passed the Alaska Lands Act.

16   Roth, *The Wilderness Movement and the National Forests*, 58.

17   Roth, *The Wilderness Movement and the National Forests*, 59.

18   Turner, *The Promise of Wilderness*, 191.

19   Telegram to President Carter from Conservation Groups, April 10, 1979.

to add to the areas recommended for Wilderness.[20] Unbeknownst to us was that the Administration through Interior Secretary Cecil Andrus was romancing the timber industry to back moving the Forest Service out of the Department of Agriculture to Interior for a new Department of Natural Resources. Carter wasn't going to queer the deal by overruling the Forest Service to give conservationists millions more acres of Wilderness. Moreover, unknown to us and even unknown to Cutler, was the bloody fight in the White House with the EPA and CEQ arguing for more Wilderness and the OMB and Department of Energy for less Wilderness. Also, Vice President Walter Mondale had long been a friend of the timber industry and logging unions in his state of Minnesota. Who knows what he was doing? The Forest Service and the timber industry had won, notwithstanding Cutler's honorable intentions.

THE UPSHOT OF RARE II

Jimmy Carter stands very high in the hall of wilderness heroes for his stalwart work on Alaskan National Parks, Refuges, Wilderness, and Wild and Scenic Rivers, but he let the Forest Service have their way in RARE II, and there he stumbled. Badly. RARE II is an ugly blotch on his record.

James Turner writes, "RARE II represented a high point of liberal faith in the role of the federal government and citizens to advance protection for the public lands." He further writes that the "failure" was "of a liberal political formula that invested its faith in the federal government, which had been central to the wilderness movement and American environmentalism since the 1960s."[21]

Many of us wilderfolk were so disheartened in the failure of this "liberal formula" (even if we didn't recognize it as such at the time) that we began talking about new strategies. As a pusher of moderation, I

---

20   Statement by the President, The White House, April 16, 1979.
21   Turner, *Promise of Wilderness*, 191.

did a lot of soul-searching. Hell, why hadn't we asked for all roadless areas to be recommended for Wilderness? Why did we feel that to be credible we had to compromise before we ever opened our mouths?

Some of us no longer believed the system worked. Some of us no longer bought multiple-use/sustained yield as the guiding principle for the public lands. The Forest Service with RARE II created Earth First and the new conservation movement—it made more and more wildlovers see the Great Conservation Divide that had been there all along.

A year after the RARE II results were announced, some veterans of the RARE II disaster started Earth First.[22] In our first public announcement, we called for Wilderness protection of all 80 million acres of National Forest roadless areas. If the other side could be uncompromising, we could be, too. If the other side could be tough, we could be, too. The 1980s were going to be nastier than any other time for the Great Conservation Divide.

---

22 Earth First did not have the exclamation mark in its name for the first year or two. See Dave Foreman, *Confessions of an Eco-Warrior* (Harmony-Crown, New York, 1991) for more on how RARE II led to Earth First.

CHAPTER 20

Down in the Dirt

LINKED TO THE AGENCIES' DISLIKE of Wilderness Areas was their foot-dragging to clamp down on land-scarring motorized recreation by off-road vehicles (ORVs). In 1971, President Nixon straightway told the federal-land-managing agencies to look at their lands and close or open them for off-road vehicle play. ORV areas and routes were to be:

> located to minimize damage to soil, watershed, vegetation, or other resources of the public lands....to minimize harassment of wildlife or significant disruption of wildlife habitats.... to minimize conflicts [with] other... recreational uses....[1]

The agencies did their best to overlook Nixon's ORV Executive Order. The Forest Service's ORV issue paper in 1974 said that "the question should not be, should we close an area to ORV use? but—can

---

1   Richard Nixon, "Executive Order 11644 Use of Off-Road Vehicles on the Public Lands," February 8, 1972, *Federal Register,* Vol. 37, No. 27— Wednesday, February 9, 1972.

ORV use, in some form, be permitted on the area?"[2] The Bureau of Land Management held like beliefs at odds with the Executive Order. Their behavior was on the edge of willful disobedience to the President. Heads of federal agencies have been fired for lesser misdeeds. Nixon, alack, had other things on his mind by then.

Hard-set as they were against the Executive Order, the agencies did only slipshod studies to weigh how ORVs harmed the land. In a report for the President's Council on Environmental Quality (CEQ), David Sheridan quoted Dr. Howard Wilshire of the U.S. Geological Survey and the acknowledged scientific expert on ORV harm to the land. After studying sixty-two Forest Service environmental analyses of ORV plans, Wilshire found that sixty were "virtually worthless when it comes to assessing the impact of ORV use on soils due to their lack of specific criteria and data."[3]

In April 1974, BLM put out regulations leaving its lands wide-open to ORV careless play until open or closed designations were made. However, in willful violation of the Executive Order, BLM did not "set a date for completing the designation of its lands."[4] The National Wildlife Federation sued the BLM, and Federal District Judge William B. Jones found BLM in violation of the Executive Order. Even after this judgment, BLM did its best to sidestep its stewardship.[5]

The Council on Environmental Quality drafted language to strengthen the Executive Order in March 1977, after Jimmy Carter became President. It called for shutting public lands to ORVs "except areas and trails which are suitable and specifically designated as open." After the CEQ issue paper went out to federal agencies, it was leaked

---

2   *National Forest System Off-Road Vehicle Management Issue Paper*, U.S. Forest Service, Recreational Management Staff, December 1974, 8. The USFS seems to have a love for weird punctuation.

3   David Sheridan, *Off-Road Vehicles on Public Lands*, Draft Report to the Council on Environmental Quality, August 1978, 97.

4   Sheridan, *Off-Road Vehicles on Public Lands*, 89.

5   Sheridan, *Off-Road Vehicles on Public Lands*, 90-93.

to motorcycle clubs, who bellowed to the dirt-biker and snowmobile gangs that ORVs were going to be banned from federal lands. This was a lie; indeed, it was a knowing lie. It was also a wickedly helpful ploy. Wilderfolk—deep into the Alaska Lands Act campaign and the beginnings of RARE II and the BLM wilderness review—were asleep on this issue; motorcyclists and snowmobilers were wide-awake. The federal government was swamped with howls against the executive order. Of the 80,000 letters and telegrams that poured in, 78,000 backed wide-open ORV play on the public lands since conservation outfits could not organize in time. Never mind that most of the "comments" for wide-open, hands-off motorized play were signatures on petitions, form letters, and coupons clipped from ORV, dirt bike, and snowmobile magazines, while the comments to hem in motorized play were mostly true letters. After this kick to his backbone, Carter then put out watered-down Executive Order 11989, pretty much only stapling a new section onto Nixon's order that told federal agencies to at once shut areas if they found that "the use of off-road vehicles will cause or is causing considerable adverse effects on the soil, vegetation, wildlife, wildlife habitat or cultural or historic resources." It also authorized agency heads "to adopt the policy that portions of the public lands...shall be closed to use by off-road vehicles except those areas or trails which are suitable and specifically designated as open."[6]

Secretary of the Interior Cecil Andrus sandbagged any meaningful implementation of the new ORV Executive Order by waving a white flag to ORVers in a Department of Interior news release. It gave the wink and nod that the government wasn't going to be tough on implementing the Executive Order.[7] I think that conservationists'

6   Sheridan, *Off-Road Vehicles on Public Lands*, 103-105.
7   "Interior Secretary Says Off-Road Vehicle Use Will Continue," Department of the Interior News Release, May 26, 1977. Andrus also helped to weaken the BLM wilderness inventory and spoke up for the timber industry in RARE II—hoping to gain their support to move the Forest Service from the Department of Agriculture to the Department of

feckless work on Carter's Executive Order is one of the worst blunders we have ever made. There is no excuse for our mistake of not making a bigger deal of this—of not rolling out everything we had to get more backing for the Executive Order than the letters against it. I blame myself as much as anyone.

Agency managers pretty much threw their lands wide open to dirt bikes, all-terrain vehicles (ATVs), four-wheel-drive rigs (4x4s), and snowmobiles, and shut down few areas. In his thorough look at ORV management for CEQ, David Sheridan wrote, "The Interior and Forest Service's reluctance to apply the available facts [numerous scientific studies quantifying ORV damage] may arise in part at least from *a reluctance to take actions which are necessary to protect public resources but would cause all manner of political headaches.*"[8] (Italics added.) This verdict could be given against the agencies for all kinds of pussyfooting.

The BLM in California was so chickenshit on ORV harm to the land that they gave dirt bike clubs permits to run the Barstow to Las Vegas race in the 1980s. Hundreds of dirt bikes roared cross-country, shredding the landscape and running down wildlife such as desert tortoises, for dusty thrills. Your great-grandchildren will be able to see the scars from this knobby-tire landscalping. Howard Wilshire said that General Patton's tank tracks from training in the California Desert in the early 1940s were still plainly visible in the late 1970s. Indeed, I have heard from those who have lately visited the areas—*seventy* years later, the tank tracks were still visible.

As the Southwestern Representative for The Wilderness Society in the 1970s, I worked hard to get National Forests and BLM Districts to let ORVers drive *only* on ways specifically open. I could not understand why Forest Service and BLM staff would not follow the Executive Orders. Letting ORVers have free run led to anarchy, harm to wildlife, erosion gullies, and clashes between hikers and dirt bikers

the Interior.
8   Sheridan, *Off-Road Vehicles on Public Lands*, 110.

and between cross-country skiers and snowmobilers (and between grazing permittees and ORVers). Later it led to near riots and death threats against rangers dealing with big ORV mobs.[9] Following the orders, it seemed to me, was not only good management, but would lessen headaches for the managers (after the first bloody fight with the motorcycle and snowmobile freaks). Only later did I understand why agency managers did not follow the orders; because they were ORVers themselves. Few Forest Service or BLM line officers were ever hikers or backpackers, but, until the 1970s, many had been wilderness horse packers. Those in the new crop of managers in the 1970s were not even that. They liked dirt bikes and Jeeps for getting around the backcountry.[10]

There is also a darker reason: if motorheads laced wildlands with their tracks, it would help shoot down any Wilderness Area proposals by wilderfolk. By shoving Nixon's ORV Executive Order into the darkest, dustiest corner of their offices where spiders spun webs over it, the USFS and BLM had a new tool to monkeywrench wilderfolks' Wilderness Area proposals: *It's not wilderness. Look at all the roads! Besides, there are a whole lot of voters who want the area for motorized recreation.*[11]

---

9   Since then, ORVers have gotten even more baneful and threatening. Heavily armed "militia" yahoos are now showing up to protest closure of lands to vehicles and staging illegal ORV rides through closed areas. Moreover, in many areas ORVers of all kinds from dirt bikers to snowmobilers have become the strongest foes of Wilderness Area designation and other protection.

10   Other staffers were hikers and backpackers, though.

11   *The Great Conservation Divide* as a book ends in 2001. But in the 21st Century, the USFS, BLM, and now the National Park Service are doing the same thing with mountain bikes. Some National Parks are even opening trails to mountain bikers within areas proposed for Wilderness by the NPS. In some places, mountain bike thrill-seekers have been the biggest stumbling block to setting aside Wilderness Areas, and have even begun a campaign to open new and existing Wilderness Areas to mountain bike play. Let there be no question: some mountain biker thrill-play wrecks the land as bad as motorized thrill-craft.

Since the Executive Orders, conservationists have been stretched to deal with travel management plans for each National Forest and BLM District. Such work, although burdensome, is among the best ways to shield wild things. Had we given it our all when Carter first offered a strengthening of Nixon's ORV Executive Order, much of this threat from ORVers and now mountain bikers would not be so much of a problem for conservationists. There is a great lesson to be learned here.

CHAPTER 21

Wilderness for the Drylands

BUREAU OF LAND MANAGEMENT IN THE WILDERNESS ACT

Howard Zahniser and other wilderfolks wanted to have all four federal land managing agencies in the Wilderness Act, but one did not make it. This was the Bureau of Land Management. Although it oversaw more land than the other three agencies, it had drawbacks insofar as Wilderness went. For one, BLM had never administratively set up primitive areas of any kind. Doug Scott writes:

> BLM... had not administratively designated any areas equivalent to the national forest primitive areas. That made it prohibitively difficult to require a formal wilderness review for BLM-administered lands. There would have been no way to circumscribe the extent of initial wilderness reviews.... Suggesting an inventory of all BLM roadless lands in that era would have been politically unacceptable.[1]

---

1   Doug Scott, *The Enduring Wilderness* (Fulcrum Publishing, Golden, CO, 2004), 84.

Moreover, it was still a bit up in the air whether the public lands BLM cared for should and would be kept as public lands. That was not settled until 1970; BLM had no "organic act" until the Federal Lands Policy and Management Act (FLPMA) in 1976.

The second drawback was that pretty much the only folks who knew about BLM and its lands were those who had long ruled them for the good of their pocketbooks. We can put them into four cubbyholes. 1. Grazing permittees, some of whom overlorded the public land in "their" ranches and did not let the public in, even though that public had every right to go in. 2. The mining industry, which believed that the 1872 Mining Act gave them the freedom to do whatever they wanted on public land and not worry about any land they scalped or banes they left. 3. Energy corporations (oil, gas, and coal), which shared the miners' beliefs, but who were under the Mineral Leasing Act instead of the rootin', tootin' 1872 Mining Law. 4. Utilities, which saw BLM land as a blank canvas on which they could draw lines for power and telephones, and for pipes carrying oil, gas, and water. These four might bicker among themselves a little, but they did not fuss that the BLM worked for them. The poor sister to these mighty four were hunters since BLM land was wide-open for lawful hunting and, notwithstanding widespread overgrazing, often had good hunting for birds and pronghorn. Others, such as poachers, trappers, pothunters and other archaeological site looters, and jeepers, who liked to wander about the outback, also prowled BLM land as country where there were no laws. Many times, such desert rats did not even know something like the Bureau of Land Management existed.

The third drawback was that darn few wilderfolks knew that there was any good wilderness in the wide sweep of lands BLM oversaw throughout the Western states and Alaska. Drylands, unless they had amazing rocks, were as yet not loved, but by a few oddballs, such as Edward Abbey, who had not yet written *Desert Solitaire*. Even the small bunch of good BLM staffers didn't think there was much wilderness on their lands. Chuck Stoddard, a top resource economist and director of BLM under Interior Secretary Stewart Udall, was one such BLMer. In the late 1970s, he was on The Wilderness Society's Governing Council and warned Debbie Sease, who was overseeing the startup of the BLM wilderness review for The Wilderness Society, that he did not think there was much land at all under the BLM that had Wilderness worth. Debbie sat him down for a slideshow of wild BLM lands that her grassroots helpers were finding. Chuck was blown away by the slides he saw. He couldn't believe they were from the lands he had once had under his wings.

What this all means is that The Wilderness Society, Sierra Club, and friends wanted BLM put in the Wilderness Act, but they had neither the knowledge nor the fired-up grassroots in 1964 and before to make much of a fight about it.

So. Public lands under the Bureau of Land Management were dropped from the Wilderness Act and from being in the National Wilderness Preservation System. One stalwart soul fought to have BLM in the Wilderness Act from early on and afterwards was untiring in singing the wonders of BLM wilderness and other outstanding areas: the amazing Charlie Watson of Nevada.

FEDERAL LAND POLICY AND MANAGEMENT ACT (FLPMA)

That BLM was left out of the Wilderness Act was only put right in 1976 when Congress pulled together an organic act for the BLM called the Federal Land Policy and Management Act (FLPMA). The Wilderness Society worked hard throughout the cobbling together of FLPMA to get a Wilderness Area review and recommendation process. John Melcher of Montana was chair of the House Subcommittee on Public Lands and took the lead on FLPMA. Melcher was not always a friend to conservationists, but he did us right insofar as a Wilderness review and recommendation process went into FLPMA. He should therefore be acknowledged as one of a few who helped to shape the

National Wilderness Preservation System into a truly nationwide and ecologically representative system. Harry Crandell of TWS wrote the Wilderness section (called "602" for its section number in FLPMA). He also rode herd on The Wilderness Society's field representatives so that we would put BLM Wilderness high in our to-do stacks.

I don't recall the BLM brass naysaying a Wilderness review. Likely they saw it as a way to jack up their status and visibility (and budget) and to show off a few wonders as good as anything the other agencies had. I do recall one meeting in Washington with top BLM staff to talk about the Wilderness review, though. I was likely a bit over-the-top in what I saw as the potential for BLM Wilderness until Roman Koenings, an old-time BLM bureaucrat and associate director, exploded, "How many millions of acres of sagebrush flats do you want in the Wilderness System?!" I calmly said back to him, "Why, as many as qualify, sir," and left him utterly befuddled. I don't think he had ever talked to anyone who thought mile after mile of flat sagebrush country was good for anything but grazing. (The biggest standalone BLM Wilderness Area today is Nevada's Black Rock Desert of over 300,000 acres–totally flat with lots of sagebrush.)

Melcher held field hearings around the West. I had the job of turning out lots of BLM wilderness backers to the Albuquerque hearing. Other Wilderness Society field reps and I did good work. Throughout the western states we showed Melcher and other subcommittee members that many folks were behind BLM wilderness. We field reps had another job, too, and that was to show the subcommittee members that BLM lands held likely Wilderness Areas of the "quality" of what the National Forests and National Parks had. Some worried that this would not be easy, and Melcher was straightforward in telling conservationists we had to "wow" congressmembers with eye-popping, breath-taking scenic beauty. We had little time to come up with such lands before the hearings.

I recall that work with a happiness that nothing else has ever matched. It was the unknown we had to explore. For many years the National Forests had been ridden, hiked, mapped, looked at; the great spots named. We had nearly none of that background for BLM. Only a few standouts, such as southern Utah's Escalante River and some mountains in the California Desert, were known. Otherwise, it was the great unknown. And it was holy bliss to come to know it. In New Mexico, with Debbie Sease (my wife at the time) and Sierra Club leader Wes Leonard from El Paso, I came up with a good list of de facto BLM wilderness. Climbers in the New Mexico Wilderness Study Committee already knew a few peaks, such as Ladron Mountain south of Albuquerque. The main wit for likely BLM wilderness, though, was a somewhat shadowy retired CIA operative, Col. Henry Zeller, who looked like someone from the best days of Her Majesty's British Empire. He would have looked good in a pith helmet and with a pipe. Zeller then lived in Silver City and was in the local Audubon Society in that heaven for birders. He drew up a list for us that to this day has the "best" of the BLM areas in New Mexico. How he came up with his list of the best, I had no clue.[2]

Work in other Western states followed a like path, with more and more wilderfolk falling in love with the out-of-the-way, overlooked wilderness of the drylands.

THE BLM WILDERNESS REVIEW

Section 602 of FLPMA bade BLM to undertake, with widespread help from the public, a three-stage Wilderness review process:

1) Inventory all roadless areas of 5,000 acres or more on BLM lands (smaller areas alongside roadless areas in National Forests, Parks, and Wildlife Refuges were also to be inventoried).

2) Evaluate all the identified roadless areas to determine if they had

---

2   I recently learned more about Zeller and how his list came about, but that's a tale for another time.

wilderness characteristics as set out in the Wilderness Act. If so, they were to be designated as formal Wilderness Study Areas (WSAs); if not, they were to be dropped from further weighing.

3) Conduct detailed studies of the WSAs and make Wilderness Area designation or release recommendations to Congress by 1991.

FLPMA recognized one special landscape overseen by BLM: the California Desert, which it designated as a standalone 12.1 million-acre Conservation Area. BLM was mandated to draw up a management plan with Wilderness Area recommendations by 1980—the "expedited" review. Interior Secretary Cecil Andrus signed off on a thoroughly lousy plan. BLM had inventoried 5.7 million acres of land qualifying for Wilderness, while conservationists had found over 8 million acres. Of the 5.7 million acres, only a piddling 2.1 million were proposed for Wilderness. Andrus may have helped on the Alaska Lands Act, but when it came to Wilderness for BLM or in RARE II, he was no friend to conservationists. But Ronald Reagan's Interior Secretary, the creepy James Watt, made Andrus look like John Muir. Watt straightaway cut the 2.1 million acres to 1.8 million and illegally went against nonimpairment for WSAs by offering energy leases, proposing to build roads, and allowing other landscalping.

The strong bunch of desert rats in the Southern California Sierra Club and California Desert Protection League went around BLM and to their Senator, Alan Cranston. Jim Eaton, then with the California Wilderness Coalition, remembers how the grassroots activists put together their bill for Cranston:

> My recollection is that the conservationists were fine-tuning a 3.2-million acre bill. At a meeting at Mabel Barnes' house, where we were going to make our final proposal, I pointed out that the bill never would get bigger, only smaller. One by one, folks decided this area and that one deserved to be added until we got

to nearly 9-million acres.... I think the California desert story is important, because it is perhaps the last time the mostly volunteer conservation force developed the proposal. Although there were increasing numbers of paid staffers involved, it was the volunteers who developed that great wilderness bill.[3]

Jim offers one of the great lessons for conservationists here: ask for what you want; don't compromise before you go to Congress. Had Jim not spoken up, think what a dinky little California Desert Wilderness bill we would have gotten. Conservationists went to Cranston with what they truly wanted and in 1986 he introduced an outstanding bill— maybe the strongest single Wilderness bill introduced in Congress up to that time. Much of what conservationists wanted as BLM Wilderness was added to Joshua Tree and Death Valley National Monuments, which would become National Parks as would a new East Mohave National Park. Cranston's bill would designate 4.3 million acres as Wilderness in the three new Parks and eighty-one BLM Wilderness Areas with 4.5 million acres—8.8 million acres of Wilderness in all. Desert rats who loved Wilderness and desert rats who wanted to go everywhere by gasoline fought it out with their chosen members of Congress until Cranston left the Senate. California's new Senators, Diane Feinstein and Barbara Boxer, picked up the fight from Cranston. In 1993, they offered a watered-down 7 million acre Wilderness bill. After much political jockeying and more compromises from Feinstein, the bill passed the House and then Senate (fourteen Republicans voted for it) before the election in 1994. Though whittled down from Cranston's original vision, the California Desert Protection Act was the greatest legislative win for Wilderness since the 1980 Alaska National Interest Lands Conservation Act. The BLM's pissant 2 million acre proposal had been long forgotten.[4]

---

3   Jim Eaton, email, September 23, 2014.
4   I draw on three books for the California Desert: Dave Foreman and

By 1976, BLM had administratively set aside a few "Primitive Areas" and "Outstanding Natural Areas." FLPMA made all such areas Instant Study Areas (ISAs) that were to be treated as WSAs. Recommendations for or against Wilderness designation were due by July 1, 1980 for ISAs. For other Wilderness Study Areas, recommendations were to be given to the President by 1991 and the President had until 1993 to send recommendations to Congress. These deadlines were met. Moreover, all WSAs, whether recommended by BLM for Wilderness or not, were to be kept "unimpaired" until Congress put thumbs up or down on each. Thanks to congressional foot-dragging, most WSAs picked thirty years ago, other than those in Arizona and the California Desert, where thorough and pretty darn good Wilderness bills were made law, are still on the books to be kept unimpaired.[5] In the late 1970s, conservationists, led by Debbie Sease of The Wilderness Society, and BLM went back-and-forth on how tough the interim management standards to keep WSAs unimpaired should be.

Even after the interim management standards were finalized, such stewardship has been sometimes seen by BLM and wilderness lovers in unlike ways; watchdogging what happens in WSAs is a key job for wilderness clubs and wilderness-loving desert rats. Too often it is overwhelming work to keep an eye on every WSA. (In one case, a power company built a hulking power line across a WSA in Nevada without the agency even knowing about it!) Roads and sundry other wounds have a way of creeping into unwatched WSAs. Wilderness Study Areas are not necessarily closed to off-road vehicles and bicycles—they can be allowed on primitive routes where such use was established before

Howie Wolke, *The Big Outside* (Harmony/Crown, New York, 1992), 156-158; Dyan Zaslowsky and T. H. Watkins, *These American Lands* (Island Press, Washington, 1994), 220-221; and James Morton Turner, *The Promise of Wilderness* (University of Washington Press, Seattle, 2012), 255-259.

5   Southwestern Idaho and some regions of Nevada have also had BLM Wilderness bills where some WSAs were released.

designation of the WSA. Under BLM regulations, there is a bit of wiggle room for local managers. Moreover, there is much ORV and mountain bike trespass into WSAs with little enforcement or even surveillance from the short-staffed BLM. Such vehicle use (including bicycles) is a main threat to keeping WSAs unimpaired and staying wild enough to be made Wilderness Areas by Congress. New leasing for oil and gas exploration is banned in WSAs, but leases issued before WSA selection are grandfathered in. However, potential for energy and mineral resources led to roadless areas not being recommended for WSA (even if such potential was not a legitimate reason—other reasons were found), and many WSAs were not recommended for Wilderness because of potential energy resources. Some ranchers have done their best to ignore interim management for WSAs they lease for grazing, and have bladed roads, dug stock tanks, laid water pipelines from springs, and so forth without asking for authorization from BLM.

Nonetheless, nonimpairment standards for WSAs until Congress signs off on their release from Wilderness designation are a great boon to conservationists. All WSAs—whether or not recommended by BLM for Wilderness Area designation—have to be kept unimpaired (undeveloped) until Congress releases them if it does not designate them as Wilderness. So, there is no need whatsoever for wilderfolk to accept a lousy bill that designates a few BLM Wilderness Areas but releases many.

Roadless Area Inventory

Even to long-on-the-job BLM staffers, a roadless area inventory of their lands was almost as much of a trip into the unknown as it was for wilderfolks. For one thing, professional BLM staff moved from state to state quite a bit. For another, some of the BLM land was truly the back of beyond. The wilderness review began in the Carter Administration and overall was run more truthfully and thoroughly than the Forest Service's RARE or RARE II undertakings, in part because FLPMA was much tighter and more straightforward on the BLM Wilderness Review than were the shady in-house guidelines the Forest Service had for the RAREs.

New staff was hired to do the overwhelming job of fieldwork, mapping, and analysis. Overall, they were good, hard-working, young folks who liked wilderness and who took their work and mandate earnestly. Many were just out of college with outdoor recreation and resource management degrees. Some of them became strong wilderness backers, and several I worked with back at the beginning are still good friends. They had a big impact on the culture of BLM because they did not come from ranching or mining backgrounds, and many of them were women. As some of them moved up the BLM ladder, they had even more of an impact. Conservationists and the new BLM Wilderness Review staffers often went together to find roadless areas or to see if they had "wilderness characteristics." I checked out roadless areas all over New Mexico with BLM staff. I even did a four-day backpack through the quarter-million acre West Potrillo Mountains with Donita Cotter, the Wilderness Coordinator for the Las Cruces BLM District. We wanted to show the Las Cruces District Manager that it had "opportunities for primitive recreation or solitude."

With BLM, there was somewhat less bickering over what a road was than we'd had with the USFS. The House Committee Report on FLPMA gave the definition:

The word "roadless" refers to the absence of roads which have been improved and maintained by mechanical means to insure relatively regular and continuous use. A way maintained solely by passage of vehicles does not constitute a road.

Notwithstanding this clearly stated description of what was a road, there was still some head banging between wilderfolks and BLM managers (rarely Wilderness staff) on whether something was a road or just a way. Sometimes, the bickering became absurd (or at least funny): "Okay, was the rock moved out of the track by hand or a shovel?" "Is this little cut on the uphill side of this slope from tires or did a blade do it?"

Out of 175 million acres of BLM land in the lower 48 states, 49 million acres were identified as roadless.[6] It is likely that 10 million or more acres were not identified as roadless that should have been. The Utah BLM, for example, identified a little less than 6 million acres of roadless areas in the late 1970s. One Utah BLM District Manager told his staff, "If in doubt, throw it out." In an overwhelmingly thorough re-inventory in the late-1990s that brought in 500 trained volunteers under the leadership of Jim Catlin, the Utah Wilderness Coalition identified over 9 million acres that were both roadless and qualified for Wilderness.[7] In New Mexico in the early 2000s, trained field workers for the New Mexico Wilderness Alliance found hundreds of thousands of acres earlier BLM and conservationists' inventories had missed. Likewise, later fieldwork by conservation teams in Colorado and Nevada found many roadless areas earlier missed or overlooked.

WILDERNESS STUDY AREA SELECTION

While there was sparring over the roadless inventory, overall BLM did a sounder job than had the Forest Service in the RAREs. Selection of Wilderness Study Areas was another deal, however. While the Wilderness staff wrote descriptions and analyses of whether roadless areas had wilderness characteristics and should become WSAs, those were edited and revised by higher-ups. The decisions to make an area a WSA were done up the chain of command to each state director. Among the area managers, district managers, and state directors were some who had no personal feeling for wilderness or disliked it.

6   Secretary of the Interior James Watt dropped BLM lands in Alaska from Wilderness Review in 1981.

7   *Facts About America's Redrock Wilderness*, Southern Utah Wilderness Alliance, April 1999.

Many shared the purity and quality mindset of their counterparts in the Forest Service, but at least no one argued that the alpine aesthetic should work in the drylands of the BLM. There were darn few glacial tarns and heaven-scraping peaks on BLM land (though one Colorado WSA has a 14,000 foot peak).

Nonetheless, there were some nasty little twists taken by antiwilderness BLM staffers to keep the WSA acreage small. Utah stands out. The BLM State Director in Utah, Gary Wicks (whom Interior Secretary Cecil Andrus seemed to think could do no wrong), did all he could to undercut the Wilderness review.[8] Of the six million acres found to be roadless by the BLM, Wicks let only 3.2 million acres become WSAs. Debbie Sease, by then The Wilderness Society's BLM watchdog, flew over some of the WSAs and unselected roadless areas with Wicks. She would say, "Okay, the area on the right you've picked for wilderness study, but just next to it on the left, you say it doesn't qualify for wilderness study. It all looks the same to me. Why is the part on the left not suitable for wilderness study? Where's the line between them?" Wicks would say, "Because I say so." So it went as they flew over much of southern Utah.

Later it was shown that the dropped roadless areas met all Wilderness Act and FLPMA criteria but were overlain with mining claims—not a lawful handle for yanking roadless areas from wilderness study. Former BLM Wilderness staffer Clive Kincaid wrote that "no fewer than 60 instances have been discovered" where BLM's recommended boundaries excluded mining claims and other potential conflicts. That was the only ground for exclusion. Kincaid's article in *The Earth First! Journal* should have been on the front page of the *New York Times* and sent Wicks to the gallows, but by that time, wilderness-hater James Watt was Secretary of the Interior.[9] Later in 1996-1998, the

---

8   BLM, unlike the other federal land managing agencies, is administered on a state-by-state basis.

9   Clive Kincaid, "Something Rotten In Utah: The BLM," *Earth First!*, Vol. III, No. I, November 1, 1982.

BLM reinventoried 3,107,070 acres beyond Wicks' picked Wilderness Study Areas in Utah and found that 2,606,990 more acres met the mark for Wilderness study, jacking up the Utah WSA acreage to 5.8 million.[10] While this was a big step in the right way, the Utah Wilderness Coalition, after doing a new standard-setting field study, said 9 million acres of BLM land in Utah should be Wilderness.[11]

In other states, BLM officials often held to old-fashioned yardsticks of Wilderness "quality" and "purity" and tossed wild and roadless areas because they were too flat in topography (not scenic enough) or too dry (not good for backpacking without water). I had the Wilderness Study documents from every state and found again and again that a desert area was rejected for WSA because it did not have enough "vegetative or topographic screening to provide opportunities for solitude." Never mind that when you are out in the middle of such a place there is likely not another human being for twenty miles. I wrote more than a few comment letters saying, "Flat is beautiful!"

Moreover, agency officials often overlooked ecological hallmarks as they emphasized primitive recreation or solitude opportunities. This was the reason for the four-day backpack Donita Cotter and I did in the waterless West Potrillo Mountains. We proved it had both primitive recreation and solitude opportunities. Though, to be truthful, I don't know of anyone else who has done that backpack in the thirty-five years since.

In Nevada, BLM cut a big area west of Searchlight from WSA consideration saying that it had no remarkable scenic features and was characterized by rabbitbrush. They failed to even note an outstanding ancient Joshua Tree Forest—one of the best in the US. Fortunately Nevada Senator Harry Reid liked Joshua trees and got the area designated as the Wee Thump-Joshua Tree Wilderness in 2002 after

10   Utah Wilderness Inventory 1999, USDI Bureau of Land Management.
11   *Facts About America's Redrock Wilderness,* Southern Utah Wilderness Alliance, April 1999.

much criticism from the BLM and others that the area didn't qualify because it wasn't a WSA first.

BUILDING A GRASSROOTS BLM WILDERNESS MOVEMENT

Conservationists were a bit overwhelmed by ranchers, drillers, miners, and ORVers at the beginning of the BLM Wilderness Review. The great Alaska campaign and RARE II were sucking most of the energy out of conservationists, and there wasn't much of a constituency among conservationists for the Bureau of Land Management. We had little experience dealing with BLM and few wildlovers knew the land overseen by BLM. The challenge was to ride herd on the BLM as a few staffers put together regulations on how the review would be done, and—at the same time—build a strong grassroots throng of dryland wilderness lovers and activists. Both those tasks fell mostly on Debbie Sease's shoulders. Moreover, the new executive director of The Wilderness Society, Bill Turnage, was busy tearing down the organizing team of Brandborg and Merritt and replacing it with cloistered economists and other "professionals" from Yale. In 1980 he fired Debbie along with nearly all the rest of the old TWS staff. She was left without an organization and a paycheck. It is a testament to her character and true wilderness heart that she kept on working. First, she was given a temporary home by Friends of the Earth and then finally hired by the Sierra Club. Along with a handful of grassroots BLM activists, such as Jean Herzegh in New Mexico and Karen Tanner in Nevada, Debbie built a grassroots constituency for BLM Wilderness from the ground up. I don't write this because she was once my wife, I write it because I watched it at the time and because I have fat file folders with the raw history of that landmark organizing. From time to time, there has been an essential person for the conservation movement. From 1978 to the mid-1980s, that person was Debbie Sease. I truly don't know how badly we might have done on BLM Wilderness without her at the center of a web of only two-dozen or so hardcore activists in the West. Jim Eaton writes, "The nationwide BLM campaigns were developed mostly by volunteers. Debbie was perhaps the last professional staff person to direct such a grassroots campaign."[12]

UPSHOT

Notwithstanding weak Wilderness Area recommendations from BLM and some head-butting with mostly the brass in BLM, I have to say, overall the BLM ran their Wilderness review more fairly and above-the-board than the Forest Service ran the RAREs and their aftermaths to the late 1990s. Since *The Great Wilderness Divide* ends in January 2001, I won't go into all the dirty dealing by Bush's Interior Department with BLM Wilderness. Even so, many good BLM staffers did their best under Bush to do the job the law told them to do, just as they did under Jim Watt in the Reagan years.

The following summary shows how BLM Wilderness has fared. It is a strong example of how a few folks can have a mighty influence.

---

12   Eaton, September 13, 2014.

BLM WILDERNESS SUMMARY*

Total BLM acreage outside Alaska	175 million acres
Roadless Area acreage selected	62 million acres
Wilderness Study Areas designated	23 million acres

Wilderness Study Areas recommended for Wilderness

9,720,490 acres; 328 areas

Designated Wilderness by Congress as of 2014

8,710,640 acres; 221 areas**

WSAs still left under interim management

12,760,472 acres; 528 areas

TOTAL BLM Wilderness Areas and WSAs

about 21.5 million acres

(Note: state wilderness groups propose much more Wilderness than the 12.7 million acres of remaining WSAs. The Utah Wilderness Coalition alone proposes over 9 million acres of BLM Wilderness in Utah.)

*As of Summer 2014

** Mostly in California, Arizona, and Nevada, though nearly all Western states have some BLM Wilderness Areas.

CHAPTER 22

After RARE II

RESOURCISM AND CONSERVATION FULLY SPLIT

After RARE II, the United States Forest Service and conservationists found themselves far apart—the Great Conservation Divide shone brightly as a high sharp ridge above ragged clouds.

Many think the USFS was prodded further by the politics of the Reagan Administration. In the heat of the 1980 presidential race, Ronald Reagan, who had been somewhat okay on conservation as California's governor, came flat out to say he was a "Sagebrush Rebel," tying himself to anticonservation ranchers and other resource-grabbing industries. It was not just campaign rhetoric to highlight his unlikeness to Jimmy Carter. After the nasty 1976 Republican presidential nomination fight where Reagan lost to Jerry Ford, the radical right took over the GOP and began to apply a litmus test on whether Republican candidates were "real Republicans" or not. The Sagebrush Rebellion hitched its wagon to this narrow-minded wing, marking the beginning of the end of bipartisanship on conservation and environmental issues.

Reagan owed the anticonservationists much after the election and had no misgivings about thanking them in a big way. He appointed a lobbyist for the timber industry, John Crowell, to oversee the Forest Service, and a BLM-hating rancher, Bob Buford, to be Director of the BLM. Then he shot for the moon and appointed James Watt as Secretary of the Interior. Watt wasn't just a landscalper like Crowell and Buford, he thoroughly loathed wild things and, as a nutcase evangelical, believed that Christ was coming back soon and we should gobble up all of Earth's wealth before He got here or He would be pissed. I do not make this up.

Though I wrote above that many believe John Crowell and the politics of the Reagan Administration prodded the Forest Service even closer to landscalping, I don't believe timber beasts in the USFS needed Reaganite commissars like Crowell to set their course in the 1980s. After playing RARE II winningly and being rid of a tree-hugger like Rupert Cutler, the Forest Service timber beasts felt free and ready to finally go for it and liquidate decadent, unmanaged old-growth forest along with laying down a road network to make all National Forest land except for a small acreage of Wilderness Areas accessible by vehicle.[1] Crowell, as a former lobbyist and lawyer for the timber industry, was more an enabler than director of the Forest Service's 1980s War on Wildness. Crowell and his appointed underlings also helped the old Forest Service timber beasts hunt down and kneecap truehearted staffers.

Moreover, the chainsaw-and-bulldozer Forest Service came under more heated word slapping from conservationists—even once polite ones. This led to an ingrown and under-fire mood, and then to even greater quashing of staffers who tried to follow the law and do a good job. In the next chapter, I'll look closer at this repression of Forest Service staff. Alas, so much went on in the 1980s War on Wildness that I can offer only a glance. I am sorry to leave so much out of this chapter

---

1   I write "liquidate" because I heard and read USFS timber beasts slinging the word.

but I would have to write a whole book to fully cover the 1980s fight between wildlovers and timber beasts.[2]

RARE II LEGISLATION GAMES

My target here is the fight in the woods between wilderfolk and timber beasts; but first I need to spotlight the fight on the Potomac since much arm-wrestling was going on in Congress and between conservation groups. Tom Foley, a New Deal and sawlog congressman from western Washington and the Speaker of the House, right away in 1979 put up a bill to implement the RARE II decision. It would designate as Wilderness the Forest Service's recommendations and "hard release" all other roadless areas. Hard release meant not only that areas so released were available for logging, roading, and other development *right now*, but that they could *never* be considered for Wilderness again. Foley's bill made a lot of conservation group staffers change their underwear.

Lead staff from the Sierra Club and Wilderness Society—the so-called Gang of Four, who took over leadership on post-RARE II strategy—worked closely together to manage this crisis, which they saw as the greatest threat to a growing Wilderness System. Although they and other conservationists knew that the RARE II Final Environmental Impact Statement could not stand up in court, they did not want a lawsuit against the RARE II decision. They thought such a suit would grease the passage of Foley's bill or other legislative hard release. The tough Oregon Wilderness Coalition (OWC) and some other conservationists, however, were thinking of calling Foley's bluff and filing suit. The Gang of Four, led by Doug Scott, came down hard on OWC and others to stifle talk or thought of a RARE II lawsuit.

Notwithstanding the mainstream conservationists' browbeating, a RARE II lawsuit was brought. But not by a conservation group. Huey

---

2   For more detail, see James Morton Turner, *The Promise of Wilderness* (University of Washington Press, Seattle, 2012).

Johnson, the übertough Secretary of Resources for California Governor Jerry Brown, filed it.[3] Johnson, who had been the first Western Director of The Nature Conservancy, was a diehard, unflappable political tough guy who wouldn't be shoved around. He is still one of the great conservationists of our time. The *California v. Block* suit only dealt with forty-seven California RARE II areas, however. U.S. District Court Judge Lawrence K. Karlton ruled for California, saying the RARE II FEIS was insufficient, and enjoined development in the areas until site-specific environmental statements were done. In 1982 the Ninth Circuit Court of Appeals upheld the lower court's decision, thereby saying that in the Ninth Circuit, which included Oregon, RARE II did not pass NEPA muster. But to protect any areas other than the forty-seven California ones, another lawsuit would have to be filed.

There was mad scrambling on the Potomac over release. In 1979-1980, state-specific RARE II bills were being drafted. The timber industry and their friends demanded that any bill establishing new National Forest Wilderness Areas would have to release all other RARE II areas to "multiple-use" and prohibit later consideration for Wilderness: hard release again. Some bills were better than others insofar as how many areas were designated as Wilderness, but conservationists were united against any bill with hard release. Our best hope for stopping hard release was the matchless John Seiberling, chairman of the House Committee on Public Lands, and his whiz of a committee staffer Andy Wiessner. They did the lion's share in working out a middle ground— so-called "soft release" or "sufficiency language," which stated that the RARE II Final Environmental Impact Statement was sufficient for the released areas, that they were available for development, but could be reconsidered for Wilderness recommendation in the next round of

---

3   Jim Eaton, then the California representative for The Wilderness Society remembers being ordered to visit Huey Johnson and talk him out of the suit. But Huey could tell that Jim didn't agree with the no-suit message he had to deliver.

Forest Plans. Only two state RARE II bills passed in 1980, New Mexico and Colorado, both of which had this soft release.[4]

ANCIENT FOREST

In April of 1983, Mike Roselle and three other men stood before a bulldozer on the Bald Mountain Road in southwestern Oregon's Siskiyou National Forest. Their stand was the Lexington Bridge in the fight for ancient forests that goes on to this day. It was necessary because after RARE II the Forest Service reckoned that, while their hands were no longer tied, they were not going to take any chances at being stymied. So their foremost goal was to swiftly whack the roadless areas with big trees. The goal of the Siskiyou National Forest managers was to get the cut out, as it had been for the after-World-War-Two Forest Service. Liquidation of old-growth forests was straightforward now. There was no shamming of sustained yield or professional, scientific management. It was cleaning out a tangled, messy wildwood as the first step in making a tree farm where the crop marched in rows to the drumbeat of bulldozers, spray planes, and chainsaws. Senator Mark Hatfield, who did the bidding of Oregon's timber overlords, goosed the Siskiyou NF foresters along.

The logging road that Roselle and other Earth First!ers blocked was being bladed into the heart of the biggest unprotected roadless area and swath of old-growth forest left on the Pacific Coast south of British Columbia—the Kalmiopsis. Up until the 1980s, the Forest Service had nibbled away at the edges of roadless areas with roads and clearcuts. However, after RARE II, the Forest Service wittingly put timber sales in the middle of roadless areas, with roads that would cleave roadless areas on one side from Wilderness Areas on the other—called "backing out" by timber beasts. The Forest Service willfully, with malice aforethought, targeted the biggest of the last wooded roadless areas for strikes at their

4　Again, I draw on my own experience here, but also see Turner, *Promise of Wilderness*, 198-199.

hearts so wilderfolk could never ask for these lands as Wilderness. Rupe Cutler meant RARE II to be an honest inventory and evaluation that would shield Wilderness and give the timber industry firm footing. Some in the Forest Service, however, twisted RARE II not to find new Wilderness, but to find the lands they thought should be roaded and logged so that conservationists could never ask for them as Wilderness Areas. That thinking was given words by a timber staffer on the Rio Grande NF (Colorado) in the 1990s when he told conservationists that the official definition of a roadless area was an area needing road construction.

Roselle, Bart Koehler, Cecilia Ostrow, and I learned about the Kalmiopsis crisis as we came through southwestern Oregon on an Earth First! Roadshow in January 1983. There Chant Trillium and other local conservationists told us about the Siskiyou National Forest plan to cut the Bald Mountain Road along the ridge between the Kalmiopsis Wilderness Area and the 130,000-acre North Kalmiopsis RARE II area. Conservationists had long wanted to add the heavily forested North Kalmiopsis to the Wilderness Area, but had been thwarted in legislative games by Senator Mark Hatfield. The Sierra Club had appealed and then sued over the Bald Mountain Road but lost. Bitterly unhappy Oregon conservationists saw no hope for stopping the road and the timber sales to follow. We also learned that national conservation groups had pretty well given up on protecting old-growth forest and were going to instead work to designate Wilderness Areas in less-forested areas.

We stewed on this while drinking much beer and talking with Chant and other local wilderfolks. Roselle and I decided it would not happen, that we would be back after spring snowmelt when the bulldozers began anew on cutting the road. We called for the local folks to stand with us in nonviolent civil disobedience to block the bulldozers. That is how Roselle and three others came to stand in front of Les Moore's bulldozer in April 1983. "Shut 'er down. We ain't moving," said Mike.

The campaign for Ancient Forests, which would go on for the next score of years, had begun.

The 1983 Earth First! Round River Rendezvous (RRR) over the Fourth of July was held in the Siskiyou National Forest. Forty-four of us had been arrested blocking the 'dozers and we hoped to find many more for blockades until snow shut roadwork down. But now, it was a time to merry meet and merry make. On June 30, Roseburg, OR, ("timber capitol of the world") attorney Neal Kagan, on behalf of Earth First!, the Oregon Natural Resources Council (ONRC, formerly the Oregon Wilderness Coalition), and nine Oregon citizens, had asked U.S. District Judge James A. Redden for a Temporary Restraining Order (TRO) against the Forest Service and Plumley Construction Company (which had the road-building contract). In a lightning-fast move, Judge Redden in Eugene issued the TRO on July 1 just as the RRR was getting underway. It was a party—but one that planned for further action. After a July 6 hearing, on July 13 Judge Redden issued an injunction against construction of the Bald Mountain Road. His decision was based on the Ninth Circuit Court's decision in the *California v. Block* case.

Mike Roselle, Earth First!, and fellow activists right away went to work on blockades and other action against timber sales in other RARE II areas and in old-growth stands outside of roadless areas. For another ten years, thousands took part in civil disobedience and hundreds went to jail in defense of the great forests, some a'growing since before Columbus sailed. And the Forest Service went on hacking roads through the wildwood, felling mighty trees, and using every tool they had against Earth First!. Even SWAT-clad snipers threatening tree sitters.

In September 1983, I wrote every forest supervisor in the country asking them to abide by Judge Redden's injunction (which legally applied only to the Bald Mountain Road) and to send me notices of every development planned for RARE II areas on their forests. Peter Kirby, an attorney with The Wilderness Society (but whose heart was in wilderness), helped me draft a one-page, fill-in-the-blanks letter that could be sent to National Forests planning development in RARE II areas. It appealed such actions on the grounds of the Ninth Circuit Court decision. I would then receive a letter back withdrawing the proposed action until a site-specific EIS could be done or until a Wilderness bill for the state with sufficiency language passed. I have an old file of more than one hundred such winning appeals.

Meanwhile, Andy Kerr with the Oregon Natural Resources Coalition was busy laying the groundwork for a statewide Oregon lawsuit. It was filed on December 13, 1983. Two months later, Jeff Sirmon, Regional Forester for Oregon and Washington, halted all development in RARE II areas in the two states. Then one of the big national groups broke ranks and went against the Sierra Club/ Wilderness Society's gainsaying of RARE II suits. It was the National Audubon Society and six of its Oregon chapters joining the ONRC suit. This was the work of Brock Evans, a long-time Sierra Club staffer in the Northwest who was now head of Audubon's Washington, DC, office. I tip my hat to Kerr and Evans for being the farsighted conservation leaders who brought what they called *Ancient Forests* and a nationwide campaign for them into the mainstream.

I had by then ferreted out a Forest Service planning document called DARN—Development Activities in Roadless Nonselected for 1979-1987. When I first got the computer printout, it had 8609 miles of road planned in RARE II areas. By 1985, that was up to 75,000 miles. It was clear for anyone to see what the U.S. Forest Service was doing. Most states (other than Montana and Idaho) had gained National Forest Wilderness bills with sufficiency language by the end of 1984, and Reagan had signed them. And before long, Forest Plans with adequate NEPA compliance had been done in Idaho and Montana. The short window in which we could stop timber sales and roads in nonselected roadless areas by trotting out *California v. Block* was over.

The fight against the Forest Service was no longer grounded in RARE II.[5]

But the Ancient Forest war in the woods was not over. Conservationists used every other tool in our box from appeals and lawsuits on other grounds to legislation to trying to cut appropriations for USFS roads, to blockades, tree sitting, and other steadily more sophisticated actions, to the old bugbear of monkeywrenching. Though we were losing overall, we were making the Forest Service feel bullyragged—and were truly saving much ancient forest.

One of the best wins against the Forest Service timber beasts, the timber industry Godzilla, and rape-and-scrape politicians in the 1980s happened in the Tongass National Forest in Southeast Alaska, where the world's greatest temperate rainforest grew and where the Forest Service and industry ransacked the wildwood like nowhere else. The 1980 Alaska National Interest Lands Conservation Act (ANILCA) sacrificed the Tongass as a hush puppy thrown to the whiny Alaska congressional delegation. The scrappy Southeast Alaska Conservation Council (SEACC) was gobsmacked and wroth at national conservation groups and House Interior Committee Chairman Morris Udall for hanging them out to dry. Logging blazed into a stonyhearted blitzkrieg against the greatest coniferous ancient forest in the world. Bart Koehler left Earth First! in 1984 to become executive director of SEACC. No better person could have been picked than the master strategist, organizer, and lobbyist Koehler. I think him the best good-old-boy, folksy lobbyist the wilderness team has ever had. He had plenty of help from commercial fishermen, homesteaders, hunters, guides and outfitters, and others in the Alaska Panhandle. In 1990, SEACC gained the Tongass Timber Reform Act, which did much to undercut the ANILCA sell-out.[6]

---

5   This history and much more is held in the pages of the 1980's *Earth First! Journal* edited and published by John Davis and me and with many articles on the Forest Service written by Howie Wolke.

6   The best source for the Tongass battles is the SEACC newspaper, *The Raven Call.*

And Then Along Came the Owl

It was a hell of a load to put on the tiny shoulders of a forest-dwelling nighthunter like the little spotted owl. The Forest Service's own researchers found that the liquidation of old-growth forest was threatening the survival of species dependent on the big, dark woods. Foremost was the spotted owl. Lawsuits using the Endangered Species Act (ESA) and National Forest Management Act (NFMA) were the new tool conservationists wielded to fight logging. In 1991, Judge William Dwyer in the Ninth Circuit enjoined old-growth forest timber sales until an effective spotted owl habitat protection plan was issued. In 1983, after taking office Bill Clinton and Al Gore hosted a summit on ancient forests drawn around the spotted owl. A comprehensive Forest Plan for the Pacific Northwest setting aside Old-growth Forest Reserves for the owl and other old-growth dependent species came out in 1994.

Out of the 1990 breakup of Earth First!, new groups, making up what I called the New Conservation Movement, came to the fore. Some, such as the Center for Biological Diversity, were started by Earth First! veterans seeking tough but legal paths for defending wild things. Such groups were overall grounded in two big shifts within the grassroots conservation movement: embracing conservation biology and spurning the old acknowledgment of multiple-use as guiding light for resource agencies.[7] Two initiatives I helped start and lead helped to give a voice to the New Conservation Movement and to lead the way through applied conservation biology. They were *Wild Earth* magazine, which John Davis and I first published in Spring 1991 on a dime and prayer, and The Wildlands Project, which was brought together by North Face/Esprit tycoon Doug Tompkins. Both had activists and conservation biologists such as Michael Soulé and Reed Noss.

---

7   In other words, we went back to John Muir and friends with the Forest Reserves in the 1890s.

It would take many more pages than I have to do the 1990s right, but Jay Turner looks at all of it well in *The Promise of Wilderness*.[8]

THE UPSHOT

The mindset of the Forest Service in the years 1945 to 2000 was that their job was to give timber to America and job and community stabilization to mill towns only kept alive by National Forest timber and other federal welfare. To do this, they needed to scalp and snuff wild, roadless, old-growth forests and remake them into managed tree plantations. In other words, to turn wilderness into tree farms. They saw conservationists as outsiders meddling with their professional responsibility to do this on the lands handed over to them to manage— not leave alone. Foresters believed that conservationists swayed members of Congress to unseemly thwart their management by making areas that should be tree farms Wilderness Areas. Therefore, it was the holy calling of foresters to work swiftly to block Wilderness designation through thoughtful road building and logging. They found in forest fires an opening to call for "salvage logging" to keep Wilderness at bay. What wilderfolk saw as dirty dealing, such Forest Service leaders and timber staffers saw as the only way they could fulfill their professional responsibility—hearkening back to Gifford Pinchot's belief that trained technicians, not politicians, should make resource decisions.

So great has been the drive of the Forest Service to tame the backcountry since 1980, that the agency has become the world's mightiest road-managing agency. There are some 440,000 miles of roads on the 157 million acres of National Forests that are outside of designated Wilderness Areas.[9] Even using a lower reckoning of 378,000 miles of road from 1997, the road density on National Forests is 1.5 miles of road per square mile of land, while the road density in the rest

8   James Morton Turner, *The Promise of Wilderness* (University of Washington Press, Seattle, 2012.

9   Associated Press, "Clinton moves to halt construction of new forest roads," *The Albuquerque Tribune*, February 11, 1999.

of the United States is about 1.1 miles per square mile. In Washington and Oregon, the NF road density is a whopping 3.5 miles per square mile.[10] In a careful 1997 study, The Wilderness Society found that "in just a little more than a decade, the total acreage of roadless land in Idaho's national forests has dropped by one million acres"—from 9.4 million acres to 8.4 million acres. Over 200,000 acres had been roaded and logged on the Boise National Forest alone. Of the roadless areas left, "only 1.3 million acres are administratively protected from logging and other development."[11] In California, 675,449 acres of Forest Service roadless areas were lost between 1979 and 1998—more than 10 percent of the roadless acreage in RARE II. The Modoc NF lost 53 percent of its roadless lands.[12]

Much has been made of the drop in how much is being logged yearly on the National Forests. The American Lands Alliance found late in 1998 that the timber cut in 1997, 3.4 billion board feet (bbf), was the lowest since 1950.[13] As much as the logging industry and Forest Service would like to tar conservationists, and as much as conservationists would like to take thanks, this steep drop in sawlogs going to the mill is mainly owing to most of the best timber being cut already.

Since the 1970s, the Forest Service has chopped up hundreds of thousands of acres of de facto wilderness a year through logging and road building. They have hacked away at ancient forests, leaving only

10   Western Ancient Forest Campaign, *Report From Washington*, Vol. 7, No. 2; April 7, 1997.

11   Michael Anderson, *Idaho's Vanishing Wild Lands: A Status Report on Roadless Areas in Idaho's National Forests,* The Wilderness Society, July 1997.

12   Paul Spitler, Ryan Henson, Danielle Weintraub, Catriona Black, and B. Delbert Williams, *California's Vanishing Forests: Two Decades of Destruction* (California Wilderness Coalition, Davis, 1998), xiv-xv.

13   American Lands Alliance, [formerly WAFC] *Report From Washington,* Vol. 8, No. 4; October 20, 1998.

scattered bits. They have ransacked critical habitat for Endangered and Threatened Species. They have left wild rivers bleeding with the silt of wrecked and plundered watersheds. All to get out the cut. All to further the professional culture and custom of the Forest Service: build roads, cut trees, and turn wild forests into tree farms.

No wonder Oregon Earth First!er Marcy Willow called the Forest Service an outlaw agency.

CHAPTER 23

Repression and Corruption in the Resource Agencies

AGENCY REPRESSION OF EMPLOYEES

A mark of the Forest Service's ebb as a professional agency from 1980 into the 1990s was the increased crushing of employees who tried to follow the laws and shield land and wildlife from the harm of go-for-broke logging and road-building. Even Forest Service line officers who were not wilderness conservationists but were good professional resource managers, such as former Nezperce National Forest Supervisor Tom Kovalicky and former Northern Regional Forester John Mumma, were shoved out of their jobs for not getting the cut out enough to keep Idaho politicians happy. Some pressure on the Forest Service came in the 1980s from timber industry lawyer John Crowell as Assistant Secretary of Agriculture (Rupe Cutler's old job), and on Interior agencies from Reagan's ideological hacks, such as Interior Secretary Watt and Watt's less creepy but still landscalping successors. But resource agency leaders from within did not truly need the outside political diktats; they were even more eager to cut the last of the ancient forest, drill de facto wilderness, and fight the listing of Endangered Species. The fight became even hotter within the Great Conservation Divide frame, between resourcists in the agencies and wilderfolks in grassroots clubs. Dedicated agency staffers who tried to follow the law and do what was right were more than ever before under close watch, bullying, and worse from the hard resourcist leadership.

This browbeating of employees who do their best to follow the law went beyond the Forest Service. *The Christian Science Monitor's* Montana correspondent, Todd Wilkinson, shone a floodlight on the widespread crushing of truthful resource agency scientists in his 1998 book, *Science Under Siege*. His book is must reading to understand the shape of natural resource management in America today. He wrote:

> *A campaign of stifling attacks on the essence of scientific truth is present and thriving both within the ranks of the nation's largest employer, the federal government, and among natural resource agencies in most of the fifty states.*[1]

As Wilkinson began work on his book, he was warned by an agency official, "*If you print what they* [government whistle-blowers] *say,* it may be difficult for you, Mr. Wilkinson, to get our cooperation on stories you write in the future."[2]

An "Iron Triangle"—the timber industry, Forest Service bureaucrats, and politicians—dampens truthful scientific research in the Forest Service.[3] Elsewhere, this triangle of crookedness and cracking the whip on staff is made up of other extractive industries and agency apparatchiks. Wilkinson tells how agency scientists in the Forest Service, BLM, Park Service, Fish & Wildlife Service, EPA, U.S. Geological Survey, and state game and fish agencies have been

1   Todd Wilkinson, *Science Under Siege: The Politician's War on Nature and Truth* (Johnson Books, Boulder, CO, 1998), 4.
2   Wilkinson, *Science Under Siege*, 5.
3   Wilkinson, *Science Under Siege*, 22.

bullied—or worse—by their supervisors to fake and twist facts so that they back logging, livestock grazing, road-building, and the like. Wilkinson names names, quotes from secret recordings, and tracks down files that draw a picture of agency managers wedded to doing the bidding of the resource extraction industry even if it means breaking the law and crushing scientists who try to do their jobs. Keep in mind that Wilkinson's book was written in 1998 before the Bush Junior crowd came to power.

Since the 1970s, wilderfolks have worked hard on National Forest management plans and on reform legislation like the National Forest Management Act. Upstanding and steadfast USFS staffers have done their best to make the agency better from the inside, even going so far as to form the Association of Forest Service Employees for Environmental Ethics (AFSEEE, now FSEEE). In their publications, *Inner Voice* and now the magazine *Forest*, FSEEE has dug up dirty dealing by the Forest Service brass. As an organization, FSEEE has steadfastly come to the aid of Forest Service whistle-blowers and staffers told to break the law or cook the books. Nonetheless, the Forest Service still doesn't play by the rules. Why do Big Timber senators work to shield Forest Service timber sales from all conservation legislation? Because the Forest Service time and again loses in court when conservationists sue. The Forest Service breaks the law, conservationists sue, federal courts rule against the Forest Service, then sawlog senators slip through riders sparing the Forest Service from following the law.

U.S. FISH AND WILDLIFE SERVICE AGAINST ENDANGERED SPECIES

Given the holiest trust in government—stopping the extinction of species at Man's hands—the United States Fish & Wildlife Service has badly botched the job. In 2000, the conservation team American Lands put out a withering once-over of the Fish and Wildlife Service's work on Endangered Species throughout the Clinton Administration: *Broken Promises of Recovery: The Clinton Administration's 10-Prong*

Attack on Endangered Species. [4] It tallies how the agency and Clinton administration were shamefully slipshod in their fulfillment of the Endangered Species Act.

The ten prongs were:

- Pretending species aren't Endangered
- Ignoring species' Critical Habitats
- Failing to develop and enforce basic habitat protection measures
- Regulatory giveaways and business as usual for big industry
- Business as usual for the Forest Service and other agencies that destroy habitat
- Failing to take recovery planning seriously
- Removing protection for species that haven't really recovered
- Underfunding their own programs
- Supporting legislation that would weaken the ESA
- Ignoring, marginalizing, and destroying its own biologists [5]

In 1997, then University of Michigan professor Steven Yaffee wrote that over:

the 23-year history of the Endangered Species Act (ESA)... the U.S. Fish and Wildlife Service (USFWS) has sought to maximize organizational flexibility, avoid controversy, and offset the impacts of actions on constituent groups by delaying or not listing species—

4   American Lands, *Broken Promises of Recovery: The Clinton Administration's 10-Prong Attack on Endangered Species,* January 2000.
5   American Lands, *Broken Promises of Recovery,* 2. After 2001, right-wing hacks in Bush's Interior Department pushed the USFWS to do even worse on Endangered Species. In the Obama Administration, the USFWS is back to doing its own dirty work as in the Clinton Administration. Witness the unscientific "delisting" (dropping Endangered and Threatened Species status) for the gray wolf in the Northern Rockies and Great Lakes regions and allowing benighted states such as Idaho to institute wolf slaughter plans.

activities that often resulted in court actions that forced the agency's
hand.[6]

Yaffee's study is bedrock for understanding why government
agencies go out of their way to keep from doing their jobs as mandated
by controlling laws.

Rob Marshall, a former biologist with the USFWS, warned, "The
Southwestern willow flycatcher [an Endangered Species] is being
piecemealed to extinction, the service is turning a blind eye to the
aggregate effects of its own (actions)."[7]

Federal courts in the late 1990s found the Fish and Wildlife Service
"to be arbitrary and capricious in refusing to list [as endangered] ... the
Canada lynx and the Barton Springs salamander." After this, John Sidle
(who worked for the Forest Service) wrote:

Some political appointees in government think mostly in terms
of politics and have little or no field experience in fish, wildlife,
and plant conservation. Many are attorneys bound for high-level
positions inside and outside government. Moreover, upper-level
USFWS administrators and others a little way down the ladder
often view themselves as entry-level political appointees and behave
accordingly.

Sidle went on to write that "the federal courts have recognized
that USFWS biologists were trying to do their job correctly but the
biologists and the ESA were being illegally undercut by political actions
of USFWS and Department of Interior officials."[8]

---

6   Steven L. Yaffee, "Why Environmental Policy Nightmares Recur," *Con-*
      servation Biology, Vol. 11, No. 2, April 1997, 331.
7   Steve Yozwiak, "Songbird's future in peril, group says," *The Arizona*
      Republic, September 3, 1998.
8   John G. Sidle, "Arbitrary and Capricious Species Conservation," *Conser-*
      vation Biology, Vol. 12, No. 1, February 1998, 248-249.

Most often, the Fish and Wildlife Service has not listed and shielded Endangered Species until made to do so by conservation groups and private citizens winning lawsuits. Art Morrison, with the Southwest Region of the Forest Service, gave an odd twist to such suits. "It's not that they're winning lawsuits. It's because they're getting friendly courts." Sort of like saying, "It's not that I got a sunburn. It's because the sun came up today." The director of the Fish and Wildlife Service at the time (1997), Jamie Clark, whined, "If they would quit suing us so much, maybe we could take some actions." But Kieran Suckling of the Center for Biological Diversity straightened things out for poor Clark, "The reason we win [with lawsuits] is because before we go through the door of the courthouse, we have all the scientists behind us."[9] More often than not, the scientists on board are also the USFWS's own scientists who have had their recommendations to list species as Endangered or Threatened snubbed by their politically driven bosses.

The federal judge in the 1990s who was ruling for conservationist lawsuits against the USFWS in the Southwest was no flaming liberal. He was Judge Robert Parker, a Republican appointed by Reagan.

In short, the Fish & Wildlife Service has been more worried about its own bureaucratic welfare than with that of plants and wildeors. Aware citizens might think that, of all the agencies in government, the FWS would be the most scientific and the most steadfast for keeping wild things healthy. They would be wrong. Throughout the Clinton Administration and under the Interior secretaryship of Bruce Babbitt, the Fish and Wildlife Service too often shunned its trust under the Endangered Species Act, shut up its truehearted biologists, and undercut conservation.[10] Even under this somewhat enlightened administration, the political leadership of the Fish and Wildlife Service and the Department of Interior worked harder for the well-being of

9   Mike Taugher, "Activists' Suits Stir Talk of Species Act Changes," *The Albuquerque Journal*, August 24, 1997.

10   Though, as we shall see, Babbitt did the right thing on recovery and reintroduction of the Mexican wolf (Lobo) in Arizona and New Mexico.

extractive industries and developers than for the birds, fish, mammals, and plants it is called on by law (and goodness) to care for. Putting the lie to those who say that conservationists' lawsuits keep the Service from doing its job, Public Employees for Environmental Responsibility (PEER) writes, "Blaming budgetary limitations, USFWS has ceased review of almost all new listing petitions yet is spending millions of dollars to fight lawsuits brought by environmental groups to force listing. Citing the work of USFWS's own biologists, environmental groups are winning lawsuits to force Interior to list endangered and threatened species."[11]

As for the Canada lynx, the federal court "ruled that the USFWS Director, by refusing to list the Canada lynx, was ignoring the 'overwhelming consensus among the [agency's] biologists...that the lynx must be listed.'"[12] The agency's work on the lynx was so bad that Ronald Nowak, a top-level zoologist in the USFWS, left his job. In *High Country News*, he said that the FWS has "fought tooth and nail to avoid doing its job."[13]

Another way to weigh whether the FWS leadership is fulfilling its duty under the Endangered Species Act is a document entitled "Director's Priorities FY 1999-2000." Nowhere in it was a word about implementation of the ESA.[14]

THE LOBO

Dave Parsons is one of the bravest and most dedicated biologists to work for the USFWS. Indeed, had he not gotten the job as Mexican Wolf Recovery Coordinator for the Southwest Region, the Mexican wolf (Lobo), the most Endangered and genetically distinct subspecies

---

11 *PEEReview*, Fall 1997.
12 *PEEReview*, Fall 1997.
13 Michelle Nijhuis, "Zoologist says listing process is endangered," *High Country News*, February 2, 1998.
14 Jamie Rappaport Clark, *Director's Priorities FY 1999-2000* (U.S. Fish & Wildlife Service).

of gray wolf, would never have been reintroduced into the wild and would be languishing in zoos and other captive breeding facilities where it would lose its wildness. By the time Parsons took the job in October 1990, regional directors of the Southwest office of the USFWS had cut under-the-table (and illegal) deals with Arizona, New Mexico, and Texas state game agencies that the Lobo would be released into the wild only in White Sands Missile Range, a 3-million acre military installation in south-central New Mexico without any cattle grazing. The problem was that White Sands did not have adequate habitat or prey base for a viable population of Mexican wolves.

Moreover, the incoming commander of White Sands, Gen. Thomas Jones, removed the range from consideration. Thereupon, the USFWS Regional Director Mike Spear announced that the Mexican Wolf Recovery Program was dead. The Wolf Action Group and other conservation groups filed a 60-day notice of intent to sue. Not only did the Endangered Species Act (ESA) mandate the USFWS to work to recover the Mexican wolf, but also, the groups argued, USFWS had illegally given the states and other federal agencies "veto power" over the program. They also demanded that a biologist be hired to manage the reintroduction program.

Spear knew USFWS would lose the lawsuit. He twisted Gen. Jones's arm to offer the missile range as a reintroduction site—but Jones insisted that alternative sites also be considered under the National Environmental Policy Act (NEPA). Spear then asked the states to suggest possible sites (although he likely told them the reintroduction would be at White Sands). Arizona offered four sites, including the Blue Range Primitive Area and Apache National Forest on the New Mexico border.

Parsons was then hired as the Mexican Wolf Recovery Coordinator, not knowing any of the shenanigans his boss had been carrying on in clear violation of the ESA. Parsons ran a professional, science-based, legally sufficient NEPA study that evaluated the White Sands Missile

Range and the four sites in Arizona as possible recovery areas for this critically Endangered wolf. The evaluation showed that White Sands was not suitable and that the Arizona Blue Range country and the adjoining Gila National Forest in New Mexico was far and away the best site for the first reintroduction to begin recovery of Lobos in the wild.

The next step was to brief Interior Secretary Bruce Babbitt, who would make the final decision. Immediately prior to briefing the Secretary in his opulent briefing room, Parsons had his ass chewed out by the Director of the USFWS for having followed the law and rejecting White Sands as the preferred reintroduction site. Babbitt arrived and Parsons was sent up to stand at his side with the briefing materials. Babbitt turned to him and said, "So, I hear we are going to the Blue Range with these wolves." Parsons, after glancing at the USFWS Director whose head was down, said, "Yes sir," and proceeded with his briefing. Babbitt was from Arizona, knew the Blue Range, and was a fan of Aldo Leopold's. He endorsed the preferred alternative in the final Environmental Impact Statement and signed a Record of Decision to reintroduce Mexican wolves in the Blue Range. Babbitt even helped carry the cages of the to-be-reintroduced wolves to their temporary acclimation pens in the snowy high country of the Blue.

Though hated by the USFWS brass, Parsons continued to shepherd the program over the irrational and threatening opposition of ranchers and other yahoos in the recovery area in both Arizona and New Mexico. The new Regional Director then set him up. When he was eligible for early retirement, he was told that he could retire and then under a special classification called a rehired annuitant come back to his old job as Recovery Coordinator. Parsons believed the scam, retired, applied for the job, and was turned down. He won the reintroduction of the Lobo in the wild, but the USFWS got even.

It would take many more pages to tell the many tales showing the wrongdoing of resourcism at the end of the twentieth century. In this book I haven't laid down a point-by-point indictment of the resource agencies, but have shown that resource agencies, far from being the friends of conservationists in keeping land and wildlife wild, have had an ideological—almost theological—mission to stamp human will on the land. Overgrazing, overcutting, dam building, roading of the backcountry, and slaughter of wildlife have been underwritten by government agencies. Lately, the "in group" of agency leaders has worked hand in hand with the landscalpers. Even more than did Gifford Pinchot, they see conservationists and their own righteous staffers as the enemy.

Epilogue

Hope at the End of the Clinton Administration; Dismay After 2001

So. We are done with the Public Lands Century. What comes next? Even into the second decade after the Public Lands Century, it is tough to say. I see two possibilities, both summed up in a name:

The Rewilding Century
The Anthropocene Century

I put "Century" after each, more for the sake of consistency than by foresight. The second could end well before a hundred years have gone by, almost surely by crash. Though a crash in the History of Man is not always bad for the Tree of Life.[1] The Rewilding Century would mean that our population growth halts and our ecological footprint lessens as we return more land and water to other Earthlings.[2] The Anthropocene

---

1   Barbara A. Tuchman, *A Distant Mirror: The Calamitous 14ᵗʰ Century* (Alfred A. Knopf, New York, 1978).

2   E. O. Wilson, likely the best-known conservation biologist and champion of biodiversity in the world, recently called for returning half the

Century would mean that we wrap up the Human Project of fully taking over the world with little thought and no love for the millions of other kinds of Earthlings who belong here.[3] In other words, the Great Conservation Divide carries on its struggle to the end. In the first choice (and they are indeed choices), John Muir wins; in the second the uttermost nightmare side of Gifford Pinchot wins, but in winning, everything else loses.[4]

In the last two or three years of the Clinton Administration, at the end of the Public Lands Century, I began to see new agency leaders bring in a land ethic and take steps to live it. Mike Dombeck was the best Chief the Forest Service ever had. With strong backing from conservationists, on January 5, 2001, President Clinton signed the Final Rule for the Forest Service's Roadless Area Plan. This plan, with unwavering backing from Dombeck, pretty much shielded 58.5 million acres of inventoried roadless areas from road-building and most extractive use, such as logging. It was the greatest deed in Forest Service history to shield de facto wilderness and to keep open the likelihood for more Wilderness Areas. It also kept what conservation biologists call a "permeable landscape"—one in which manmade barriers to roaming wildlife are not overwhelming, and where a rough framework for Wildways between Mexico and Canada holds together. By the way, it

surface of Earth to other Earthlings. Tony Hiss, "Can the World Really Set Aside Half of the Planet for Wildlife?" *Smithsonian Magazine,* September 2014. About twenty years ago, Reed Noss said we needed to set aside 50-percent for wild things, so it's good to see someone with worldwide name recognition get behind it, too. Withdrawing the Man Swarm and its works to one-half of Earth would be a key step for The Rewilding Century.

3   In my next book, *True Wilderness,* I will rip into the arrogance of the Anthropocene.

4   I do not think Pinchot would still be driving extreme resourcism or the Anthropocene were he alive today. When Bob Marshall was dating his favorite niece in the 1930s, he was showing signs of rethinking how far resourcism should go.

came only a bit more than twenty years after Howie Wolke and I first called for keeping all roadless areas roadless.[5]

Also on January 5, Chief Dombeck signed the National Forest System Road Management Strategy, which called for "decreasing road construction and increasing road decommissioning."[6] Then Dombeck told the Forest Service to stop cutting old-growth forest. Whew!

Moreover, Park Service Director Robert Stanton in 2000 set up a NPS task force to look at Richard Sellars's book *Preserving Nature in the National Parks* and make recommendations for shifts. In the 1990s, the four land-managing agencies set up two institutes on wilderness: The Arthur Carhart National Wilderness Training Center and the Aldo Leopold Wilderness Research Institute, both in Missoula, Montana. I know outstanding conservationists and resource professionals in all the federal land and wildlife managing agencies and in some state wildlife and land agencies.

In the 1990s, we saw wolves move into their old homelands in northwestern Montana from Canada and into northern Wisconsin and the Upper Peninsula of Michigan from the Boundary Waters country in Minnesota. Furthermore, Americans wittingly brought Red Wolves home to eastern North Carolina, Gray Wolves to Yellowstone National Park and the great central Idaho Wilderness, and the Lobo (Mexican Wolf) to the Blue Range-Gila Wilderness landscape on the Arizona-New Mexico border.

Interior Secretary Babbitt emboldened President Clinton to wield his Antiquity Act authority to set up new National Monuments on some of the wildest and most outstanding Bureau of Land Management landscapes.

---

5   Dave Foreman, *Rewilding North America: a Vision for Conservation in the 21st Century* (Island Press, Washington, 2004), 158.

6   *Skid Marks*, Wildlands CPR email newsletter, January 17, 2001.

I truly thought that Al Gore would be elected President in 2000, Dombeck would go on as Forest Service Chief, and other good agency heads would build lasting reforms that would see conservation biology edge out multiple-use as the frame for the public lands and for wildlife stewardship and recovery. For once my scorn for the wisdom of Americans (and other *Homo sapiens*) left me. I could not fathom American voters choosing a cheery goof such as George Bush over a thoughtful, sturdy fellow like Gore (even if he was seen as overstarched). Nor could I dream (as in a nightmare) the United States Supreme Court pulling off a coup to install Bush.

With the "election" of Bush-Cheney and their taking office, the Public Lands Century ended, as did the timeframe of this book. Nonetheless, epilogues are where books look ahead. Bush-Cheney was worse for the public lands and wild things than Reagan on three grounds. First, the agencies were on the cusp of true reform in 2001 unlike in 1981 when they were itching to get back on the road of liquidating old-growth forests. Second, far more than in the early years of Reaganism, moderate, proconservation Republicans were almost as hard to find as passenger pigeons or great auks. More than ever before, landscalping and Dark Age "science" were key chunks of the Republican platform. There were no mighty Republicans to soften or slow the Bush-Cheney overthrow of public land reform (though, thank goodness, the Roadless Area Rule outlasted their onslaughts).

There was a third why and wherefore, too. Big national conservation and environmental corporations lost their nerve and their moral backbones.[7] This became even worse with the election of Barack Obama, clearly the Democratic President least concerned with Nature and least beholden to conservationists and environmentalists since Woodrow Wilson. Obama delisted wolf populations in the North from Endangered Species Act protection and threw them to the benighted

---

7   Dave Foreman, *Take Back Conservation* (Raven's Eye Press, Durango, CO, 2012).

landscalpers of states mired in the 19th Century who rekindled the
Great Barbecue with wolves on the spit. Moreover, there is no leading
Democrat with a strong oar in the River Wild. No great champions like
John Seiberling and Frank Church in Congress fighting for wild things.[8]

So. *The Great Conservation Divide* has been a history book that
ended in January 2001. My goal has been to briskly tell the tales and lay
out the lessons the next generation of wildlovers needs if they are to be
stronger and more winning warriors for the Wild Earth. It is a sibling to
my 2004 book, *Rewilding North America*, which lays out the policy and
science for a hopeful, workable, scientifically grounded vision for the
21st Century.[9] Truly, more than ever before, the fate of Earth is in the
hands of the generation now coming to the fore.

It's up to you, my young friends and fellow Cannots. Don't let the
wild things down.

---

8   There are a handful of members of Congress that have what it takes to
    become mighty champions for wild things. They need to be always
    reminded of how key they are and how we need them to work to gain
    leadership and power.
9   Foreman, *Rewilding North America: a Vision for Conservation in the 21st
    Century.*

ABOUT THE AUTHOR

For forty years, **DAVE FOREMAN** has been one of North America's leading wilderness conservationists. He is the author of *Rewilding North America, Man Swarm, Confessions of an Eco-Warrior, The Big Outside* (with Howie Wolke), the novel *The Lobo Outback Funeral Home,* and other books. He was the lead author and designer for the Sky Islands Wildlands Network Vision

photo by Nancy Morgan,
Noatak River

and the New Mexico Highlands Wildlands Network Vision. Among the wilderness outfits with which he has worked as a staffer or volunteer leader are The Wilderness Society, New Mexico Wilderness Study Committee, Earth First!, *Wild Earth Journal,* The Wildlands Project, New Mexico Wilderness

Alliance, Sierra Club, and now The Rewilding Institute. *Audubon magazine* picked him as one of its "100 Conservation Champions" of the last 100 years. He has canoed and rafted some of the wildest rivers in North America, and is a hiker, birder, and photographer. He lives in his hometown of Albuquerque, New Mexico, with his wife, Nancy Morton, who is a nurse and wilderness activist, and a cat named Blue (after the Blue Range Primitive Area in Arizona).

ABOUT THE EDITORS

JOHN DAVIS co-founded *Wild Earth* and The Wildlands Project (now Wildlands Network) with Dave Foreman and other conservation friends. He later served as Biodiversity Program Officer at the Foundation for Deep Ecology, then as Conservation Director of the Adirondack Council, before leaving office work to trek the Appalachian/ Atlantic and Spine of the Continent

photo by Nancy Morgan, Noatak River

wildways outlined in Dave's book *Rewilding North America*. John is now a fellow of The Rewilding Institute; Wildways Advocate for Wildlands Network; board director of RESTORE: The North Woods, Eddy Foundation, and Wild Farm Alliance; and volunteer land steward in Split Rock Wildway, a wildlife corridor linking Lake Champlain with the Adirondack Mountains. His book on TrekEast, *Big, Wild, and Connected*, was published in 2013 by Island Press.

SUSAN MORGAN, PhD, began her conservation career in 1968 with The Wilderness Society where she worked for over ten years, and she subsequently worked with various conservation outfits (Earth First!, LightHawk, NM Environmental Coalition, Washington Wilderness Coalition, Forest Guardians, and others) that focused on wilderness, wildlands, and public

photo by John Miles

lands conservation. Currently she is an editor and is president of The Rewilding Institute. She and husband John Miles are retired and live in Arroyo Seco, New Mexico, and Bellingham, Washington.

To order copies of *The Great Conservation Divide* and other books by Dave Foreman, please go to www.rewilding.org.

CPSIA information can be obtained at www.ICGtesting.com
Printed in the USA
LVOW10s2036260115

424408LV00002B/691/P

9 780990 782612